THE TRUE NORTH DOJO

THE CANADA'S BEST KARATE STORY

CANADA'S BEST™
KARATE

BOB MUELLER

"The True North Dojo"

The Canada's Best Karate Story

First Published in Canada November 2021

For information about booking Bob Mueller for Keynote speaking, art purchases, personal training and coaching please contact:

www.bobmuellerart.com

www.canadasbestkarate.com

www.findingyourbutkus.com

bmue51art@gmail.com

ISBN: 978-0-9938086-3-0

A special thanks to Scott Bullard for his long dedication, and superb efforts to CBK. His advice and editing skills in the production of this work have been invaluable.

Forgiveness is the fragrance
that the violet sheds
on the heel that has crushed it.

Mark Twain

Note to the Reader

While this book had been imagined for almost a decade, the principal writing took place during the 2020 - 21 Covid 19 global pandemic. Millions died and much of the world's modern economy of travel, trade and export was effectively shut down.

Given this worldwide issue, I once again found myself lucky and grateful to be born a Canadian, as this birthright provided me the time and patience to create this work. If you lived during these times, you know what I mean, and if you are reading this book some years or decades from now the scope of the 2020 pandemic will give you some context about the times.

Perhaps the trauma of the times was also a motivating factor for me to record the history and legacy of Canada's Best Karate. My hope is that future generations will know the incredible people from the past and good fortune that helped make my journey possible.

THE TRUE NORTH DOJO

CONTENTS

DEDICATION

Dedication is - *"The willingness to give a lot of time and energy to something because it is important"* Cambridge Dictionary

Dedication is probably the most important concept you'll find throughout this book. It is first and foremost that I thank, and recognize the abilities of all the teachers, students and contributors who have dedicated themselves to their study of the martial arts, and specifically to helping me tell the stories and history of Canada's Best Karate.

Your personal efforts, time and energy over the years has helped me live a wonderfully full, and colorful life. Whether you've pushed or pulled me, fueled or drained me, helped or hurt me, loved or left me; ironically, you contributed to who I am. Your stories have become my stories, and together we, each in our own way, have contributed to creating something bigger than ourselves.

I am grateful for my many loves, and my children: Leigh, Brittany, Drew, and Kieran. Additionally, thank you for the nine grandchildren (as of this writing) you have provided and numerous gifts your efforts and lives have given me. My hope is: through my many missteps and mistakes, I cleared the path just a little, so you might find your journey a little easier.

To paraphrase my beloved Sensei, I say, *"I love my family and all my sons and daughters, everyone whose path I walked on, sometimes very briefly and sometimes for many miles. I love you all. You made me."*

If you have ever stepped on the mat, the hardwood or concrete of the Dojo floor then you will recognize the unusual dedication and accomplishments of the many men and women that populate these pages. I recognize and thank you, as you have inspired me with your efforts.

If you have not had the opportunity to experience the Dojo for yourself, then I hope to inspire you to take the floor and become part of our incredible story and history.

I was once told that the most important element to being successful was to be willing. Be willing to take a chance, willing to extend an effort or be willing to offer a helping hand. If you are willing to give of yourself then you are likely to find the people, places and things that are willing to help and enhance your life.

My willingness to do rather than to try has made for many memorable life experiences, and it is my goal that by reading these stories you'll find the extra inspiration to be equal to your challenges. May your willingness to give your passions a lot of time and energy serve you as they have served me, and you too will enjoy a similarly bountiful and fulfilling life.

FORWARD

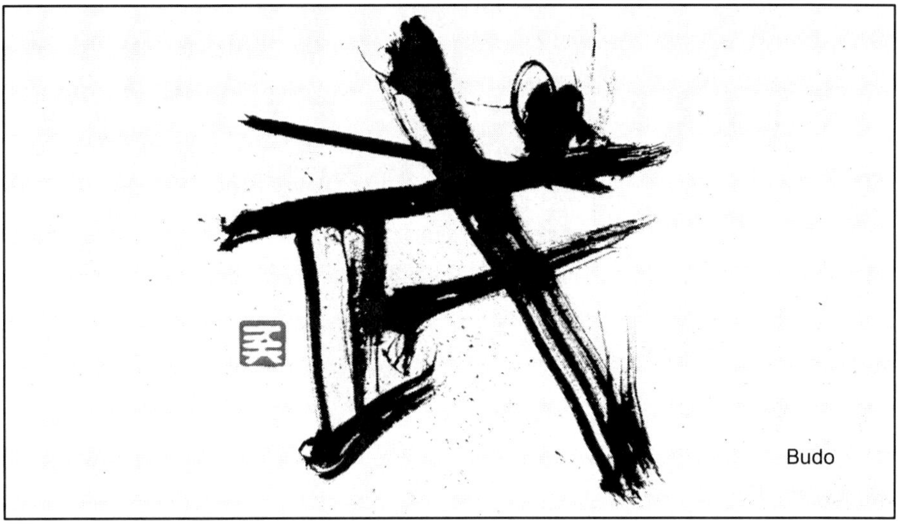

Budo

When you spend your life traveling the world researching martial arts efficacy and traditions you see a lot of things. In my travels, I have literally seen *"the good, the bad, and the ugly"* of Karate organizations, teachers, and participants. If you put styles and systems aside, the true measure of Martial Arts is about the integrity and truth of its participants. The sad truth is: while using respect and honor as its martial arts maxim, Karate is also full of frauds, fakes, and charlatans. Thankfully, I have also found many gems and experienced high-quality programs in very unexpected places.

Bob Mueller of Vancouver Island Canada is a classic case of, *"unexpected gems coming from unexpected places."* Despite being a fit, functionally competent, and a wonderful instructor, he, in his own self-deprecating words, was *"never God's gift to athletics"*, rating himself as a very average Karate-ka. However, I doubt there's a person who knows this gentleman who would argue that he is an exceptional *"artist of life"*, as so wonderfully described by the late, Richard Kim Hanshi. For me, I believe he's a gifted artist, storyteller, and a wonderfully inspirational leader.

His book, *"The True North Dojo – The Canada's Best Karate Story"* is entertaining and enjoyable to read. I can identify with the many stories of travel, trials, and tribulations. As you will read, the journey to success is full of bumps and bruises; or to paraphrase Robert Browning: *"Ah, but a man's reach should exceed his grasp, Or what's a (Dojo) heaven for?"*

Whatever your idea of average is, the writer's "Bushi" mentality is exceptional. Mueller's tales reflect a man who has *"walked his talk"* and reached many through his efforts.

Patrick McCarthy 9th Dan Hanshi

I'm an insider. One who has intimately viewed the people of CBK as a daughter, student, sister, and a Black Belt. I'm also an outsider who has successfully made their way in life away from the Dojo. My view, while the vantage point as an adult is 180 degrees from that of my childhood, remains the same. All martial arts are good, but when something good is taken to a higher level it transcends from being good to being the best. Many people view Karate as recreation, but I know from the inside out that the families of Canada's Best Karate see it as RE-creation.

It's well-known that recreational sport creates healthy bodies and healthy minds. Karate is no exception, as the physical demands to perform a proper punch, a thrusting kick or guttural Kiai brings an exertion of effort and sweat like no other. It is truly a different sense of sport that you experience when you enter a Dojo. The bare feet, a shapeless uniform, and the beginner's white belt all create a humbling feeling of equality for all who take the floor. The bowing is a symbol of respect.

The Mueller family is about respect. It began with my father, and I now see how my brothers have developed and transformed their karate. Their way of life is also inspiring. Together, for over 40 years they have changed this traditionally individual sport into something far more. The CBK belt testing system not only transforms people to achieve their personal best, but more importantly, it enables individuals to succeed while also raising their peers. Success, when shared, lifts the entire group to achieve more than they could as individuals. It's the essence of the CBK Dojo.

I have consistently witnessed the "I Can" attitude from those who take the challenge to make the Dojo part of their life. If you are not successful in your first several attempts, the spirit to persevere is cultivated in the hearts of all who take the floor.

The result is the creation of a new family within your dojo experience that creates a level of comfort that you can carry with you throughout your life. From the Sensei to the beginner white belt, the Dojo manages to shape a society of people who choose respect for one another, respect for authority and sometimes the most important of all, respect for themselves.

What I see today is what I experienced decades ago with my own training and, believe me, what is gained is never lost. I'm proud of my family's good work and everyone who wears Canada's Best Karate crest with pride. They are my family inside out, both on and off the Dojo floor.

Brittany (Mueller) Adair.

Sensei - Teacher, Master. Of all the Japanese terms adopted by Karate Dojos around the world, it's this one word - *Sensei* - that is universally recognized and respected.

In no small part due to Bruce Lee movies of the 70's, the Karate Kids series of the 80's and 90's on up to animated films featuring Ninja Turtles and Kung Fu Pandas, the idea of a mythical master who embodied all the traits of a great leader was central to the main character's development. In many ways, this same relationship has occurred in martials arts schools for countless millions of people, young and old.

You may have been fortunate to have had a schoolteacher or coach who made a positive impression on you, who helped direct the course of your future. For reasons I don't fully understand, a karate sensei seems to exert a tremendous amount of influence on their students. That was certainly the case for me when I met Bob Mueller. Which surprises me a bit, when I think back on the early days of our relationship.

Good fortune favors the bold. I often think "what if" I had walked into a different dojo? Looking back almost 40 years later, I wonder "what if" I had joined a karate club that had either poor instruction or worse, was unethical? There was no internet for information about what or who you were joining. As a novice, beginning karate meant you had to take what you were taught on blind faith. Looking in the rear-view mirror, I see my good fortune to have walked into what was the beginning of something special.

I took my first class at Bob Mueller's Martial Arts Academy in September 1985. It was only a couple of years later, after opening a second dojo, that Mueller moved back to

Vancouver Island to start a new dojo there. Even though he left his Ontario students in very capable hands, I've still never quite forgiven him for abandoning me during my early karate years. Despite the great distance, we managed to maintain a connection and as the years passed, this bond has only grown stronger.

It is a given that a karate sensei must be a great fighter and technician, but I have always felt that a sensei must also be a storyteller. Stories inspire us, they ignite our imagination, and they educate us. Through the art of storytelling, we get to live vicariously through the journey of the Hero and, perhaps, see the hero we can become in our own story.

It's appropriate that the story of Canada's Best Karate be told by Mueller. Not only is he a consummate storyteller, but his influence on so many karate students, many of whom have also pursued a path of leadership and teaching in the martial arts, is the keystone to the CBK legacy. It's what keeps us together.

If a Sensei is "one who came before", then his journey and the teachers he encountered can be thought of as "the dojo that came before".

I have had many great teachers throughout my years of martial arts training, but Bob Mueller was the first one to inspire me to strive for more in my life. He has been my teacher, my mentor, my friend, but first and foremost, he will always be my *Sensei*.

Scott Bullard 6th Dan Shihan

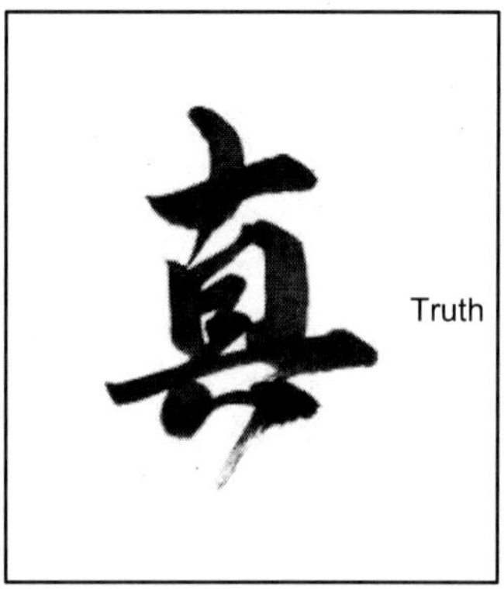

INTRODUCTION

Since you are picking up this book, I am guessing you are interested in learning more about the Martial Arts. You might be curious about training and wanting to give it a try, or you might already be a student who is eager to learn more. Either way, this book is your first step. Welcome!

As your guide, along with several key contributors, I will lead you through a series of stories on a journey through the Martial Arts. Our objective is to share the history of Canada's Best Karate through the eyes of the people who have lived it. The True North Dojo includes a cast of characters that could make movie mogul Steven Spielberg envious. You may know or may have heard of some of these people but sadly, most now live on only through history.

If you are a CBK student or family I highly recommend that you read the entire book so that you learn something about your history. But, if you're unsure, do what I do, and read the last chapter first! I always find that it makes me curious to read more so I can discover how the author got there.

However, to get to the end you'll need to start at the beginning. The father of modern-day Karate, Gichin Funakoshi, said, *"The ultimate aim of Karate-Do lies not in victory or defeat, but in the perfection of the character of its participants."*

Learning the physical "how to" of martial arts techniques is of little value if it is not accompanied by a moral code; a Budo code of conduct. Budo is a Japanese term that means "martial way". It refers to those martial disciplines in which the goal is spiritual, ethical, and/or moral self-improvement.

Learning and living the Budo code has been the core of my lifelong journey in self-education. Though there are many benefits to being "book smart", you simply cannot learn Karate from a book. You need a *Sensei* to weave the physical, mental, and spiritual/artistic lessons into the philosophy of the training. The word Sensei is Japanese for teacher. (The literal translation is one who has "gone before".) In this book, you will meet the Senseis who introduced me to this way of learning, and, through their roots, you will be led all the way back to the origin of modern Karate.

While martial arts can be traced back thousands of years, it may surprise you to know that what is commonly acknowledged as traditional Karate is only about 100 years old. My involvement dates back to the early 1970's, so I have actually been involved for about 50% of the entire history of modern Karate! My direct teachers have legacies that take us right back to the beginning.

That beginning was in the spring of 1922 when Funakoshi Sensei introduced Okinawan Karate to Japan. He adapted his traditional Ryukyu training to create modern Karate. What had been an obscure, almost secret practice became a much sought-after exotic oriental fighting art. It spread to every corner of the world. What made Funakoshi unique among his peers was how he focused on the philosophy of character-building by making self-improvement the purpose for training. Instead of simply focusing on the "how to" of practicing physical karate, he injected a "why" into his Shotokan system. It's this "why", the philosophy of improving one's character, that makes learning Karate different from other fighting arts.

Unlike boxing, wrestling, and other combat sports where fighting techniques were the primary focus, Karate took a different path. Funakoshi's emphasis on self-improvement is what gave Karate the potential for lifetime study, rather than a fleeting youthful sport or some elite warrior/soldier training.

Learning life skills through physical training develops strength and delivers personal power for its participants. The lessons involve instructions on what to do and how to do it, but the primary focus is on who you might be, inside and outside the dojo.

The True North DOJO is not a "how-to" instruction book. Knowing something is useless if you don't know how to apply it. This is a book about people. How they developed themselves through Karate and how they took various inspirations and paths to teach others. Some of these people are famous, some not. But each one is interesting and has directly or indirectly assisted the growth of this organization.

The stories in this book demonstrate how others have shown up in the world and how they have faced challenges, accepted defeats, and engaged in success. Some of these people were my heroes. Others have proven to be scoundrels. As in all walks of life, these characters are human beings - full of both good and bad deeds.

My promise to you is to tell you these stories accurately. I hope to inform and inspire by telling you about CBK's people as I knew them, and the impact they had upon me and the history of Canada's Best Karate - both positive and negative.

Bob Mueller.   Sōsetsu-sha – Founder

BOOK ONE

一

HAJIME

THE IMPORTANCE OF BEGINNING

"The beginning is the most important part of the work." Plato

Hajime is the Japanese word for beginning. Hajime!

Imagine if, on your very first day of doing something new, you were equal to everyone else. For a single moment, right at the beginning, you are equal to every other person *in history* who had ever started!

Sensei Richard Kim, 9th Dan Hanshi, always began his training camps with a lecture about the opening bows in a traditional karate dojo. One of the key points was equality. Kim stated: *"You will only have two true moments of equality during your lifetime; the first is the day you are born; the second is your first day on the dojo floor. It does not matter who you are. You could be the richest person in the world or the president of the U.S.A. - on your first day at the Dojo you start at the end of the line, and at the back of the room. Everyone starts at the beginning, as a white belt. Everyone is equal for one moment. After that, where you line up depends on you, your effort, and your dedication to the work."*

The dojo is a true meritocracy – you get what you deserve. Everything is earned. You can reinvent yourself by simply doing the work - a powerful thought! In the dojo, everything has a sense of purpose, propriety, and organization.

Many people ask, "What is the difference between starting at the dojo as compared to other gyms such as those in weightlifting/fitness, boxing, gymnastics, or even with other team sports like hockey, basketball, or football?"

The difference: The smell!

The "smell" can be the actual aroma of the place, but it can also be the feeling you have upon entering. How does it feel when you enter something new? If you have ever walked into a boxing club or hardcore weightlifting gym, you will notice right away that you are being eyed up and down. Not being welcomed there is a normal feeling. No empathy whatsoever! You are seen as "meat" or as competition. The eyes of the wolves are wondering how they will deal with you. You are fair game. Typically, many trainers are called coaches and they are usually very good on a one-to-one basis, but they also run with the pack. The strong get stronger, and the weak are usually swallowed up. This kind of attitude, given that the ultimate aim is competition, is not unfair. But it's not a good place to start and it's not for everyone.

When you enter a traditional karate dojo as a new person, you will also feel somewhat awkward, and likely full of anticipation and expectation. However, unlike the Gym, the eyes watching you are warm. Because you have a uniform, you have already been pre-qualified and thus accepted. The smell of a good dojo is clean. Everything about it - from the bowing to enter with your bare feet, to your new clean white uniform - gives you a sense of acceptance. The hierarchy of a dojo has a structure and a feeling that immediately supports you as belonging.

Another concept that you should know when entering a traditional dojo is the "Sempai/Kohai" relationship. This means Senior and Junior. Sempai or Kohai infers the relationship you have with every other person in the dojo. It is not a title. It is a state of mind. As a new beginner, a white belt, everyone in the class is your senior. As you progress and begin to earn colored belts, everyone who holds a lower belt to you is your junior/kohai. Everyone who holds a higher belt is your sempai.

To add a little confusion to the terms, there are two types of *Sempai*. As described, there is the Sempai/Kohai relationship, as well as a senior student who is called Sempai. The term Sempai literally means "number one student". They typically have authority as the second in charge to the Sensei of the dojo.

The junior/senior status is very important culturally in Japanese Karate. This special relationship creates a daisy chain of respect and gratitude. You are assumed to be in the middle and as such, you are required to give respect to your Sempai and compassion to your Kohai. You are expected to help anyone junior to yourself and be helped by anyone senior to yourself. The dojo seeks to be a perfect ecosystem of respect, compassion, and gratitude.

"Sometimes you need a helping hand and other times you need to lend a hand." J.R. Biden

This is the major difference between a gym and a dojo. By rule, you are obligated to assist your fellow students. This dojo structure makes interpersonal competitiveness secondary to personal self-improvement.

The Obi, Belts, and Ranks

"I had my white belt so long it turned black" I lamented playfully to the class of 7- to 9-year-olds. Today's lesson was about patience. The kids loved hearing how I had struggled to learn the art that I was now teaching them. As such, I continued by telling them a fairytale about the Obi, the Karate belt.

Once upon a time there were just two belts, one white and one black. Way back in old Okinawa, Karate was very secretive and learned in private. Most Karate training was done outdoors, so over time a lot of sweat and dirt was ground into the obi. The beginner's white belt got darker and darker until it turned black. To make matters worse, Karate students were not allowed to wash their belt for fear of removing the skills they had learned. The belt represented everything, and it became a legendary because It was more than just a piece of cloth. The Black Belt became a symbol of wisdom, patience, and most importantly your personal power!

Great story, but like most fables, most of it isn't true.

In actual fact, the Karate Belt wasn't even invented by Karate Masters. In 1883 Jigoro Kano, the founder of Judo, created the concept of recognizable ranks and the first version of the "belt system". What's true from the fable is: Kano only had a White and Black Belt, with nothing in between. White Belts were worn by students, while keeping the Black Belts for teachers.

Karate's Funakoshi Sensei met Kano during his first demonstrations in the 1922. He liked the Judo belt system so much that he later added it to his Shotokan Karate Clubs of the 1930's. The belt system quickly caught on and was adopted by most of the other Karate Masters of the day. It became the main way to identify the status of the participants. A few decades later, coloured belts were introduced in Europe, and the classic carrot on a stick motivational belt was born. In the old days, because the training could be quite severe, there was definitely more stick than carrot!

Time, and interest evolves everything. Understanding the carrot approach began in earnest during the early 1980's. Our original program began teaching children in a big way when we helped introduce a program called Superkids Karate. As part of Bob Mueller's Martial Arts Academy, Superkids was the first program in Canada created exclusively for kids. At the time, switching from teaching adults to children was a huge shift. Everything we knew about how to teach had to be adapted, but our goal was to maintain our entire curriculum and standards, while making it effective for kids. To make classes interesting and fun for kids the training needed to be age appropriate,

The main difference is to understand this simple fact: children thrive and learn when taught on a macro level. They need constant movement, big concepts, and very demonstrative teachers. Too much detail or depth, and you will lose them. Kid's imaginations are fertile, and their minds are open, so any philosophies need to be entertaining and be taught in story form. The ideas of good vs bad concepts are kept simple, as well as the moral lessons for children. When presented properly children will soak it up – but beware. Kids will show you right away if they are unmotivated by your teaching – no they don't complain, they just look out the window!

Adults on the other hand love detail! The more micro you can make your instruction the more involved, and fascinated adults become. Unlike the children, visualization doesn't come easily to adults so giving them small details helps them learn to feel of the techniques. I believe that adults are mostly motivated by the rediscovery of their own potential! Brian Tracy states, *"If it's to be, it's up to me!"* Like the kids, adults also love stories and enjoy martial arts philosophies, ethics, and mind training.

One of the key things to remember with all training is that everything is a combination of age and belt appropriate instruction. Your age and your belt level determine the level of expectation regarding your technique and decorum.

There three distinct group levels within the dojo: beginner, intermediate and advanced. The first two categories fall into the KYU or coloured belt groups and the third is for the DAN or Black Belt group. There are 10 KYU levels: White Belt 9th KYU through Brown Belt 1st KYU, followed by 10 Dan levels, 1st DAN to 10th DAN. Beginners from White Belt to Red Belt are followed by Intermediates Green Belt to Brown Belt.

Black Belts of all Dan ranks train together, with 1st, 2nd and 3rd degree or in Japanese: Shodan, Nidan and Sandan being the majority of participants. Collectively these ranks can account a lifetime of learning / teaching or as Sensei Kim liked to say: *"From womb to tomb!"*

Karate training consists of learning basics (Kihon), forms (Kata) and sparring (Kumite). These three modalities all lead to learning systemized self-defense and ultimately understanding yourself, as outlined by Funakoshi Sensei in the *"meaning of kara".* Now that you are acquainted with basic ranks and class structures of the dojo, we can discuss the actual training.

Focus and concentration are everything.

"Your ears hear in all directions and your eyes notice everything!" said Sensei, *"Be aware all the time, listen to the commands and then do them with 100% of your ability."* Learn to react, not just from what you see, but what you hear and what you feel. This open concentration is what builds your martial arts foundation. We say, *"Karate training begins and ends with courtesy."* As such, you will be asked to bow upon entering and leaving the dojo. As well, additional bows of respect are required when you engage with a partner or demonstrate your techniques.

Everything in the class and the dojo is organized. Harmony between teacher and student is calibrated to create a sense of discipline and respect. It isn't an accident that much of the training schemes and space seems somewhat militaristic. For decades, our dojos were affiliated with the ButokuKai, an ancient Japanese Martial Arts Organization. The meaning of the ButokuKai is "military virtue" with its tenets going back to feudal Japan and the Code of Bushido (The Way of the Warrior).

The best advice I can offer a beginner is to be patient with yourself and add practicing at home. Even 5 or 10 minutes a day can make a huge difference. The more you practice at home the quicker your mind and body will grasp the techniques. Don't worry about doing things incorrectly, as you will quickly fix your techniques by attending classes. If you plan training in 2 classes per week and then practice 2 or 3 times at home, you'll be surprised how quickly you progress.

Learning from your teacher gives you the knowledge you need but practicing on your own teaches you how to self-evaluate. Making your own corrections is what creates real abilities and develops a true Karate skill. The most important skill in becoming good at Karate ... is to practice your Karate. Or to be as blunt as a Japanese Sensei, *"No Practice, No Good!"*

Another sad truth I will share is that you do not develop "super-powers" when you become a Black Belt. Sorry to disappoint; but everyone who has ever earned their Black Belt has had to face this harsh truth. The good news: the effort and perseverance it takes to accomplish this goal is priceless. It will likely affect you positively in every other aspect of your life. The rewards are immense. Having your Black Belt tied around your waist for the first time is just about the most amazing, exhilarating experiences you will ever have. I know it was for me.

Earning your belt and appreciating your accomplishment, is the part of the fable that is true! While it wasn't my white belt that turned dark, I can say that earning a Black Belt is a step from the darkness towards the light.

Or as Sir Paul McCartney once wrote, *"And in the end, the love you take, is equal to the love you make."*

Finally, the structure of belonging to a dojo is summed up by these three tenets as outlined in Peter Urban's definitive 1967 work called the "The Karate Dojo". This famous 1960's Goju-Ryu Karate Sensei wrote:

"Everyone Works.
Nothing Is Free.
All Start at The Bottom."

The dojo creed underscores Richard Kim's lessons. The dojo floor is a place of ethics and equality. We are all measured by what we do, not by who we are. Everyone starts in the same place – at the back of the line and at the beginning.

Or as one of the great leaders in modern history once said:
"Now this is not the end. It is not even the beginning of the end. But it is, perhaps, the end of the beginning." Winston Churchill

Hajime! Let's begin.

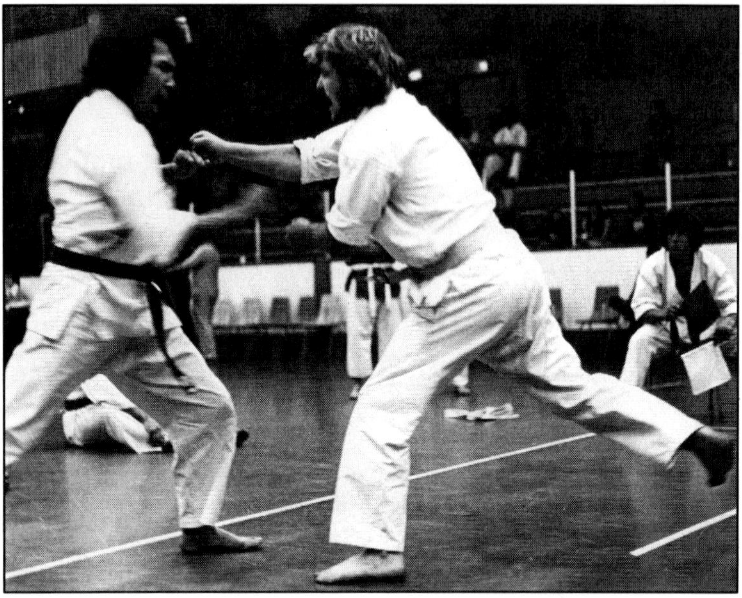

Hajime: My first Karate Picture
(Bare Knuckle Tournament as a Yellow Belt)
Circa 1975

YOU ARE WHAT

YOU THINK YOU ARE

Sensei asked, *"What are the three most famous words in philosophy?"* The vacant looks on our faces left the question unanswered.

Then he answered himself with a smile, *"I - don't - know!"*

"OK, what are the second most famous psychological words?" he continued and, without waiting replied, *"I think, therefore I am!"*

In 1637, philosopher Rene Descartes coined the phrase *"Cogito, ergo sum"*, as a first step in demonstrating the attainablility of certain knowledge. His curious answer helped lead the European Renaissance of art, literature, and thought. He created his famous saying during a session of self-contemplation and self-doubt when he answered his thoughts with three famous Latin words that translate as: *"I think, therefore I am."*

My thoughts about the "importance of being" have routinely gone to these kinds of ideas, especially when introducing new people to the art of Karate-do. I love witnessing young and old students take the floor with looks of anticipation. It's a particular mix of uncertainty and great bravado. Learning something new teaches you a lot about how you feel about yourself - your fears, your doubts, and your ambitions are often exposed all at once. For most, regardless of why you began training, martial arts becomes learning how to be responsible for yourself and your lot in life. I see it as life-affirming. This is my favorite way to teach.

Years ago, I created a series of Kata affirmations that are said aloud before performing a Heian Kata. One of my favorites is said before performing the Kata form called Heian Yodan.

I practice peace through my actions.
I must know myself before I can understand others.
I accept who I am, and the reality in which I live.
Through patience, I achieve all that I desire

For me, the idea of linking a good thought with a highly physical demonstration seems to be taking responsibility through action. It's not enough to think about doing good - you must act to empower the thought. *"I think, therefore I am – I take action!"*

This is not to say that you won't ever fail or have difficulties, as that is impossible. However, the willingness to act, along with the persistent patience to understand your reality, combines your mind with your body. Everyone suffers from their own "dark ages" from time to time, and while it may not be as profound as Descartes, doubting yourself is full of deep and damaging issues.

I agree it may appear to be an odd subject for a Karate class. After all, what does this deep thought have to do with punching and kicking? On the surface – not much! But it leads me to the importance of subliminal confidence in your life. If you could look in the rearview mirror, how old were you when noticed your confidence, or lack thereof? What was the event or activity that either built you up or tore you down? Then ask yourself what might have been different if you were more confident at a younger age.

The question routinely asked and answered at the dojo is: *"Does learning Karate improve self-confidence and self-esteem? If yes, then why is punching and kicking so effective to develop self-esteem in children?"*

The answer is yes! For as long as I have been involved with martial arts training, I have known that confidence is a cause-and-effect condition. The truth is that just about any physical sport or activity where you succeed can create confidence. The question is: "Can you succeed at what you are doing?" Team sports and games are about winning. In general, they are very "hit and miss" at creating confidence for their participants. If winning is your only cause, then the likely effect is that you will lose far more than you win. The lack of winning robs participants of their confidence.

Paraphrasing the famous football coach Vince Lombardi: *"Confidence isn't everything; it's the only thing."*

Martial arts training, at its core, does not require an opponent to be effective in developing confidence. You quickly learn that the obstacle to overcome and succeed is yourself. The act of beating someone else doesn't do much for your self-esteem; rather it breeds uncertainty. If you are always looking for something outside of yourself to affirm your confidence, you will constantly be in flux. You'll always find yourself lacking if you only measure yourself against others. The sooner you become self-reliant, the better. So, what is the best age to engage in confidence-building activities? The sooner you begin, the better.

Early education experts state that much of your self-esteem is formulated at a very early age. It's during your childhood that you confirm your self-esteem by how you think about what happens to you. I also believe that your nature is a combination of your upbringing and god-given genes. After that, exposing children to positive growth situations and experiences is the best way to ensure the seeds of confidence. This is where the punching and kicking of Karate comes in.

While it was years before I found punching and kicking training for myself, my confident nature had the gift of good genes and yes, a few great experiences. I was reminded of my good fortune while assisting an electrician fixing a light at the dojo one afternoon.

The electrician was, like me, an Esquimalt B.C. alumni. While I had never met him before, Ron had grown up a few blocks from my childhood home near the Work Point Barracks at the Naden Naval base.

"When did you graduate Esquimalt High?" I asked.

Ron looked down from his stepladder with a half-smile saying *"Well, actually I didn't. I quit school in grade 10, but if I had it would have been 1971."* His timeline made sense to me as to why I didn't know him - he was 3 or 4 years older than me.

"Me too!" I laughed *"But I made it to grade 11 before the world called on me."*

Standing there in conversation, I couldn't help but notice how powerfully built he was. I put him at about 5' 6" tall and perhaps around 220 lbs. His thick legs, large chest, and ripped arms told me he had spent a lot of time in the gym. Our conversation moved from various people we knew in common from the old days to something deeper. We made a fast connection.

Stating the obvious, I commented on his physique, *"Looks like you have put some time in at the gym!"*

Stepping down from the ladder he confirmed, *"Yea, you could say that I've seen the inside of a gym or two. I was a world-class bodybuilder at one point. At the peak, I weighed 267 lbs. But it was amazing and terrible all at the same time. I never won any big championships, but I did make it to the Mr. Universe and the World's Strongest Man Tournament. I met all the big guys: Franco Columbo, Lou Ferrigno (TVs Incredible Hulk), and yes, Arnold."*

"Wow! That's amazing – I knew you were well put together, but that's too much!" I retorted.

"Thanks, but I have to tell you I wish I had done what you did. I wish I had trained in Martial Arts instead. The bodybuilding, for me, was unhealthy in every way," he admitted.

Now relaxed, he began his account as a small, skinny kid who lacked confidence. Ron told a familiar story of being bullied and feeling powerless because of his size. How, as a teenager, he started lifting weights to build his body and, more importantly, to gain confidence. Then, as he began to succeed at becoming big and strong his story took an unexpected turn.

Before carrying on with his tale he asked, *"Did you do some gym work too?"*

" Yes, on and off, but mostly to augment my Karate. I, as a kid, was kind of the opposite of you. Growing up I was always relatively strong and a good-sized kid. When I played football as a 12 –13-year-old I was one of the biggest kids on the team. At twelve, I was about the same 5' 8" height and weighed 155 lbs. It was a problem, as the league weight limit for Jr Bantam Football was 150 lbs. However, size is a good problem if you're going to be a football player. My Saanich Hornets coach, Roy Volinger, would take me and a couple of the other guys to the steam room and sweat off the extra pounds so we could make the league weight!"

Now it was his turn to be amazed. *"Man, that's great. Once I started getting big, it became an addiction. At one point I was squatting over 700lbs and my bench was close to 500 lbs. I ruined my body, broke my back, and destroyed my knees. But I was obsessed with getting bigger, no matter the cost. You know, it didn't matter how big I got - I felt small. When I went to the Mr. Universe competition every other guy I met there, except one, felt the same as me. To a man, they were guys with a small man psyche or syndrome. All they talked about was how they might get bigger, all to mask their feelings of inadequacy. Do you know who the only exception was? Schwarzenegger! Arnold's the man - that guy was all confidence."*

Ron's honesty and admission were amazing. The depth of his feelings of inadequacy was something that even at that time, in his mid-thirties, he still suffered from.

"I never shook my lack of confidence. No matter what I did I was always that small, skinny kid. But I'm pretty sure that if I had done Karate or some kind of martial art it would have been different. It's almost like smaller guys there are celebrated – I think it's a great equalizer." he said.

That's when it occurred to me. While Ron began his life feeling small, I had started as a big guy – at least in my mind. Perhaps my temperament and natural gifts would have made me into a confident man regardless, but because of Ron, I saw this special insight for the first time. You see, at twelve years old I thought I was going to be 6' 4" and 250 lbs. I dreamed of being a professional football player. Everything I did, I did like a big guy. The fact is I never really grew much past that time. I stayed about the same height, and rounded out as an athletic adult at about 185 lbs. I developed a big, "can-do" personality. While I didn't dwell on it, I always felt confident and ready to take a chance or follow a dream. Anything I imagined I wanted to do - I could do.

Ron, on the other hand, lived to this day as a small person. He was always looking for some outside thing or force to embolden him. He had some great successes in sport and his work, but he could never shake the childhood feeling of being small and helpless.

I had been fortunate. Playing football at a formative age, on a good team, and with an extraordinarily great coach was good luck. Had I started that same competitive sport a few years later I wouldn't have experienced the same size advantage. There is

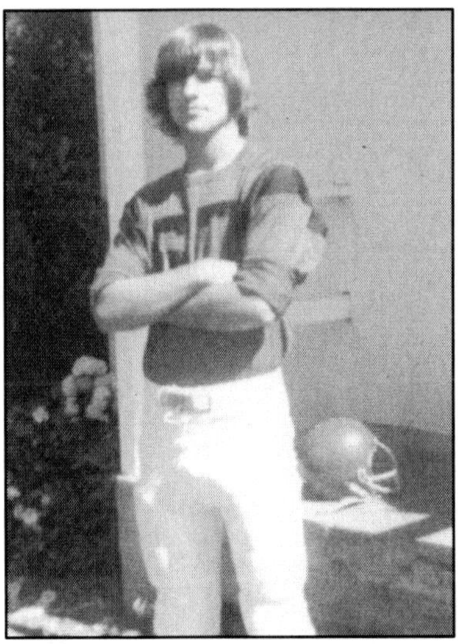

always a thin line between success and failure. In football, like most competitive team sports that focus on winning, you only get to play if you are the best at your position. Don't get me wrong – I believe team sports can be great at building character, but it is not their mandate. It is a by-product for the fortunate few who succeed on the field. For every childhood success, there are a hundred failures.

My size allowed me a wonderful start at an early age. From that, I imagined myself successful, even though I wound up very average in height and ability. Through my actions, I didn't need to compare myself with others. I retained the idea that I was big, in every way. Ron's size caused him to feel lacking at a young age, and regardless the evidence of how big he became, it did not benefit him. He compared himself to others and felt small.

Comparing team sports to martial arts, particularly Karate-do, is like comparing night - to day. Right from the start, whether you are naturally talented or not, your focus is directed to your abilities, not others. Every little action, technique, and effort is noticed and rewarded. The reward is not winning something or even receiving praise - *"the reward of working hard is more hard work!"* The martial arts mandate is always character building first.

When, at an early age, you are exposed to the rewards of working hard to accomplish a task, you find confidence in your abilities. A dojo maxim states: *"Everyone works, nothing is free."* Karate training involves thousands of small building block tasks that are both action-oriented and require mental concentration. If you listen to the instruction and move your body to understand, then your mind focuses your imagination so you can feel yourself succeed. As Sensei might say, *"Don't just do the punch – become the punch. Use your mind, body, and spirit with everything you do!"*

Teaching young children the tools of focus and concentration creates a direct link to their self-esteem. It's an "I Can" attitude of how good they can become that is an incredible gift. And it's not just for a few. It's an experience that works for most kids who train in martial arts.

If Descartes were alive today, perhaps his three words might be, *"Just Do It!"* or *"Do the Work!"* You become what you focus on. You are what you think you are. Think Big.

You think, therefore you are!

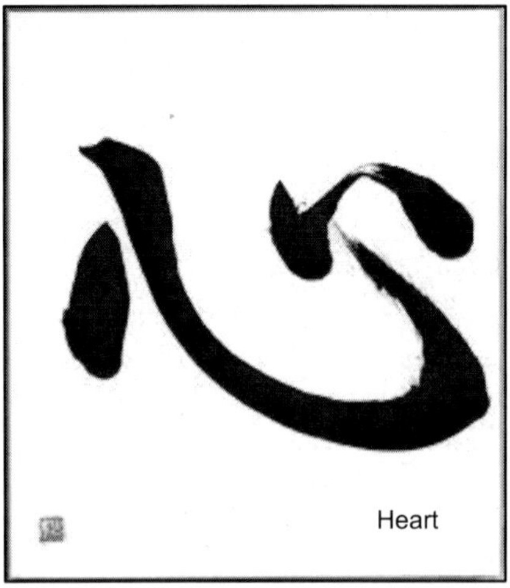

Heart

THE POWER OF EMPTINESS

"Nature abhors a vacuum." - Aristotle

I lost count a long time ago of how many students had come through the door to train at my dojo. When compounded by a dozen or so affiliated schools over forty years, the number of those served is impressive. An easy estimate would be tens of thousands of children, women, and men who have found their way to our CBK dojo floors. Empty spaces became fulfillment places.

Roy Kinsella is a fictional character from the movie, "Field of Dreams." In this movie, Roy heard a voice from a cornfield stating, "If you build it, they will come." This thought is also a central theme of my life and something I have repeated many times. I built places for myself and for others to benefit from.

Buddha *said "What you think - you become, what you feel - you attract and what you imagine - you create"*

As a lifelong builder, I can state unequivocally that having a strong belief in the completion of a project creates the desired outcome. Faith, much of which is visualization, is seeing the finished product before you begin. The possibility of seeing a dojo from an empty space requires both a lot of visualization and a great deal of faith.

The ideas and belief of building something from nothing is not exclusive to leaders and risk-takers. They are for everyone. They apply to each student and Sensei who takes their place on the dojo floor. Through our actions, we think, attract and create ourselves anew every day. A good question to ask yourself is *"I wonder what wonderful thing is going to happen to me today?"*

One of my mentors, Harold Warden, said to me once after watching a beginner white belt class, *"Just imagine what it took for each person to come to your class. Most of them probably spent months thinking about trying Karate. They then investigated, researched, and compared you and your programs to those of your competitors. To choose your school, they left their warm homes and fought traffic to get here. They took their first step by removing their shoes, dressing up in white pajamas, and stepping onto the dojo floor. They did all of this to learn from you."* Then, looking me straight in the eye, he said pointedly, *"Do you think any of that was by chance?"*

Nope! Each person went through a similar process to find a way to our dojo doorstep. They put their time, money, and efforts into what was, at the time for them, just an idea - an empty space. This is fascinating to me! There are no accidents in life, only outcomes. This brings me back to the power of emptiness and what it means in the dojo and to Karate training.

Before Kara-te-do was called Karate, its name was *Toude*, which meant "Chinese Hand." Funakoshi Sensei changed the name when introducing his Okinawan art to the Japanese. The new word meant "empty hand way." Why did he change the name? There are several reasons, but to put it into today's terms, he did it for commercial reasons. History books say that, in Okinawan, "toude" sounds like "kara." In Japanese, the Zen idea of emptiness aligned seamlessly with other traditional martial arts like Kyudo (archery-way) and Iaido (sword-way). Additionally, the Japanese looked down on the Okinawans as they considered them lower class. Thus, a Japanese-sounding name uplifted the Okinawan art to be more acceptable to its new patrons. Politics!

Regardless of the politics, the art of Karate-do, the Empty Hand Way, became popular with the Japanese. In 1935, Funakoshi, who was a schoolteacher, wrote a master text, "Karatedo Kyohan". The following are the key elements of the meaning of kara (empty):

"*The first connotation of 空 indicates that karate is a technique that permits one to defend himself with his bare hands and fists without weapons.*

"Second, just as it is the clear mirror that reflects without distortion or the quiet valley that echoes a sound, so must one who would study Karate-do purge himself of selfish and evil thoughts, for only with a clear mind and conscience can he understand that which he receives. This is another meaning of the element kara in Karate-do.

"Next, he who would study Karate-do must always strive to be inwardly humble and outwardly gentle. However, once he has decided to stand up for the cause of justice, then he must have the courage expressed in the saying, "Even if it must be ten million foes, I go!" Thus, he is like the green bamboo stalk: hollow (kara) inside, straight, and with knots, that is, unselfish, gentle,

and moderate. This meaning is also contained in the element kara of Karate-do.

"Finally, in a fundamental way, the form of the universe is emptiness (kara), and, thus, emptiness is form itself. There are many kinds of martial arts: judo, kendo, sojitsu ("spear techniques"), bojitsu ("stick techniques"), and others, but at a fundamental level, all these arts rest on the same basis as Karate-do. It is no exaggeration to say that the original sense of Karate-do is at one with the basis of all martial arts. Form is emptiness, emptiness is form itself. The kara of Karate-do has this meaning."

Emptiness also relates to the Zen Buddhist idea of detachment. It is a process of clearing space and emptying your mind. Being detached does not mean you do not experience the pleasure or pain of life. It is quite the opposite. You tend to experience each emotion more deeply. The difference is that you do not get stuck in the experience. You observe, experience, and move on.

Perhaps, at this point, your head is spinning a little! Mine was, and it took decades for me to appreciate the value of emptiness in my Karate practice. Some simple ideas can be learned and implemented on your path of developing these qualities.

The easiest and most profound way is to empty your stomach! No kidding! Notice your own physiology after eating a big meal. What happens to 99% of people after enjoying a large turkey dinner is that they fall asleep! Alternatively, if you train yourself to lean out or be empty before you eat, you will notice enhanced physical energy and mental sharpness.

Another way is to develop a minimalist lifestyle. No, you don't need to sell all your stuff, but you do need to clean it up. Organizing your possessions will help prevent you from being owned by them.

Finally, while nature does abhor a vacuum, learning to detach yourself frees up the space to deal with life. Nature always wants to fill up that space, so you need to guard your mind against thoughts and actions that do not serve you. The way of Karate practice is a means to quieting your mind while building your body. At the dojo, and in karate classes, you begin to practice emptiness. Learning to move your body in a precise way, a martial way, requires total physical focus. The result of moving your body dynamically, with total commitment, is that you find stillness. Your mind purges its thoughts to engage in the action. For a moment, while executing your technique, you are empty.

The concept of kara (empty) is a powerful one. Here is a famous Zen story that tells about the wisdom of emptiness:

Once upon a time, there was a wise Zen master. People traveled from far and wide to seek his help. In return, he would teach and demonstrate the way to enlightenment.

On this particular day, a scholar came to visit the master for advice. "I have come to ask you to teach me about Zen," the scholar said.

It soon became obvious that the scholar was full of his own opinions and knowledge. He interrupted the master repeatedly with his own stories and failed to listen to what the master had to say. The master calmly suggested they have tea and began pouring a cup for his guest. Although the cup was full, he kept pouring. The cup overflowed onto the table, then onto the floor, and finally onto the scholar's robes. The scholar cried, "Stop! Can't you see that the cup is already full?"

"Exactly," the Zen master replied with a smile. "You are like this cup. You are so full of your own ideas that there is no room for anything else. Come back to me when your cup is empty."

If you want to learn, be teachable.

If you want to be successful, work.

If you want to be happy, just be.

Empty your cup and nature will fill you with the knowledge and wisdom you desire.

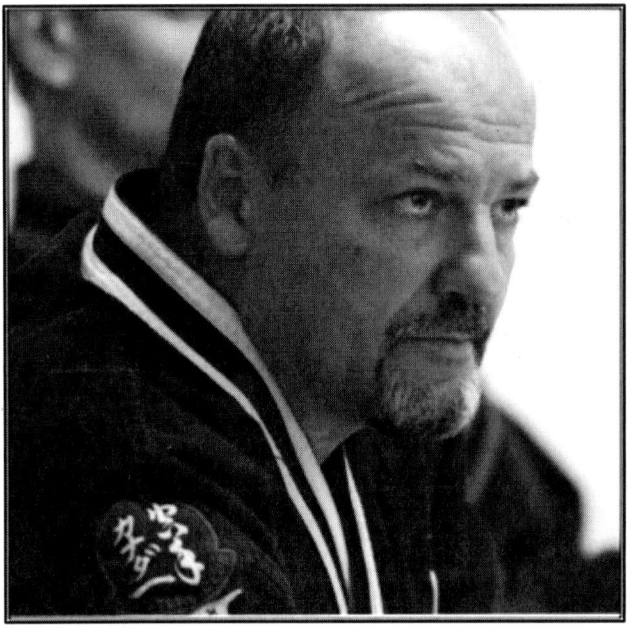

The eyes notice even the smallest movement
- the ears hear well in all directions.

THE LAST INTERVIEW

LINDON BATESON

Knock, knock, knock.

My heart was pounding unexpectantly with anticipation. A quick cascade of good memories showed that I still revered this man. Those inspired thoughts had prompted me to reconnect with him and ask for this interview. What I was hoping for was a bit of a long shot, as I knew before I knocked on the door that his life had not been easy. Still, I wanted to see and interview the Sensei of my youth.

When Lindon Bateson opened the door, the reality of what I saw replaced any delusions I might have.

His thick, silver-grey hair seemed younger than his weathered, unshaven face. The deep lines and dark circled eyes revealed a lifetime of cigarettes, alcohol, and dissatisfaction. His home, like him, was disheveled. Numerous small dogs roamed the house unchecked, leaving an unclean smell. It was overwhelming, but I took it all in as we began to record the session.

"Do you want my teeth in or out?" asked the old man.

"Teeth in, please," I answered, as a practiced smile helped his eyes come to life. His look encouraged me to start.

"What do you remember about the beginning of your Karate career?" I asked.

Sensei Bateson's face dropped, and his mind went blank. The simple question created a dark mood as he struggled to find the answer. He couldn't remember and it was a foreboding beginning.

"You started on the Prairies, didn't you?" I asked *"It started in Calgary with Dr. Olaf Simon during the mid-1960s. He was a master of Karate, yes ... he was a master, but his background was somewhat vague. I also trained with Dwight Scheer in Saskatchewan and Emil Repack from the BC interior. They were big influences. I respected Scheer. He was a big S.O.B. and Repack, like me, was a small man. It's good to learn from someone the same size as you, but big or small it's all about how you do things that matter. I learned a lot from them and I wanted to teach what I had learned."*

"Good, tell me more about that" I encouraged.

"I was about 25 years old when my girlfriend, Arleen Hill, and I came to Victoria. It was September 1970 when we opened the first professional Karate School on Vancouver Island. At that time if you were a Sensei you were like a God - people really respected you."

"What was your favorite part of teaching?" I asked as he began to open up.

The old Sensei began to find some joy and started to talk freely.

"My goal was to teach something that anyone could use. It was called Shotokan because I liked the power of the Japanese style over the Chinese stuff. But I learned and used techniques from anywhere. If I thought it was effective, I taught it. I liked to entertain people and I liked to fight! It was pretty brutal in those days. They called it "point" fighting but it was bare knuckles. Like real fighting, and although being called "non-contact" you got hit a lot more than you would think."

"Yes, I remember," I added in agreement.

"It's not as fast when you are actually on the inside, but it sure looks fast from the outside watching in ... and it's a lot rougher."

"How about your teaching? I remember that you had a huge presence in the dojo. Is that something you consciously worked at?" I asked.

"No, not really. I had a certain presence when I came into a room, but it was earned - it wasn't anything I put on. I earned the respect. I was only 135 lbs, a small man, but I had a big punch. It surprised people. How was I able to punch so hard? - total commitment, I guess. I just totally believed in what I could do."

Bateson was a maestro on the dojo floor. His presence was so complete that you felt like he was always talking directly to you. He noticed everything. He somehow controlled and conducted the class like he was leading an orchestra – Every note and detail seemed to fit together perfectly. There was humor, tempo, pace, and an omnipresent vehicle of fear. That is, the fear of displeasing him. It impelled every dojo-dedicated soul to strive to do their very best. Sensei pushed and cajoled. His favorite saying, "You can't shoot a howitzer out of a palm tree!" stressed the importance of your foundation and the basics. You never took a moment off in his class. I know many times he got more out of me than I knew I had. It was this style and persona that, years later, I adopted in my dojos.

"What were some of your successes? What was your Everest moment? The pinnacle for you?" I pushed.

"Beating Super Dan Anderson in the BC Open when he was rated as one of the best - 9th in the world. I only fought him once. Good thing, 'cause I might have lost if we fought again." His body raised and his eyes twinkled. *"Haha. That was tops and I retired shortly after that,"* he stated proudly.

He continued with some enthusiasm, "*And teaching, I had a knack for knowing what someone needed, then I helped them to learn it. I liked that. I just wanted to bring the best out of people. I had lots of great students. Tom Callahan was my first Black Belt here in Victoria, then Don Arnott. I had about 25 top Black Belt students - guys like Larry Mutter, Bob Allen, and, of course, Jim Mac Donald. Bob Mueller and Stan Peterec came from Jim MacDonald – lots of very good guys went through the Bateson Karate School on Yates St. I was in business for 15 years ... I guess. But it's Mike Puckett who was the best - my best friend. Stan was a great fighter and good friend – so talented."*

His smile gave way to a painful expression as his eyes looked up searching. The darkness returned and the energy left him. Overwhelmed again, he mumbled quietly.

"They kept me alive." He confessed.

I had a sense, by Sensei's demeanor, of where his mind had gone to at that moment. Bateson's original school, the one that cultivated so many talented martial artists, had failed in the mid-1980s. A combination of a young man's poor choices, failed marriages, drugs, alcohol, and an oblivious ego had taken him down. The truth is when you fall from a great height - you fall hard.

"In the end, I got too involved in the kickboxing and other things that took me away from the dojo. Nothing good came from it. People got hurt - I got hurt. It was a mistake that I regret. I should have stayed with the Karate, but I let it go. There were so many good people over those years, so many gone now. Almost 50 years ago," The old man lamented as his eyes lowered and his chin dropped.

The last interview, one meant to create a lasting record to celebrate the old man, had fallen like him into a desperately dark place. The camera doesn't lie and neither did Sensei. Despite the many successes he had experienced in his life, all he could truly remember was the failure.

"Is there something you'd like to say?" I asked gently.

He couldn't shake the bitter remorse. Eyes bloodshot, Lindon Bateson teared up. The original Island Sensei looked into the camera and said, *"I just don't want to own up to the success you are looking for me to say. You know, humility comes into play. I knew I could lead, and yes, I was a good leader. But I got overwhelmed. I felt like I was being pulled in so many directions at the dojo and in my life. I had to shut the school down. I failed. I feel sorry for the people I let down. I'm sorry."* Although it had been 35 years, the tears flowed.

"Sensei, you didn't do anything wrong," I said as I consoled him. *"You did a lot of good for a lot of people."*

"Yeah, I know." he nodded without belief.

Reality bites hard.

I knew this man during the peak of his potential, and I know there were mistakes. That said, his ability and brilliance were something to behold. He had been lightning in a bottle. Unfortunately, in my opinion as a young man, Mr. Bateson only really learned the physical, competitive side of Karate. He had missed the internal work, not learning the Budo philosophies of building a resilient character. The toothless man I interviewed had lost himself, now barely retaining his accomplishments. All he could remember was the overwhelming feeling of failure.

Sensei Bateson's confidence and presence taught me a virtual kaleidoscope of the mechanics of leadership. From Lindon, I saw firsthand how personal power could corrupt - turning winners into losers. To that end, I carried these lessons forward, always mindful to keep some kind of balance during my own tumultuous ride. If you do not learn from the past, you are doomed to repeat its failures.

Winston Churchill said "Success is not final; and failure is not fatal: it's the courage to continue that counts".

The day I earned my Black Belt Sensei taught this lesson by stating, *"This is either the end of the beginning or the beginning of the end."* When Lindon Bateson tied the Black Belt around my waist I knew that as far as I had come there was still a lot to learn. Churchill's idea about courage says that you will experience both success and failure but the difference of how it affects you is in what you do with it.

Seeing the old man and to honor his statement I say, *"There but for the grace of God, go I."* I acknowledge his lessons and I'm grateful.

I know that without Bateson's canvas of contrast, and without this Sensei, there wouldn't be a Canada's Best Karate.

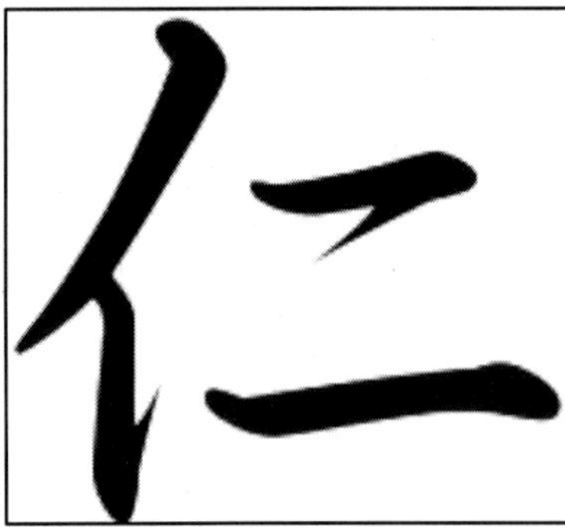

Compassion

HAVE GUN WILL TRAVEL

JIM MacDONALD

The gun rack had an empty space again. No, the replica 1892 Winchester rifle wasn't on some grand hunt; it was in hock.

The collector gun was famous as Chuck Connor's weapon in TV's "The Rifleman" in the 1950s, and by John Wayne's Oscar-winning "Rooster Cogburn" in the 1970s. Iconic for sure, the gun mechanism was symbolic for action. This rifle, his most prized possession, seemed to spend more time at Island Collateral Pawn Shop than it did at home. Perhaps it was poetic justice as I admired his willingness to trade the material things he owned for the opportunity to pursue what he loved.

Jim MacDonald (or Jimmy Mac to those who loved him) was off to another Karate Tournament. His hocked gun always paid the ticket so he could afford to compete. And during the 1970's he never missed a chance to test himself in open Kata, Kumite, and Weapons Karate Competitions. Tournaments in those days were different, as they were more for the elite, top-ranked Black Belt competitors. There was no such thing as a "participation award". You won or you lost! Traditional bare-knuckle fighting pioneers like Chuck Norris, Mike Stone, and Joe Lewis dominated the 1960's. Everyone refers to it as the "blood and guts era" of Karate – less skilled, but extremely physical and tough. A second larger wave of fighters like Benny (the Jet) Urquidez, Bill (Superfoot) Wallace, and Canada's Wally Slocki advanced the level of the competitors. It was still bare-knuckle point fights, but it also began evolving into "full-contact fighting" so hand and foot pads started appearing. Taekwondo Master Jhoon Rhee invented the rubber-coated foam pads called SafeTchop, resulting in more competitions appearing everywhere.

Jimmy Mac straddled this change, having fought bare knuckles and adopting the first SafeTchop as they appeared on the market. But, he preferred a piece of white athletic tape wrapped around his fists rather than the padded gloves. He said it helped his fist control and avoided cuts. MacDonald was a basic, but fierce fighter. His street fighting background had taught him how to be fast. He knew how to close the gaps and distance by quickly rushing and dominating an opponent. But his best skill was his timing. Karate gave him a strong base and he became an excellent counter puncher. As Sensei Bateson had taught him, he would shoot his howitzer of a reverse punch anytime an opponent came into range. He was so good at it that he could virtually drop opponents at will with a gyakuzuki (reverse punch) to the solar plexus. Everyone came to know that if you faced Macdonald, win or lose, you were in for a heck of a fight!

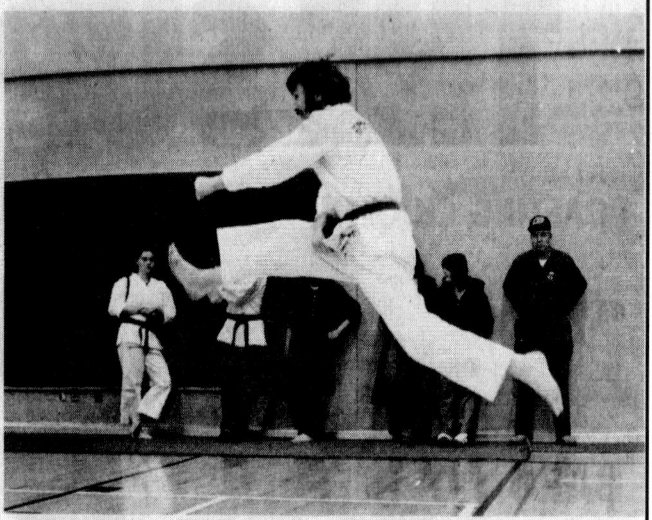

Jim MacDonald, on his way to a fourth place in the kata (form) competition at Abbotsford, displays a double front kick. MacDonald won three trophies at the Lower Mainland event.

JIM MACDONALD

Changes style, wins trophies

Jim MacDonald, the instructor for the Bateson Karate School in Port Alberni, changed his style a little and picked up three trophies at the B.C. Butoku-Kai Karate Tournament, held last weekend at Abbotsford, B.C.

MacDonald found himself having to fight under Japan

None of MacDonald's Port Alberni students were at the Abbotsford competition — either as spectators or competitors — although he feels that several of the locals would have done well had they made the trip.

"We've got some tough fighters in this club," he says, "but they seem to lack a little confidence in their abilities."

There are now 32 students at the school — 15 of which will go for their yellow belt (the first step on the long road to the black belt) this Friday. Another student, Stan Peterec, will test for his orange belt at the same time.

Many of the local fighters are expected to be in Victoria June 12 to take part in an Open Tournament, the first such event‹ that locals will compete in.

Jimmy Mac reveled in the training, and he won many tournaments. He gave most of the awards away to kids as prizes. Like the old Winchester, trophies sitting on a mantle were just things collecting dust. If you couldn't put them to use, you didn't need them. You could always get more stuff, but you could never replace a day spent at a tournament or match the thrill of the action.

A bartender by trade, MacDonald's big personality would quickly earn enough tips to rescue his gun from purgatory and have the Winchester ready to fund another trip. For him, it was a game, and it became a ritual. Whether he needed the money or not he'd trade the rifle to get the experience. It was added excitement and he reveled in the symbolism it provided.

While the rifle maintained his rebel heart, he was yearning for a less restricted living and it's that desire that brought him west. Moving from Brockville Ontario, Jimmy Mac landed in Victoria BC during the summer of 1972. Among his prized weapons he brought with him the Karate Green Belt he'd earned at Tsuruoka's Karate Dojo in Kingston, Ontario. A green belt in the '1960s / '70s was a big deal. He was so committed to learning karate back then that he routinely traveled an hour each way, over 100 miles, to attend classes.

Victoria had local training within the city, but only two choices. Korean Tae Kwon Do with Chang Keun Choi or Karate with Lindon Bateson. He chose Bateson's Karate School (at 719A Yates Street) as it was young, vibrant, and progressive. The decision was a good one for both the new student and the new teacher alike.

Jim was a few years older than Sensei Bateson, and as an older student, he brought his respect for the art and his passion to compete to his new home. Although MacDonald was an accomplished eastern fighter, the Bateson Karate School's open style methods impressed him right away.

It was the early 1970's, as the Bruce Lee phenomenon spread across North America, millions (mostly young men) became interested in martial arts. Bateson's timing, and MacDonald's interest, were two sides of the same coin. They both profited. All Dojos were packed with new students. There were line-ups to sign-up.

Stories abound of warm-up calisthenics in white belt classes were so punishing that many would quit after just one session. The reason was simple - with so many clamoring at the door to learn Karate, the general thought was to "separate the wheat from the chaff". Or, in more direct terms, "to distinguish the valuable people from the worthless ones". Your desire to learn was qualified by your toughness to endure. Jim was one of many who were humbled in his first class, finding it so taxing that he vomited during the workout. This was not uncommon at the time, but Jim MacDonald was tough, and he endured.

Born into poverty on November 2, 1944, he never met his adventurous Scottish / Canadian father. James MacDonald senior served during World War II as a sergeant major in the Canadian Army. He was killed along with his dog by sniper fire while resting in the town square of a small French village. It is important to note that his father also had another inauspicious honor. He had been a Dieppe Raider. The Canadians, known for their toughness, made up 80% of the 6100 soldiers who were assigned to attack the heavily reinforced 1942 German stronghold at the French port of Dieppe. It was one of the worst Allied battle mistakes of the war. Only 2,210 men, thrown back into the sea, returned to England from the battle. The rest were killed or captured. Sergeant MacDonald's cunning and toughness got him through. After MacDonald survived the killing fields of Dieppe, he returned to Canada to train paratroopers for D-Day. He volunteered back to active combat duty and re-joined his regiment as part of the second wave of invaders who fought their way across France. In October 1944, a month before the birth of his son, James MacDonald Sr was ambushed and killed.

Jimmy Mac never referenced his father's sacrifice without mentioning the fact the ambush happened in an unprotected village square and that he had died with his dog at his side. Because of his father's death Jim valued service, sacrifice, and had a life-long interest in history.

Fatherless, he and his sainted mother lived in poverty near Jasper, Ontario, about 20 miles north of Brockville. Iia ("Ma Mac, as he liked to call her) eventually raised them out of poverty by marrying a loveless man and becoming a nurse. Jim didn't like how his mother was treated and he took many beatings by voicing his displeasure. The ensuing chip on his shoulder took Jim on two paths. First, he developed his big personality by choosing not to be dominated. He became very independent, outgoing, and gregarious. The second path, the angry one, sought freedom in late nights and made him a fighter – a street fighter.

Willie Nelson once wrote, *"The nightlife ain't no good life, but it's my life."*

Ma's rule was "Make sure you are home before the streetlights go off!" She would use her nursing skills to patch up his fighting wounds without lecture or disapproval. She knew he had his father's spirit. Jim obliged by limiting the acting out to the dark of night and making good during the day.

The poverty, the fighting, and the nightlife could have made Jim an unsavory man. Instead, he chose a middle ground. The street fighting led to Karate as an outlet. The nightlife became a living as a professional bartender and, like his father, the need for adventure put him on the road to travel. Toughness was his heritage, yet he admired justice and simple acts of courage.

As a teenager, Jim performed his first heroic act when he noticed a small child by a partially frozen river. Seeing the danger, he immediately ran towards the toddler as the child broke through the ice. Jim's speed and quick reactions saved the child's life as he pulled the boy from the frozen water.

Another clue to Jim's compassionate nature was his admiration for the movie "Old Yeller", a sentimental story about a boy and his dog sharing both love and pain. Jimmy had the soul of a dog. He didn't dwell on any bad roads taken, he simply gave his best effort and looked for the good in what happened. Like his old Winchester rifle, MacDonald took aim at what he wanted, then used what he had to motivate others to follow his lead.

Jimmy Mac's need to compete inspired other students, including the Sensei at Bateson Karate School, to become active in the Northwest Karate tournament circuit. He also brought basic techniques like "TeWaza" ('27 Movements') and other Tsuruoka Karate forms to Sensei Lindon's dojo. His big personality had found its true purpose.

MacDonald was about 30 years old when he made the step to become a Karate teacher. Although only a brown belt, he announced his decision to Sensei Bateson and, with his blessing Jim began his new adventure. He moved in the fall of 1974, along with his wife, Beth, their two-year-old son, Travis and, of course, the Winchester. They started two Karate Clubs in the center of Vancouver Island. The first was in Parksville; the second opened a few months later in Port Alberni.

A 17-year-old Bob Mueller was the seventh person on the first day to join the new Parksville outlet of Bateson Karate School. Later, in Port Alberni, a grade 10 high school student named Stan Peterec was among the first beginners to train there. Locked and loaded for action, Jim Mac Donald's journey created a fortuitous intersection for me. As he looked forward, I never looked back as Jimmy Mac became my main mentor.

JAMES A MacDONALD

FIGHTER TURNED TEACHER

Everyone was barefoot on the cold, hard, bare concrete floor in the basement of the Parksville Credit Union. The room may have been cold, but the teacher of the hard style Karate was a fireball of energy. Within a month of starting the White Belt class, the school was at full capacity. It was the fall of 1975, and it was on that ice-cold floor that I met my first Sensei and a future I would come to love.

Jim MacDonald, the fighter, now began developing into a teacher. Unlike Sensei Bateson, he did not have an awe-inspiring presence when he taught a class. Rather than commanding, he was humble and generous. Karate had done so much to heal his past that Jim wanted the same benefits for everyone else. This desire came through in his teaching. His enthusiasm was infectious.

Classes were 1½ hours long and divided into three sections. It started with a rigorous warm-up that included strength training, followed by deep stretching and basics, and ended with kata & kumite (sparring). As soon as the White Belts were able, he had us sparring and readying for competition. According to Sempai MacDonald, class without fighting was like a day without sunshine. Thus, we got a lot of sunshine!

As mentioned, Jim was a brown belt when he started the Parksville club. Because I had begun on the very first day, I was always an advanced student. There is no question that, like a first-born child, I received the benefit of added attention plus the responsibility of becoming a leader.

As an added benefit, I had the unusual honor of attending my teacher's Black Belt Grading where he earned and received the title of Sensei. While he appreciated his new standing, he instructed us to call him Sensei in class, but Jimmy Mac outside of the dojo. He was uncomfortable with pomp and ceremony. Unlike Sensei Bateson, he did not require any titles on the street.

Bateson was Sensei no matter where he was – it was natural for him, as it is for most Karate teachers.

What one needs to understand is just how unusual this is. I have never seen anyone else successfully take this approach. While it was real and seamless for him, it also belied the insecurity he held most of his life. The fighter is typically a man insecure of his value or stature. Being fatherless and poor had left a hole in Jim MacDonald – a sense of worth that no dojo could fill. That said, becoming a teacher fuelled his desire for competition. This satisfied his need to fight, quieted his mind, and ultimately allowed him to overcome his demons.

Like all good Sensei, he combined what he had learned with who he was. He taught about the power of signs, a samurai bartender's code of service, and the honor of responsibility. Most importantly, he had rules of engagement for fighting and for life. His empathy for those weaker than himself was immense. He understood that, for him, praise was the most powerful tool in his toolbox. Jimmy Mac never missed an opportunity to notice something good about what you were doing or how you were doing it. As a Sensei, he inspired great effort and fearless action – always giving more than he got.

Here are some of the life lessons:

10 Life Rules According to Sensei J.A. MacDonald

1) Thou shall not screw Jimmy Mac.

2) It's OK to be rough & tough - but learn to be gentle, particularly with the ladies.

3) If someone steps into your zone - aggressively hit them NOW.

4) When giving someone change, fumble with it; this allows them time to give you a tip.

5) Disarm your opponent with friendliness, then overwhelm them with your aggressiveness.

6) If you are cheated, maintain your respect, bow deeply, and acknowledge your opponent; then get even and knock his head off.

7) Be a good tipper; people understand poor - but everyone hates cheap.

8) Have a healthy respect for authority - but don't trust it.

9) Notice more of what you did right than what you did wrong. If you lost, did you score a point? Was it close? Was it fun?

10) Be gregarious, be a character - chose to lead, not follow. Don't be caught watching when you could be doing.

Bonus

11) Thieves will be killed. A thief is the lowest form of criminal.

What he was not good at also provided lessons. Sensei MacDonald was a gifted teacher, but a lousy businessman. He struggled with money and lived life on the edge of what I call a "poverty mentality". Far too many people live with this affliction. Having grown up so poor, Jim was suspicious of the rich and inadvertently would create lack in his life as a means to maintain his circle of comfort. That was, as they say in baseball, "the hole in his swing".

This is not to say that he did not enjoy success from what he did, for he succeeded at everything he tried. What is fair to say is that he held himself back when it came to monetary success.

Jim MacDonald was one of the great loves of my life. He taught countless lessons about manhood, how to be, and when to act. I could share a thousand stories of his humanity, humor, and generous spirit. We crossed the country twice, sharing both fun and adventures along the way; I followed him once and then he followed me the second time.

Jimmy Mac did not like politicians, or what he called "apple polishers." He had the heart of a lion, with the touch of a kitten. He got more out of me than I knew I had. More importantly, when it was your turn to be in the spotlight, he got out of the way. He did that so you could absorb your just due and, equally as important, so he could have the joy of truly bearing witness to your success. There is not much more you can ask of a mentor.

My life changed in a moment as I was sitting in my kitchen the day I received the phone call.

The voice said, "*Bobby, it's Stan. We have lost a good friend today.*"

As it was very unusual for Stan Peterec to call me, I immediately thought something has happened to Bateson. *"Is Lindon sick?"* I asked.

"No," he replied shakenly, *"Jimmy died today."*

Immediately I felt the color drain from my face. I held my breath, then asked, "*What happened? How? Where? Why?*" trying to comprehend what I had just heard. He answered a few questions and hung up.

My wife looked at me with dread as she asked, *"What's wrong?"*

I couldn't answer. I burst into uncontrollable tears. I think I sobbed for days.

It had only been a month before that I had sponsored Jimmy Mac to come teach a seminar at my dojo. August 3rd, 2002 to be exact. At 57 years of age, he still had the "it" factor and people loved what he had to say and how he taught. He had been his usual self – full of energy with his show-stopping smile and ever-present big personality.

It was impossible to think that he was gone. I had just seen him. Stan briefly explained that he had been hospitalized a few weeks before, diagnosed with terminal cancer. As he did not want anyone to see him, he swore his beloved wife Barb to secrecy. He took no visitors, and as his personal power was so great, he wished for pneumonia and willed himself to die.

Sensei Jim MacDonald competed to the end. Once he knew the fight he was in could not provide the win he needed, he was determined not to be a burden.

He metaphorically loaded his Winchester and, on his own terms, took his shot. He died peacefully on September 15th, 2002.

As is the tradition of ancient samurai warriors, he left a death poem. To this day, Sensei's last lesson is a gift I revere. The depth of truth in his last words still gives me pause.

EULOGY
Written by James Arthur MacDonald
Born: November 2, 1944
Died: September 15, 2002
From: Smoking

I love my wife and all my sons, everyone whose path I walked on with them, sometimes very briefly and sometimes for many miles. My active enemy, who taught me much, especially that he had no power over me, not even the power to change my mood.

The teacher in Grade 4 who didn't call me stupid or careless or lazy and instead taught me to read.
All the men who were fathers to me. Mine was dead and my stepdad didn't know how.

My mother already knows how high she rates.

I won't mention any more names for fear of leaving one off and there are so many.

I love you all. You all made me. Life has been a wonderful gift and experience.

Because I have such an unshakable faith in a Universal Power (God) I look forward with great anticipation and wonder towards this next adventure.

God speed my friend and teacher ... my best friend

THE RELUCTANT STUDENT

BOB MUELLER

"Did you see the Ad for Karate in the Parksville Progress News today?" asked Mike.

Mike Rushant and I met when we rented a mobile home with a couple of other guys on the outskirts of the tiny town. We were both a little too young in 1974 when we had collectively left home. In a place like Parksville, having a social support system was important.

He was from Prince George, I from Victoria and we became fast friends mostly out of financial necessity. In a small town, people tend to be cliquey and somewhat unfriendly to outsiders. Parksville/Qualicum was no exception. Combine that with being teenagers, we were always looking for new people to meet and talking about things we might do. During one such evening the topic turned to a discussion about learning Karate.

Our conversation was of dreams and things we'd like to know. We had both been athletes - me with football and he with soccer - so when the subject of Karate came up we both agreed it was something we would like to try. Boxing and wrestling were just sports, but Karate, that was the real deal, real self-defense! Yes, if we ever had the chance, we would do Karate. At that time, in the early 1970s, Karate was the ultimate badass thing a young man could learn. Karate wasn't for kids then; in fact, you had to be at least 16-yrs old to register at most clubs. Schools teaching the "manly art of oriental self-defense" were rare, especially in small towns. But that was changing, as names like Bruce Lee and Kwai Chang Caine from the TV show "Kung Fu" had become household names. It was truly the beginning of a worldwide martial arts boom and Japanese Karate was the king.

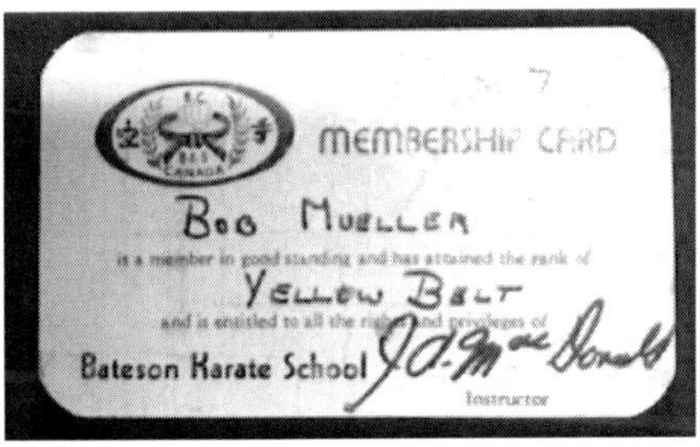

Mike continued, *"The paper said a Karate School is starting in town. Registration starts tonight, how about we go check it out after work?"*

"Tonight?" I responded ... feeling my feet get cold. He ignored the excuse, so I reluctantly accepted our agreement to go have a look.

Later that night, Mike registered as the 6th and I the 7th person to join Jim MacDonald's new club. Amusingly, being a year older, he had to sign as my "guardian" because at 17 years old I was underage. We laughed about that over a beer later that night. The cost of classes was $25 per month, and you had to commit yourself for 3 months. To put that into perspective in today's dollars - two classes per week would now cost about $300 a month.

During those years I worked framing houses. Heavy, hard work - eight hours a day, five days a week, rain or shine. Strength and work stamina were important for construction – flexibility, not so much. As such, my already football stiff lineman body did not respond well to stretching. My nick-name in those days was appropriately called "Iron Hips".

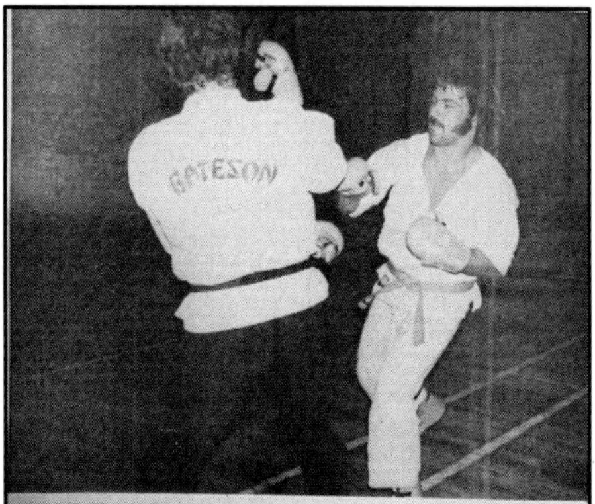

TAKE THAT...SIR. Jim MacDonald, instructor at the Bateson Karate School in Parksville prepares to block a blow from one of his more advanced students. The demonstration was part of a regular class for students at the school with MacDonald describing the exercises being performed.

Classes began with Tuesday and Thursday in Parksville. A few months later training was available 51 kilometers away in Port Alberni on Monday, Wednesday, and Saturday mornings. Mike and I attended every local class. While I liked the classes I was not committed in the beginning. My construction job left me worn out daily, so the thought of a tough Karate workout in the evening was a lot for me.

Mike, with a lighter job at a cement plant, thrived on the extra demands. He was more of a natural athlete, and he flourished with the training, always doing extra push-ups and sit-ups as well as jogging on days off. It was all I could do to keep up.

Regardless, after 3 - 4 months we both tested and earned our Yellow Belts. At that time Jim would put your name on the "Grading List" when he thought you were ready for testing. With his recommendation, you felt confident enough to go for your next belt. After getting the Yellow Belt I decided I'd keep going and see if I could get to Orange. I figured anyone could get to

Yellow, but if I could get to Orange Belt that would be a respectable accomplishment. I'd quit after that.

A few months later, something extraordinary happened when Jim posted the upcoming grading list. There were a bunch of new people going for Yellow and Mike Rushant was breaking new ground as he alone would test for his Orange Belt. I was not on the list. It made sense as Mike was always doing extra, practicing all the time and he was simply much better than me. Although I didn't say so, I was pissed! I didn't like the thought of being left behind while my buddy advanced.

I believe my need to be "one of the best" began on that day. I applied myself more and achieved my next belt on the following grading. With that I began a familiar cycle of saying, *"I'll get just one more belt; anyone could get an orange, green, or whatever belt so I'll carry on to the next one, and then I'll quit!"*

Three years later in December of 1978, I was ready to travel to Bateson's Victoria Dojo to test for my Shodan. I was the only person trying for the first-degree Black Belt on this test. It was nerve-racking, exhausting, and tough. When I passed the three-hour test, where I fought all the existing Black Belts, no one was more humbled or surprised than me. I teared up when Bateson Sensei tied the Black Obi on me, cinching it around my waist. It was a highly emotional moment for me - one that I will never forget. Jim MacDonald also cried.

The Parksville Progress published a half-page article on the front of the local sports section. The headline read: *Mueller beats 400 - 1 odds to earn Karate Black Belt.* Starting as a reluctant student, I had surpassed everyone else, including my friend Mike, who shortly after earning his Orange Belt, contracted Hepatitis B and almost died from liver disease. He withdrew from all his activities and moved back home.

My five years as a student of Jim MacDonald were profound.

He was the reason for the success of my martial arts. Not just for the skills learned (which were considerable) but for the attitude he instilled in me to be a winner. I persevered belt to belt and stuck with it simply because I did not want to let him down. It was like he wanted it more than I did! His inspired actions caused me to want to do and be more than I ever thought I could. This wasn't just on the dojo floor. The more I trained, the more the Karate mentality took over how I moved through the rest of my life.

During those years I competed in about 90 local and international tournaments, becoming a top Kata competitor and an above-average fighter. My garage became a home dojo where, no matter how tired I was after work, I would put on my Karate gi and train. Even if it was just a little, I practiced almost every day. To get extra training I would often travel with Jim to his Port Alberni school. His 1972 orange Super Beetle VW was almost like a 4 X 4. It got us safely over the Alberni Mountain Pass and through many winter storms.

Routinely, on Parksville class nights, I went early to the dojo and stretched at the back of the training room. I learned a lot about teaching by watching him conduct beginner classes. During TV commercials at home, I'd work on my splits stretch - then relax and watch the program until the next set of advertising. This was a trick I learned from Mike Pucket. It was the extra work in small bits, that made a huge difference. It was something I could do. While I never achieved the flexibility I dreamed of, my kicks became very fast and effective. My strengths: the love of basics and the ability to display my powerful persona through forms (Kata) became my passion.

Jim and I traveled across the northern USA competing in Karate Tournaments and ultimately landing in Cleveland, Ohio for the M.A.R.S. National Championships. Neither of us won there, but it was a great excuse to take a road trip on our way to spending the summer in his hometown of Brockville Ontario. Jimmy Mac was fourteen years older than me, and the summer '77 taught me about his bartender's budo code for living life. It was the greatest summer of my life, as it would foretell my future in many, many ways.

Sensei Mac became my mentor, and I was his top student. There were many more gifted students than I, but no one more loyal or committed. He was my best friend.

To that end, I experienced what the Japanese call 'Giri" - the ideals of obligation and the burden of those obligations. I will explain this later in more depth, but in its simplest form Giri can be described as: your teacher took on the burden to teach you and that you have a duty, a burden of obligation and devotion to them for their gift. It is a moral debt of gratitude. Your first Sensei is the most important one you will ever have and cannot be replaced.

I have had many teachers since Jim MacDonald. Some of them far more talented, with rich pearls of wisdom and incredible techniques, but none could ever supplant what he did for me. He was the one who saw the spark of ability, then fanned the fire until the combustion became my unique flame.

It is what a great Sensei does.

BOB MUELLER

THE RELUCTANT TEACHER

It was the next big push / pull moment in my Karate life when I answered: *"No, I'm not sure that is something I could do, but let me sleep on it."*

"OK, I understand. If you don't want the club, I'll ask Rory if he wants to buy it. Call you tomorrow." stated Jimmy Mac.

That was the first time I heard that Sensei was leaving.

He had bought a brand-new red Dodge 4x4 truck with plans to drive to Key West, Florida, buy a sailboat, and make his home on the Caribbean Sea. I hadn't noticed his restlessness of the past few months, but when I look back the signs were clear. The new girlfriend, a missed day here and there, and the big one; he sold his Qualicum home.

Jim MacDonald was ready for a new adventure.

My dreams that night were nightmares - imagining myself being in Rory's Karate class or him being in mine. Rory Lebrocq was a few years younger than me and had just got his Black Belt the year before. He was a great kid but no, I wouldn't be training in his class. Later the next day I met Jim's ask. I'd buy the club for $1000 and carry it on part-time, teaching twice a week at the Parksville Community Center.

I understood Jimmy Mac's need to evolve. Like him, continuous change had also been the only constant thing in my life. I believe I inherited my restless spirit from my grandfather Taylor who was born in South Africa and immigrated to Canada in 1905. My father was a restlessly ambitious officer in the Royal Canadian Navy. His need to achieve promotions and get ahead had us move repeatedly from posting to posting. It became a normal childhood experience for me. What other people feared, was treasured by my family. My mother said she always looked forward to a new move and a fresh posting. Even within cities, we moved many times. There were times that I changed schools within a given school year. Now I was at the beginning of a similar life, so understanding Jim's need to move on was an easy concept for me.

The 1980 summer was long and hot, and I was busy. By this time, I owned a framing company I called PB Construction. "Parksville Bob" was a joke name that had somehow stuck. I liked it because it was quirky. Other contractors liked me because, for a young guy, I was well trained, dependable, and worked hard to stay on time. Truthfully, being newly married, with a baby coming, and working full time - I was doing about as much as I could do. Being in a demanding trade I did not look forward to the added responsibility of managing and teaching the existing group of students at the dojo. Stepping into my beloved teacher's shoes was not going to be easy. Feeling like a poor carbon copy replacement, I struggled to deliver much value to those missing Sensei MacDonald. We all seemed to suffer without him. Some left, some stayed, and a few ones joined. That pathetic first year of teaching was made worse as my construction work increased. I became less interested in playing at the Dojo.

In every story, be it business or a life an event, a crisis can bring about a new beginning or a terminal end. Mine began on a hump-day Wednesday when the proverbial straw broke the Camel's back!

The part-time Dojo's side doors flew open as an overweight man in a white apron and cook's hat yelled, *"Excuse me, coming through!"*

My Community Center Karate class stopped immediately as the Chef maneuvered a hip of beef on a wagon towards me. He wheeled the cart through the middle of my class on the way to the larger room. Tonight, the local Shriners were setting up for a special Casino Night. It was bad enough that I had to teach over the growing noise in the main hall, but this insult was more than I could bear.

The symbolism of that moment told me everything that was wrong with the Karate Club. No one was in charge. Regardless of my good intentions, my half-baked efforts were not committed to any kind of success. Things needed to change. As the hip of beef moved to the big room, I moved my mind toward a big decision.

If I was going to continue, I needed help and I needed to go all in. No more part-time effort: full time meant no more accepting a hand to mouth existence. This Karate club needed a dedicated home. For me to guarantee a professional space I needed a committed Karate membership to follow suit. And I would also need the support of a partner.

Help would come in the form of an outsider from Hamilton, Ontario.

Sensei Rick Marshall had been on the fringe as a guest student for the past couple of years. Everything about us was different. He was Goju Ryu and I was Shotokan. He was reserved and quiet and I was enthusiastic and outgoing. But Marshall brought a lot to the table. He knew what a successful, professional Karate School looked like. He knew where to start. He also had connections back east to his Sensei at Don Warrener's Martial Arts Academy and exposure to the internationally celebrated Hanshi Richard Kim. Most importantly he was willing to take responsibility for 50% of the new school's operation and, as he was unemployed, run the daytime business activities.

Rick stated, *"We will no longer be a club; we will become a school."* That sounded great! We changed the name from Bateson to something we both could take ownership of. We used the Japanese name for the island and formed Shima Karate School.

I was scared and thrilled all at the same time. We signed a lease and committed to paying $168.00 per month for 850 sq ft for the next 3 years. It seemed like a lot of money at the time. The former dank concrete storage basement was pretty humble. It had an outside door, a small window, and a place to hang a sign. However, the fact that it was all ours and we could now control our space made it exciting.

No invaders with hot meat would be crashing our party!

My obligation to teach no longer felt like a burden. I found joy in leading the students and the resulting efforts filled me with satisfaction. What I discovered was I, like Bateson and MacDonald, had the unique chops to teach and inspire. Registrations filled our beginner class and, as the new students had no other reference, they thrived on my style and what I had to teach.

Marshall proved good to his word and our new commitment brought the beginning signs of success. In all respects, our poorly lit, dank school was humble, but our ambition began to put us into the spotlight. Within the year our school's membership doubled. We sponsored tournaments, got the attention of our town, and earned the recognition of international teachers like O'Sensei Richard Kim and Master Don Jacob of Trinidad.

As the local Dojo was expanding, a dark force was lurking within the Canadian national economy. The coming economic contraction that would crush my present path would simultaneously heighten my dedication to my Karate teaching and leadership. What had been a burden would become an opportunity. I would never again accept the status quo, nor would I allow others to dictate my path. I was only 25 years old, but I knew that where I had been - was not where I was going.

Philosopher, Deepak Chopra said, *"Go to the darkness, towards the unknown – for that is where the world of possibilities lies."*

Parksville had set a foundation for me but moving was my heritage and in my blood. The coming recession and losses were about to open my mind to the possibility of a different life.

I say, *"If we never experienced the dark, it would be impossible to appreciate the light."*

THE MAKING OF A SENSEI

CAMELOT ON GEORGE ST

"I know it sounds a bit bizarre,
But in Camelot, Camelot
That's how conditions are.
The rain may never fall till after sundown.
By eight, the morning fog must disappear.
In short, there's simply not,
A more congenial spot,
For happily-ever-aftering than here
In Camelot,"

So sang Richard Burton in the 1960 Broadway play "Camelot".

That same year, John Fitzgerald Kennedy became the President of the United States of America. For the next three years or one thousand days, until his tragic death, his presidency was said to be a modern-day Camelot.

As a child of the 1960's time stood still for me when, on my seventh birthday, he was buried. I remember the feeling that was JFK, and the ideals projected in his Camelot. My reflection of my time, just four and one-half years in Brockville, has that same feeling.

As Winston Churchill said, *"Never have so few, done so much, for so many!"* Equally, without enormous need, the many will not be moved from their comfort zone.

1981 was uncomfortable; it was a bad year. When interest rates peaked at a record 21% they devastated the local and national economy. My little contracting business was in trouble and it wasn't just me. Everyone I knew was out of work and going broke. I didn't understand, given my youth and inexperience, why the interest rates were so high or what to do about it. All I knew was that by June of 1981, the work dried up and stayed that way for the next year.

Like all things in life, you find a way to survive and you get through it. By the end of the year my first son, Leigh, was born. It was stressful but amazing. The following spring's business started to recover and I began thinking about making a change. The question was, could I make Karate my life?

For the next few years I saved as much money as I could by building and selling speculation houses. At the same time, I began taking business courses, learning from the best people I could find. Sensei Don Warrener taught an excellent 3-day Karate Business Course in Hamilton Ontario. His "How to be Successful Teaching Martial Arts" was the first template I modeled my Dojo operations on. I also added being a fitness instructor to my knowledge base, and then formulated a bold plan. I would sell out, give my half of Shima Karate School to Rick Marshall, and move 3,000 miles to Brockville Ontario. Why Brockville? It was my wife Paula's, as well as Jimmy Mac's, hometown. There was some support, as she had family there, but most importantly to me: Brockville did not have a Karate School.

I came to a crossroads early in my life. As Yogi Berra, the New York Yankee's great liked to say, *"When you see a fork in the road - take it!"*

In the spring of 1984, our goal was to begin operations as soon as possible. I leased a 2,500 sq ft former dance studio, located at 51 King St W. The initial business sign said Shuri Te Karate / Shape Up Shop, but it quickly became Bob Mueller's Martial Arts Academy.

My impatience, and the need to start proving myself, pushed me to open the Dojo doors on July 5th, 1984. This is absolutely the worst month of the year for the Karate and Fitness business. I mention Aerobics / Fitness because before Paula and I started the business I felt that this would be one of the keys to our success. At the beginning of the 1980s, Jane Fonda had taught aerobics classes in airplane hangers to hundreds of (soon-to-be shin-splinting) women. At the time, it was the next big thing. I quite naturally thought that with our west coast progressive ideas The Shape Up Shop would capture the market and be a huge success! And we did!

Karate enrollment in July turned out to be a surprising success, as I registered an outstanding 17 new adult students. They all paid in advance for the entire year, sight unseen and with no guarantee. Turned out they were as hungry as I was!

Within five years, eleven of the original seventeen would achieve their Shodan Black Belt. People like Danny Coles, Bob Noonan, Steve Stranges, and Laura Fry would become the cornerstones of the dojo. To put this in perspective, I was the first person from Jim MacDonald's dojo to receive my Black Belt. The headline had stated: 1 - 400, as it had taken that many karate students to have one earn a Black Belt. Perhaps I was a little better teacher and motivator than I had previously thought.

The next six months were a whirlwind of success!

If there was an "It" factor in Brockville, we were it. Within months we were not only flush financially, with everything paid for, but we were in demand. The aerobic classes were full, and my karate program had become the engine of our success. I would teach aerobics in the morning, operate the business during the day, and finally teach the Karate program at night.

To keep up, I added kids' classes and quickly had a membership pushing towards 200 students. On a whim, at the end of a karate class, I announced that we needed more space and I wanted to buy a building. I asked my students if anyone knew of an applicable building for sale?

The answer came the following day. John Hayden, one of the original seventeen who did not earn his Black Belt, presented me with "Camelot."

"The old Masonic Temple is for sale," John shared.

"Masonic what? What's a Masonic Temple?" I questioned, as I had never actually heard of the ancient European power organization. *"Where is it? How big is it? How much does it cost?... Can I afford a temple?"* I shot back.

With that, John took me one block up Broad St. towards the most prominent place in Brockville. Courthouse Square was the center of the city, complete with the statue of Sir Isaac Brock. General Brock was the hero of the War of 1812 when his small army defended Upper Canada. Although he was mortally wounded in the engagement, his troops turned the invading Americans back and they surrendered.

The Square is truly a spectacle, particularly for a small town of only 20,000 people. Beside a large parliament-like building, there were four outstanding, large churches located at each of the square's four corners. On the southwest corner stood a three-story, red brick, gothic-style castle. Built-in 1895, it had started as an Episcopal Church. The Masonic Order took over the existing church during the 1920s, making it the home for their temple for the next sixty years.

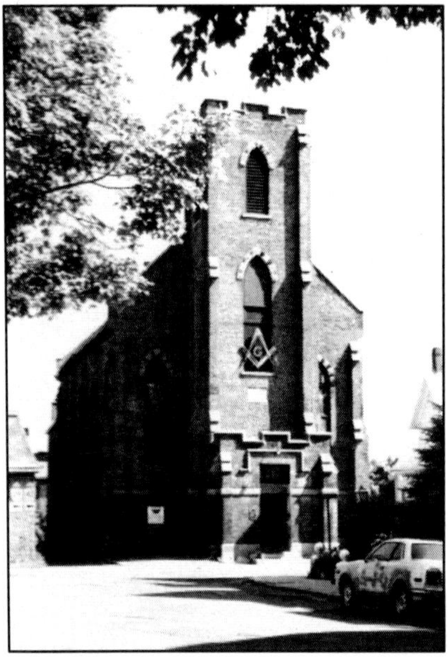

Standing in front of the 12,000 sq. ft. behemoth, I thought, *"No way... This is insane... A church? This is too much. I can't afford this!"* Although excited, I stayed calm and said nothing.

With wonder, I smelled the musty "old building smell" as I walked up 18 steps to the main floor. Before me was the expanse of a large room with lots of windows and weathered hardwood maple floors. The back stairs lead through a secondary room down to the basement and the town's bingo hall. It was rank with the smell of stale smoke and grease, but to me the whole thing smelled like opportunity. This building was gorgeous!

From the daylight-lit basement, we climbed back up three stories for the coup de grace, the actual Masonic Temple. This was the top of the church. The room was complete with an eighteen-foot ceiling, with a 12-on-12 pitched roof and huge beamed trusses. Here were some of the strangest items I had ever seen. The almost 3000 sq. ft. of blood-red carpet featured theater seating on both sides all leading up three steps towards a northern star. An ornate chair sat at the far end of the chamber. It was reserved for the Grand Master of the lodge. Symbolic eyes looked at each other from opposite ends of the room. It was creepy with skulls and bones, and even a casket (which was used for initiating new members.) It was a powerful room meant to intimidate, and it still did.

I salivated, as a former carpenter, with the thought of owning and renovating this beauty. This would be the largest dojo that anyone could imagine!

"The masons are in trouble. Years ago, the Masonic Order was a big thing in the community, but today their membership has dwindled. They don't need all this space and they cannot afford the operating costs. Just the oil bill is $20,000 per year," John said. *"I know the leadership, and I am told that they will sell the building for $50,000."*

"Fifty thousand dollars!" I blurted out loud as I reeled to take it all in. *"Fifty thousand dollars, for all this - are you kidding?"* Even if I had tried to be cool, my expressions of shock and my body language of excitement would have been impossible to hide.

"I'll buy it!" I said. No questions, no research, no nothing. I want this! The following months were filled with negotiations, zoning appeals, votes, Masonic infighting, building inspectors, and historical societies. They all needed appeasing. The price went from fifty thousand to seventy thousand, and being a small town, the gossip and rumor mills were alive with speculation.

Looking back, I realize that I was a fish on a hook and the Masons played me. They had been trying to unload the building for years, as no local business would take on this dinosaur. When I needed, as a condition of the sale, to rezone the building, I presented it to the city council. Although I think I did a good job, I'm quite sure that the masons had already fixed the 'yes' vote.

Years later, whenever a zoning change was suggested in the downtown area, the city council would be reminded of me. They had rezoned the church from institutional to commercial with only two official parking spots. Normally a building of this size would require a minimum of twenty or so parking places. I believe the City Council looked the other way to accommodate the Masons.

They didn't know what was in my heart, and they certainly didn't know the drive with which I would pursue my dreams.

Eighteen months later, with no parking, the traffic jam, particularly at class change times, was something to behold. All at once, parents were picking up and dropping off kids and karate students. Aerobics participants and gym members were coming and going. It all created a traffic gridlock at the southwest corner of Courthouse Square. So much so that we had to create procedures of how to line up on the stairs leading up to the third-floor karate classes. Students had to stand to the left side going in and come out on the right side. We tried to keep the traffic moving - inside and out.

I had a vision. I had my skill as a builder, and I had a lot of help. Students volunteered to sand floors, paint walls, build beams and assist in the creation of "Camelot."

On three floors we had martial arts training, fitness classes, and in the old bingo hall basement, a Gym/Weight Room. At the peak, the dojo had about 275 students and the total membership soared to about 1000 people. If Brockville's stated population of 20,000 people was correct, we had about 5% of them coming in some fashion or another to "The Shape Up Shop."

The mechanics, methods, and mistakes that happened to acquire and then to hold the castle, are far too numerous to mention. That would require an entire book. Safe to say, we were under-funded and over-valued. Camelot did not come cheaply, and its demands never ceased. As much as I loved the building, it was the people who came to learn, and the dojo itself, that created the magic. It was the most memorable effort of my life.

I had begun, 10 years before, with my own karate training during the Bruce Lee craze. Although I was only a decade older than most of my students, I took on my role of the Sensei so seriously, that I created an image that people still remember to this day.

Luck? Yes, there was plenty of that! The year I opened was the same year the movie *"The Karate Kid"* became a runaway hit. Millions of kids across North America clamored to "wax on & wax off" and I benefited greatly. The kids became an engine that would propel my career and my expansion for decades. Yet nothing in my martial arts experience since has ever replaced the grandeur of my Camelot Dojo.

A world-renowned teacher, O'Sensei Richard Kim, had heard of my unexpected success from Don Warrener. Kim, along with his lifetime of martial arts training, was highly educated, having earned Ph.D. doctorates in Philosophy and History. He taught me: do not be *"just a martial artist – but strive to be an artist of life"*. It was easily the most important lesson I ever learned. It was Warrener who recommended him to come and teach a seminar at my dojo during his annual spring training tour. Richard Kim always traveled with an entourage of between five and fifteen of the top Senseis in Ontario. He lectured and taught in what he called a Socratic method. As he traveled around, he would continually council his minions by telling stories on a broad spectrum of subjects. Typically, he would have a series of stories and lessons prepared, then teach them over and over to the entourage as they moved from city to city on the tour.

Although I was unaware of it at the time, it turned out I was a hot topic on this trip. As a relative newcomer to his Butoku Kai organization, and having created this dojo in a church, I became interesting to him. Sure, lots of people taught karate in church basements, but who dared to own one?

Kim liked boldness. He also liked to publicly expose his devotees who liked to talk a good game but didn't follow through. As in most organizations, there are always some flakes and hangers-on. Richard Kim's group was no exception. Outside of Warrener and few others, I found many of these characters to be small-minded, fearful, and petty.

Nothing missed Kim's eye. When he saw an opportunity to teach a lesson or to stick it to someone who was not living up to their potential, he took it. That day, I was such a lesson.

"Bob, did you buy that?" Sensei Kim questioned. The entire entourage, about twelve in all, came to a stumbling halt about half a block away from the Church. It was a cold spring day and we were all feeling the dampness. We were dressed professionally with suits and ties and O'Sensei took advantage of the cold. As we shivered, he stopped every few steps to resume today's topic: the "Samurai mentality" of overcoming fear. Classical Samurai stories and empirical studies would often round out Mr. Kim's discussions. And he did all the talking. We, the student Senseis, would listen and take notes. Kim would take it all in, creating his mental notes about us. He watched us as we watched him.

Still halted, he asked again, this time more powerfully, *"Did you buy that? Did you buy the church?"*

"Yes, Sensei," I answered with a sense of dread. Then, there was a long pause, and for effect, he gazed up at the three stories of the red brick church.

He pointed his aged finger at the church and then at me. *"You gotta lot of guts!"* he burst out.

Looking at his minions defiantly he laughed aloud.

"Boy, that's something. You know, this is the first true martial arts temple outside of the orient! How long have you been with me? Just a couple of years, right?"

"About six years, Sensei," I stated.

"You gotta lot of guts!" he declared again. *"Some of my students have been with me for decades and have nothing like this!"*

As he spoke, I felt the irritation and humiliation come over the entourage. That is, except for Warrener! He was also laughing right along with Kim, as he too loved sticking it to the hangers-on in the crowd! For the rest of the tour, be it at dinner or walking or teaching, Mr. Kim would suddenly leap into short conversations about the church and about fear. It was his lesson, and I was, for a few days, his muse.

If I wasn't sure before, I knew after Kim's visit, that this building represented something special. I had asked O'Sensei if he, being a Shinto priest, would bless the building in some "Feng Shui" type ceremony. He said it was unnecessary as churches are built on sacred ground. That was that!

Sacred ground ... Camelot does not begin to tell the story that was my time in the George Street Castle. It was not without its problems or failures, but it was incredible.

The reality is the sacred ground of Camelot only exists in our imagination. It doesn't exist anywhere, and never did.

What did exist was the work and sense of accomplishment. I had never worked so hard. In fact, I had burnt myself out. To that end, I'd challenge any other Sensei's effort and record of that time.

Starting with nothing but a dream we did an incredible amount. Within five years I had created the Dojo with three separate divisions of business, as well as completely renovating the Church. Our family added two children, moving three times, buying and renovating multiple houses. As a teacher, I guided and graded 27 students to earn their Black Belt, while maintaining about 250 current, actively training Karate students. When another opportunity presented itself, I started a second Karate School from scratch, 50 miles away in Kingston, Ontario. It also became a going concern. As well, we took on an innovative new system called "Superkids Karate". With them, we helped revolutionize children's martial arts instruction in Canada. To facilitate all this I empowered my two best students, Mike Sweeney and Dan Coles, to become leaders and wonderful teachers in their own right. Many others were also waiting in the wings at the dojo for their chance. In fact, because of the energy created during those few short years, 21 students would go on to become professional martial arts teachers and dojo owners. From all of the above accomplishments, I am most proud of inspiring others to follow in my footsteps.

Any reasonable person would have taken stock of their success and been satisfied. Perhaps I would have too, but I yearned for my west coast home. As the call to move on became stronger, I put the wheels in motion to secure my students' future and then set out for the west coast and home. I set my sights on a new adventure.

Had I never done anything more than this, it would have been fair to say that I had succeeded beyond my wildest dreams. But as my former Sensei, Lindon Bateson, often said, *"It was either the beginning of the end or the end of the beginning."*

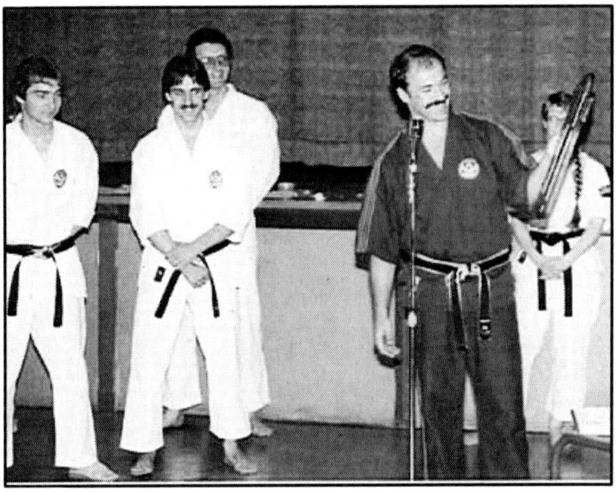

King Arthur's Castle was fictional and mine had been real. But Camelot was a dream that didn't last any longer than Kennedy's Camelot. It had been special. In the end, Camelot, the Castle on George Street, like JFK, was struck down by an assassin and burned to the ground. A few years later, the people who purchased the church from me, after three tries, destroyed the heritage building. In an attempt to collect the insurance premium, Basil Adams, the new owner set the church on fire. It was destroyed. It was disgusting and unforgivable.

It should have lasted for another 100 years. But the people, students, and teachers who came through the castle do not dwell on how it ended. Rather we remember it as a time of promise, when the dreams of what could be intersected with the reality of what was, if for just a moment.

Camelot launched the Martial Arts careers of many people and gave a special memory for the thousands who participated. The eleven students who put their money down, without so much as a class, had helped make this time memorable. Most achieved their dreams by forging the mental metal of Karate training in Camelot that had taught them. They led many others to learn the ways of the dojo and have inspired future generations to come.

Sensei Kim taught, "Be an Artist of Life," and although this was one of my first canvases, the art of this creation was undoubtedly one of my best.

Churchill was right, "A few can do a lot for the many."

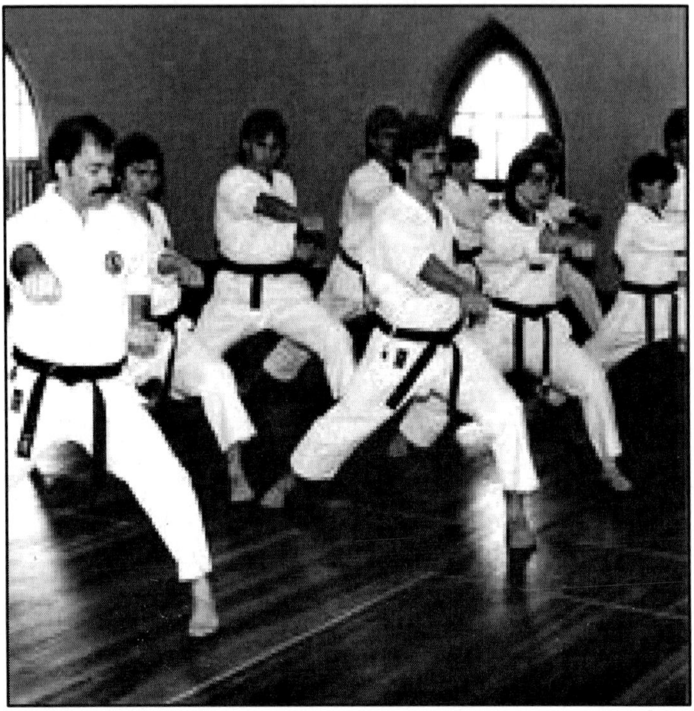

Leading my top students circa 1988

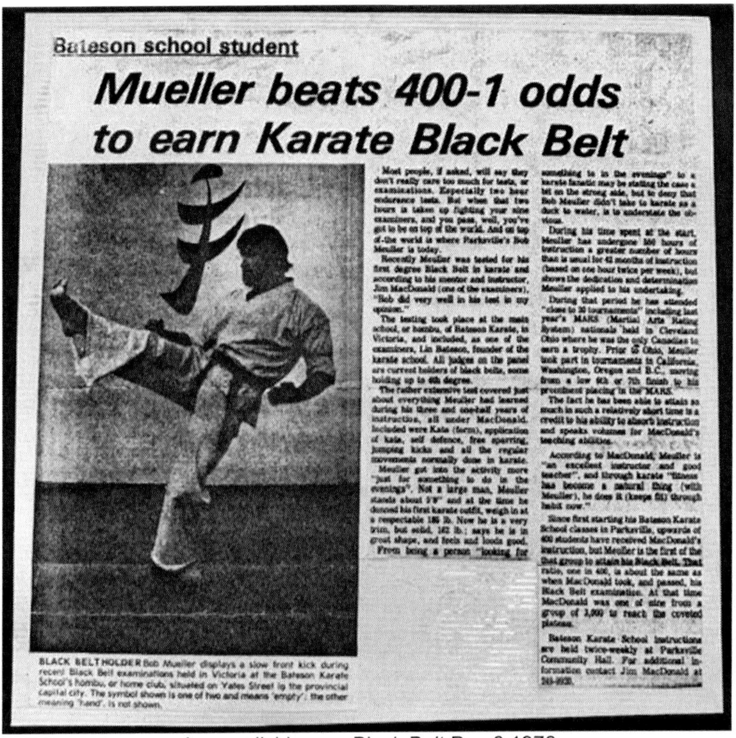

Bateson school student

Mueller beats 400-1 odds to earn Karate Black Belt

Most people, if asked, will say they don't really care too much for tests, or examinations. Especially two hour endurance tests. But when that two hours is taken up fighting your nine examiners, and you pass, well, you've got to be on top of the world. And on top of the world is where Parksville's Bob Mueller is today.

Recently Mueller was tested for his first degree Black Belt in karate and according to his mentor and instructor, Jim MacDonald (one of the examiners), "Bob did very well in his test in my opinion."

The testing took place at the main school, or hombu, of Bateson Karate, in Victoria, and included, as one of the examiners, Lin Bateson, founder of the karate school. All judges on the panel are current holders of black belts, some holding up to 6th degree.

The rather extensive test covered just about everything Mueller had learned during his three and one-half years of instruction, all under MacDonald. Included were Kata (form), application of kata, self defence, free sparring, jumping kicks and all the regular movements normally done in karate.

Mueller got into the activity more "just for something to do in the evenings". Not a large man, Mueller stands about 5'8" and at the time he donned his first karate outfit, weigh in at a respectable 185 lb. Now he is a very trim, but solid, 162 lb.; says he is in good shape, and feels and looks good.

From being a person "looking for something to do in the evenings" to a karate fanatic may be stating the case a bit on the strong side, but to deny that Bob Mueller didn't take to karate as a duck to water, is to understate the obvious.

During his time spent at the start, Mueller has undergone 500 hours of instruction a greater number of hours than is usual for 42 months of instruction (based on one hour twice per week), but shows the dedication and determination Mueller applied to his undertaking.

During that period he has attended "close to 20 tournaments" including last year's MARS (Martial Arts Rating System) nationals held in Cleveland Ohio where he was the only Canadian to earn a trophy. Prior to Ohio, Mueller took part in tournaments in California, Washington, Oregon and B.C., moving from a low 6th or 7th finish to his prominent placing in the MARS.

The fact he has been able to attain so much in such a relatively short time is a credit to his ability to absorb instruction and speaks volumes for MacDonald's teaching abilities.

According to MacDonald, Mueller is "an excellent instructor and good teacher", and through karate "fitness has become a natural thing (with Mueller), he does it (keeps fit) through habit now."

Since first starting his Bateson Karate School classes in Parksville, upwards of 400 students have received MacDonald's instruction, but Mueller is the first of the that group to attain his Black Belt. That ratio, one in 400, is about the same as when MacDonald took, and passed, his Black Belt examination. At that time MacDonald was one of nine from a group of 3,000 to reach the coveted plateau.

Bateson Karate School instructions are held twice-weekly at Parksville Community Hall. For additional information contact Jim MacDonald at [illegible].

BLACK BELT HOLDER Bob Mueller displays a slow front kick during recent Black Belt examinations held in Victoria at the Bateson Karate School's hombu, or home club, situated on Yates Street is the provincial capital city. The symbol shown is one of two and means 'empty'; the other meaning 'hand', is not shown.

Accomplishing my Black Belt Dec 8,1978,
Jimmy Mac Brick Break, Belt tying Ceremony with Lindon Bateson

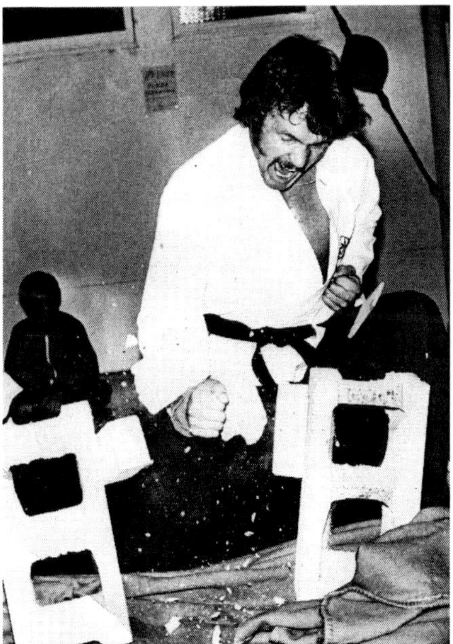

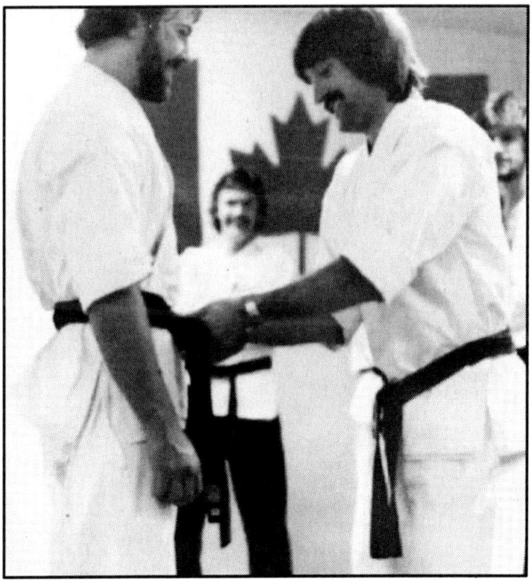

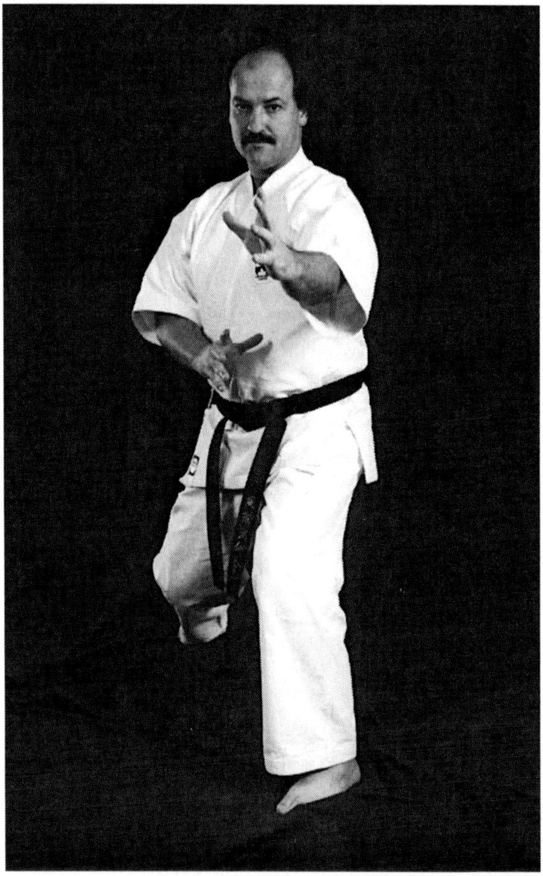

Bob Mueller circa 1995

BOOK TWO

二

ENTER THE PURPLE DRAGON

PROFESSOR DON JACOB

The year was 1980 and it was a cool September evening in eastern Canada. My new business partner, Sensei Rick Marshall, and I were invited to a home on the prestigious Hamilton Mountain.

I was a 2nd Degree Black Belt. This was my first visit to Hamilton, Ontario, and an introduction to all its martial arts characters. I was about to walk through the door that would expand my world, and my life, forever. We entered Sensei Don Warrener's home and though a little nervous, I was very excited to meet some of the famous and infamous people I had heard about.

At that time I was an "unknown" from a small town on Vancouver Island. I had little status in this world of martial arts, with a very low Karate-do rank in comparison to the 4th and 5th Dans seated there. In the living room, a dozen leaders were sitting around in a typical communication circle.

Sensei Warrener warmly welcomed his old student, Rick Marshall, and me and then introduced us to the assembled group. Warrener's major guest of the weekend, Hanshi Richard Kim, was not in attendance this evening, but there were many internationally known martial artists enjoying his hospitality. Big Phil McColl, a towering Goju practitioner, was introduced along with entrepreneur Harold Warden, and Canadian fighting legend Wally Slocki. Across the room Jim Wilson, the Captain of England's famous 1976 World Shotokan Championship team, was observing this unique mix of martial arts masters. He sat calmly, listening intently to a boisterous conversation emanating from the middle of the room.

Sitting on the floor in the center of the room were two young black men I had never heard of before. The larger man, Sensei Carlyle Thorne, sat quietly as he acknowledged the overwhelming presence of his teacher. Master Don Jacob, of Trinidad and Tobago, was of similar age to me. I thought he was too young to be a master. He had chiseled features, proud dramatic cheekbones, and a strong, sprinter-like physique. He spoke to the other senior Sensei with abundant energy and enthusiasm. He talked about his abilities and his lack of respect for martial arts politics. He proclaimed that his "Don Jitsu" style refused to be dominated by anyone, most particularly the stiff Japanese traditionalists.

What I heard was a very "Muhammad Ali-like" man who was excessively promoting himself.

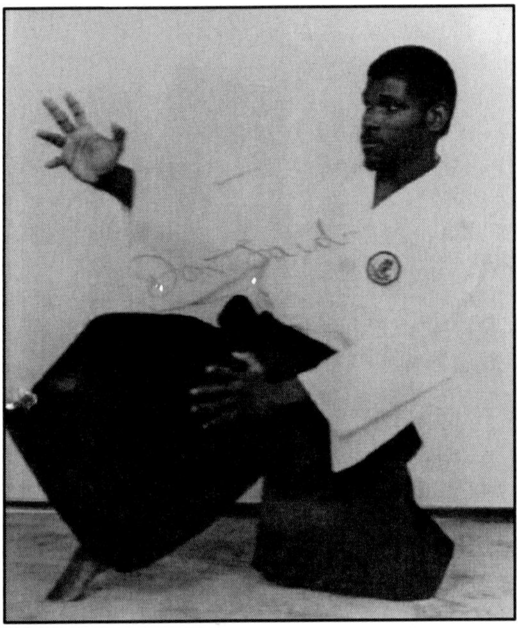

Outside of the west coast Karate tournament scene, I had never been exposed to Karate teachers of this stature and diversity. Frankly, given my age and inexperience, I had some very rigid and small-minded ideas about Karate. Although impressive, this young master seemed to have more bark than bite.

As I listened, I found myself doubting his ability.

He continued his opinionated oration and, as if to confuse my thoughts further, he caught my eye briefly then looked away. Despite his bold and self-assertive demeanor, I was surprised to notice the gentle warmth in his brown eyes. He just smiled and let me go, leaving a question mark in my mind as to who and what he was.

Good fortune was on my side that evening as I kept my thoughts to myself.

The next day Master Jacob, along with his student, Carlyle, were scheduled to do a series of Jujitsu demonstrations. It was the grand opening of a new Karate school owned by Sensei Wally Platt, with Jacob's demonstration being the day's finale. Platt's new dojo was unimpressively small and cold, with a painted concrete floor and little atmosphere. Regardless, the spectators and some local news reporters quickly filled the dojo. Several thin mats covered an area that was laid out for a small demonstration space. When everyone was seated, the two black men entered the dojo.

Master Don Jacob appeared larger than I remembered, wearing a bright purple satin Karate gi, while Carlyle was in traditional white. Jacob greeted the assembled audience with his trademarked big, gap-toothed grin and many generous thank-yous. I prepared myself to observe, siting with my legs crossed and arms folded. I had low expectations, as I had seen this "ho-hum" kind of block and punch demo a thousand times before.

The two men turned inward to each other and made ready. My attention sharpened when the intention of Carlyle, the bigger man, was revealed. He stepped back dramatically with a strong traditional block and a guttural, "*Osh!*" Immediately I was drawn in, as I sensed an unexpected presence and a dangerous chemistry between the two men. Master Jacob nodded and Thorne attacked viciously in a lunge position. Jacob defended himself fiercely, with a quickness and an explosion of power that I had never seen before! Stunned by what I was seeing, my feet untangled, arms uncrossed - falling to my sides, and I leaned forward in my seat.

The Master shifted, then struck the student with the hardest knife hand strike I had ever seen. He then followed his strike with a spin kick to the belt that catapulted Carlyle to the ground some 8 to 10 feet backward. For the next twenty minutes, I witnessed hundreds of techniques, slams, and locks - all performed with a machine gun-like precision. The shocking energy and the raw power of this young twenty-five-year-old master was amazing.

I had never seen such controlled, explosive ability in my life. He never once repeated a technique, as he appeared to deliver the beating of a lifetime to his willing student. Clumps of Carlyle's curly black Afro hair were floating in the air as he was lifted, swept, and taken down over and over again. After each engagement, the student would quickly jump up. His hands opened towards his face with a quick, but a deep bow, saying, *"Osh Master. Yes, Master."* I have never been more impressed, shocked, and surprised all at the same time.

Master Don Jacob had not been bragging the night before, rather, as he liked to say, he had been confessing. He had understated the truth about his talent, and his system. He was far better than his words and he was easily the best martial artist I had ever seen.

As I witnessed the man who would become one of the greatest martial arts masters of our time, I thought about the night before. I was embarrassed about my doubts, and I wondered if this Master had somehow read my mind when our eyes had met. I will never know what was in his mind. What I do know is, when the young Professor saw the doubt in my eyes, he responded as a true martial artist, with warmth and a knowing smile.

We became fast friends and over the years Professor Don Jacob and I have been to each other's homes many times. I know of no other man, in any field, who has walked his talk more than Don Jacob. His bite is equal to his bark, as he is the only man I have ever personally met who has lived life as a warrior - a true Samurai. From dawn to dusk, he is constantly traveling, teaching, and inspiring everyone he meets.

Professor Don Jacob is an artist of life. He trains harder, jumps higher, strikes faster, laughs louder, and lives life full out, as an example to all.

CANADIAN TWINNING

AN UNEXPECTED FRIENDSHIP
BY DON JACOB

Man, I was so cold. Winter in Canada! It was maybe the coldest I had ever been. The electric heat wasn't working, and no wood for the stove made this drafty little house and me truly miserable. I had landed in a place called Errington, somewhere on Vancouver Island. I didn't know exactly where I was, but what I did know was I couldn't get warm. Chilled to the bone! Now, I'm not a man given to self-doubt, but I was questioning why I had agreed to come to this place.

It was near the end of my 1981 seminar tour, my last stop. Admittedly, this wasn't new for me. I had demonstrated in 54 countries around the world, so going to unknown places, under strange circumstances was a common occurrence. A few days before, I had been teaching and demonstrating in Hamilton, Ontario, when I got a last-minute invitation to Vancouver Island. As I was from an island in the Caribbean called Trinidad, I thought it would be interesting to see a Canadian Island. I had no idea at the time that Canada even had Islands. I just knew it was big, it was north, and even the warmest part of it seemed to be among the coldest places I had ever been.

"Rick, if I don't get warm somehow, I don't know how I'm going to teach. My legs are frozen, and my teeth are chattering, man. I am so cold!" I said to my host.

"No problem, Professor, I'll fix this and get you warm". Rick answered. Sensei Rick Marshall had sponsored my trip here, so he, and his partner at Shima Karate School deserved my very best. Marshall recognized my need and made a call. The next thing I knew we were in his brown Hyundai Pony, heater on full, looking for the warmth of another's home.

When the door of salvation opened, my shoulders were so high on my neck that I could feel the borrowed winter coat tickling my ears. A warm smile greeted me as Bob Mueller brought me into his welcoming home and his happy life.

Have you ever had a moment that froze in your memory? My name is Don Jacob and I have had many, many good memories burned into my mind. But it's the frozen ones that I remember with clarity. Memories like my early career teaching in places like Burberry Hall in London England, Europe, the USA, and even for the Sultan's Guards in Oman. A highlight for me happened in Madison Square Garden New York, where I had demonstrated my Donjitsu Ryu for 25,000 people. It was a standing ovation I can still feel to this day. For a little black boy, it's a long way from the ghettos of Port of Spain, Trinidad to the center stage at MSG. It's true, my talent has taken me far, and my drive to teach and live martial arts had always been my lifelong dream.

I've met many fellow dreamers in my travels and many incredibly talented martial artists. So many people have opened their hearts, homes, and dojos to me that I'm truly blessed. But I'd have to say some of the warmest hearts I've ever met have come out of my cold Canadian experiences. Any doubt I had about my decision to come to this Canadian Island left when I saw Mueller's smile and roasted in his warm home. While I didn't know it then, this unassuming man would become a life-long friend.

My beloved Granny used to say, *"Show me your friends, and I'll tell you your future."* I'm also reminded that when you sow a seed you reap an intention. For me, a single kernel of kindness when I needed it opened unexpected doors. It's not a coincidence that many branches of my system have taken root in Canada, particularly in British Columbia. Purple Dragon now has schools headed up by some incredible Canadians. Sensei Amber Murphy, a 4th Degree Black Belt, distinguished herself as the first female to create a successful dojo outside of Trinidad. She was followed by Senseis Ian Shu, in Uculuet, and Ioanna Koutava in Vancouver. Anthony Phillip and Adrian Brown in Ontario also have Purple Dragon branches. Canadians also welcomed my eldest son, Shihan Daniel Jacob, to immigrate to Vancouver. He successfully anchored Donjitsu Ryu, and together with Amber and the others have created a group of incredible students. Firmly on Canadian soil, I am so very proud of all of them. My respect and belief in the goodness of Canada have been rewarded over and over.

I must say that it is not the same everywhere else in the world. In my country respect is not given. It must be earned. Our training in Trinidad is hard: concrete floors, cramped spaces, and never-ending heat. My art and my training are exacting and very physical. It has to be. The demands and dangers of living in a 3rd

World country like Trinidad mean that everything taught here has to work. In my case, I can swear that all my techniques have been ... road-tested! Donjitsu came from a combination of Judo and Karate, tied together through the teachings of Ju Jitsu Grand Master Moses Powell of NYC. Everything in my Purple Dragon Donjitsu System was built from the ground up to teach real self-defense and develop an unstoppable spirit and mindset.

That said, my experiences in Canada captivated me. Canada also impressed me as a beautiful and extremely safe country. The Bob Mueller I met in 1981 seemed to be a typical Canadian Karateka of average ability. Kind of strong, but kind of stiff. He could move, but without much flow, and he definitely couldn't roll! He was confident but unsure. Interestingly, he joked about his shortcomings, and whenever the opportunity presented itself, he laughed. I liked him right away.

Had I not been warmed in his home that day, it is possible that I might not have noticed his hunger and his willingness to learn. Looking back now, I'd say he was a kindred spirit. Something you tend to learn when you travel the world is how to read people. At first blush, Mueller seemed to be the lesser half of the partnership I encountered at the Shima Karate School. What I learned over the next few days in Parksville was that the person who commanded the respect was also the one with a warm smile.

I made a mental note to encourage my new friend and, from that simple thought, many opportunities came about to create what I call "a twinning". I like this term. The idea of linking and connecting with like-minded people is how I was able to travel the world. Along the road, I have found a few associations worthy of twinning. Bob Mueller's group, Canada's Best Karate, has always kept a special place in my heart. I have told him many times about how much I love that name. I'd tell him *"You became what you proclaim."* You must speak *"truth to power."* In that way, we became budo brothers over the past forty years.

In the early years, both hungry to expand our knowledge, we found ourselves meeting, by accident, at various workshops and self-improvement seminars. He also attended Canadian tournaments where my teams competed. His groups showed up over and over when I taught and demonstrated. Twenty years ago, we took our teams to Australia to compete at a World Championship. While the event didn't measure up, our friendship made the experience worthwhile. Perhaps that is a good analogy for our twinning. Regardless of our circumstances, we have stayed connected. I have sponsored him to teach and experience my dojos in Trinidad & Tobago many times. Once, he asked if I would teach his children. As such, he sent his eldest son to Trinidad to learn. Leigh, and his student, Eric Perkio, are the only Purple Dragon outsiders that I have ever allowed to grade and receive a Shodan, 1st Degree Black Belt Rank in my system. I did not do that lightly then, just as I don't pen this without regard. You are only as good as your word and mine is my bond. That has never faltered between us.

In turn, I have been at his dojos and homes across the country teaching my art many, many times. Whatever the place or the weather, the reception has always been warm. For me, it was another frozen moment that stands out as one of profound truth and innocence.

I don't remember the date, but it was springtime. My flight to Toronto had arrived late in the evening, making the four-hour trip to Brockville, Ontario feel like an even longer journey. Everyone was asleep in the Mueller house as my assistant, Anthony Thompson, and I joined our host to find our beds. The house was small, and our rooms were obviously the children's. The kids were elsewhere, so I assumed they had piled into bed with Mom and Dad.

Again, I was cold, but the bed was warm. I felt the joy of pulling the duvet cover up all the way up to my chin. Long travels make for wonderful sleeps! The next morning came fast as one eye opened to catch a little boy peeking into my room. I love kids! This one was a perfect age, perhaps 3 or 4 years old, and as our eyes met, I gave him a big smile and a quiet *"Good Morning."*

Having caught his curiosity off guard, the little boy's eyes got big and he dashed off. Leigh Mueller ran, yelling down the hallway, into the arms of his father, *"Daddy, daddy there's a man with a black head sleeping in my bed!"* Yes, I had been cold in Canada again. But this time it was a little boy's innocent excitement that warmed my heart. You see, children don't pretend, and they can't ignore the obvious. Young Leigh didn't see a black man in his home; what he saw was a black head, blankets up to the chin in his bed! I love kids!

It is a story I tell every single time I see Leigh and, to this day, I get the warm feeling accompanied by a big belly laugh.

I have known the Mueller's and Canada's Best Karate for a long, long time. I have seen them struggle, I have seen them succeed and I have seen them evolve. You can always tell how good an organization is by the quality of its students. They have always had good, honest, and talented students. Perhaps I have helped a little to grow their technique and expand their martial knowledge. If so, I am grateful for how our twinning has made us all better and our friendship has remained strong.

My granny taught me how to read people. If she was suspicious about someone's intention or nature she would ask *"Does he know what time it is?"*

Truth to power. She wanted to know if I saw what she saw.

Sensei Bob Mueller has always had good timing and an unencumbered spirit. I've known him as a builder, a Martial Artist, an entrepreneur, and an amazing award-winning artist and author. Yes, a kindred spirit!

All of that is great, but sometimes it is the simplest act; like someone bringing you out of the cold that makes a big difference. Time reveals the truth, and warmth is felt on the inside as well as the outside. I am happy to say that the twinning with Canada's Best continues to this day.

A CANADIAN CONUNDRUM

DON WARRENER

"I had to get out of Canada- too damn cold!" he said. With that, this unusual man sold what he had, pulled up stakes, and moved to the U.S.A. The California sunshine did a lot to heal the coldness he felt from some contemporaries as well as the Canadian winters. It also fueled the fire in his belly. Hell, if Arnold Schwarzenegger, a German man who could not speak English when he landed in America, could make it in Hollywood and beyond, so could Don Warrener.

To me, Don Warrener is an enigma. For over 4 decades I have watched him operate martial arts schools, publishing houses and real estate developments while creating intermittent businesses and motivational seminars. And that was just in Canada!

Don Warrener is a bit of a riddle and somewhat controversial. No one who has ever known or dealt with him could put him into a tidy box or paint him into a corner. He always knew, in so many different ways, how to move. Some say he is a cheat, while others call him an honorable Sensei. Perhaps a better word for him would be a paradox or a conundrum.

That aside, I can say with all truth that he helped me in many ways, particularly when I was starting my first professional Karate School. He introduced me to people, gave me advice, and for a fee he taught me the basics of the karate business with his 1980's Martial Arts Business seminar. His laugh is infectious, and he was a friend to me when others were not. On the other hand, and I say this to be accurate, outside of his many direct students, he has his share of detractors. Unfortunately, like most ambitious go-getters, he left a wake of discontent on his path to success.

If you know him, you know his favorite saying is, "NEXT!" Frankly, I can't argue with that expression. If you are in business, and particularly in the martial arts, you better develop a thick skin.

I believe it was his unprecedented determination and drive that created his thick skin. I saw it again in the fall of 2005 when I was in L.A. for a meeting with NFL great Dick Butkus's lawyer. Butkus was interested in a new art product that I had created. As part of this trip, I planned to visit Don and had brought along a piece of artwork I'd created for him. As with any meeting with Warrener, it was fun, and he was full of stories. When I asked him how his new video business was doing, he told me this origin story. His oration, and the way he practically conjured up a successful start in a very hard city, is one that the Harvard School of Business should teach!

"I got here in January, about 5 years ago, with nothing." he started.

Yes, he had a few bucks, but he didn't know anyone, not a soul. He'd sold his Canadian businesses, but with no income or prospects, he knew that the money wouldn't last long. Warrener needed to get going as fast as he could. In February, the local Los Angeles community has a big martial arts festival around Chinese New Year. Everyone who is anyone shows up to see and be seen. That year was the Year of the Dragon – a biggie for Martial Artists and the celestial beast. Don was ready.

With a big laugh, he said, *"Like I said, I knew nothing and no one, but I did have a plan. I bought an expensive baby blue suit, I mean really baby blue, and the brightest yellow tie you have ever seen. It was epic!"* He also had 1000 great-looking business cards that said, in big bold letters, DON WARRENER, Producer. The festival was about 10 days long so he committed himself that he would give out 100 business cards by meeting at least 100 new people every day.

"I would make people remember me or at the very least - that damn yellow tie!" Keep in mind, this is Hollywood. Everybody has brass balls there so he needed to stand out or he would get crushed.

His smile turned intense as he said, *"My goal was to connect with someone good. I needed to meet someone really good - a person who could help me started in this new world."* By the end of the 2nd day, he met Issac Florentine, an established movie director and fellow martial artist. They hit it off immediately and formed a studio called Rising Sun Productions. Within weeks they began creating martial arts content for every style, system, personality, and expert you can imagine. Today their studio has over 2500 titles under a new brand called Warrener

Entertainment. It's one of the largest martial arts video production companies in the country.

This isn't a rags to riches story, but it is indicative of the big personality and the force Don Warrener is, and has always been. While he had been successful at home in Canada, making the big move and putting everything on the line has created a storybook ending. These days Warrener, the Canadian Conundrum, seems almost as big as his dreams.

CANADA'S CONNECTION

TO O'SENSEI RICHARD KIM
BY DON WARRENER

I first met Sensei Richard Kim in 1973 with an introduction from my first Sensei, Benny Allen. Allen was tough as nails but kind and gentle as a feather. He was the best fighting instructor anyone could ever have wished for.

The next time I saw Sensei Kim was when I walked into the Chinese YMCA in San Francisco, California. I just knew he might be the man I was searching for, as I was looking for a new mentor, coach, Sensei, or master. He was tall for an oriental man and had an air of confidence. It was a quality unlike any man I have ever met. His bowtie and the fancy watch (that was also an alarm) made him appear to be something special to me.

Please trust me, as I have met them all.

All the great masters like Gogen "The Cat" Yamaguchi, Hidetaka Nishiyama, Morio Higaonna, Eiichi Miyazato, Shoshin Nagamine, and Wally Jay. I've trained in their dojos and have been in their classes but none of them had what he had. Sensei was not just a great fighter; he was a true leader of men. He recorded 44 fights in the ring, losing only two. I once arrogantly asked how he had lost the two fights? Without hesitation, he said, *"they cheated me by rubbing rosin in my eyes during the fight".*

After meeting him I knew I needed more, so I immediately invited him to come to Canada and teach at my school. He accepted the invitation on the spot. It was the best move I ever made.

After his first time in Canada, I invited him twice a year and every year thereafter. Although I paid him handsomely, it was the best money I ever spent. No one else had the kind of information that he shared with us. There were lots of katas - far too many to remember, but it was his personification of everything he taught that renders him in the rafters as the most complete teacher I ever saw. He was "THE SENSEI" and that is all there was to it. He knew how to handle people and how to be a leader. His lectures were second to none and as informative as any book I have ever read.

One of his skills was his detailed knowledge of body language. He could read a person as they walked by, and then tell you everything about the person. He proved it to his inner core of students not once, but on several occasions.

On one occasion, we were in Paris, France for a summer camp. We were sitting on a famous Boulevard, the Champs Elysees, sipping coffee and eating fine pastries, when he started talking of his wartime experiences and about the "Colonel".

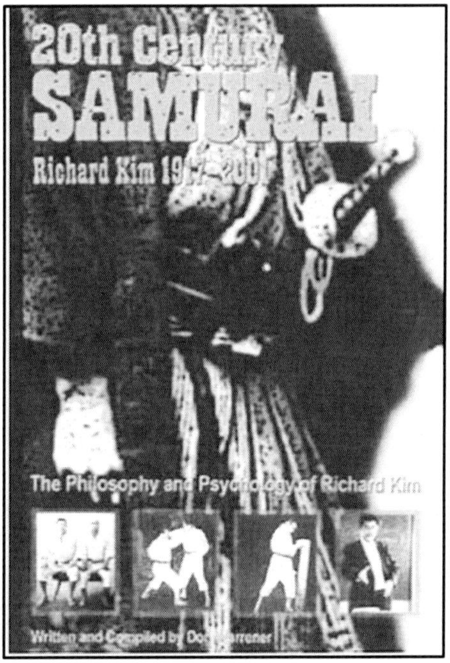

The Colonel, who I later discovered to be Kinji Doihar, was the worst of the worst of the Japanese in WW2. So terrible that he was hung by allied forces at the end of the war for his atrocities. He was Sensei Kim's mentor.

Sitting there, he told us how to read a person just by the way they walked. It was a technique he had learned at a Japanese Spy school in Shanghai. Sensei said, *"OK, the tenth person to walk by, going from there to there - I will tell you all you need to know about him."*

The people started walking by 1, 2 3....10 and then a gentleman wearing a tailor-made tweed suit and carrying a leather briefcase walked by. Sensei just sat like a guard dog poised, watching everything about him. Then he said, "OK he is a lawyer, going to court. He has a wife and two children at home. He's very wealthy and punctual, and he likes the good things in life; fine whiskey, fine women, and on and on he went.

When I asked how he knew all that he said, he replied, *"Don, did you see what kind of watch he was wearing? It was a Patek Phillipe, and his shoes were Dalkes, He's the right age to have two kids as he is about 35, wearing a men's wedding ring and the courthouse is across the street where he crossed. The expensive suit he's wearing is English herringbone and his mustache was impeccably trimmed. Plus he was checking his watch, as it was almost 1:00 pm. That is when court starts."*

Wow! He was right on every single thing he said. Things I would never have looked at, he noticed. That was Sensei Kim.

His knowledge of martial arts can only be described as significant. He was not a kicker, but his hands were strong and lightning fast. His wide range of katas stemmed back to his teachers in Japan. Yoshida Kotaro, who he always called "my Sensei", was in tight with the other Tokyo martial artists including top names like Moreihei Ueshiba. Sensei Kim trained with him and Gogen Yamaguchi, receiving his 2nd dan in 1949 along with the future Kyokushin Kai master, Mas Oyama.

Kim also received special training from Toyama Kanken in Okinawan Kobudo weaponry, memorizing over 50 weapons katas. He also learned several unique weapons, like throwing knives, that he taught us only once. This special training came from Yoshida Sensei, who was trained by Sokaku Takaeda in the ways of the Ninja in the 1800s.

It's safe to say that Mr. Kim was a walking encyclopedia of knowledge.

In summary, he was, as Black Belt Magazine once called him, the *"Pied Piper of Martial Arts"* His direct students were mostly highly educated professors, police officers, and intellectuals. Many were part of the silicon-valley elite think-tanks. Additionally, there were even some high school dropouts who were like sheep following the master. Sensei welcomed all people, men and women, who wanted to learn.

In 1998 I moved from the cold Hamilton, Ontario winters to the warm waters of Los Angeles, California. I wanted to be closer to him. Sadly, he passed away only a few years after I arrived in LA. I was able to see him in the Bay area several times and the last time still puts a lump in my throat. We were both at a Black Belt Grading in Santa Cruz, where he had invited me to join him at the head table as part of the grading board. For some reason, I was very nervous as we sat silently observing the test.

Finally, he leaned over to me and asked, *"Do you need any more Dan Gradings?"*

The question caught me a little off guard, so I just said, *"No Sensei, I am just fine, but thank you anyway."* I had received my Shodan decades before in 1968 from Benny Allen and after 30 years I was a 5th Dan with Sensei Kim.

"I didn't think so," he responded as we continued to sit there saying nothing more.

At the end of the test, I said, *"Well Sensei, I must leave now. I have a long drive back to LA."*

"OK, Don. No problem. Take care of yourself." These were his last words to me. I stopped at the dojo door to look back at the man who changed my life for the better. Somehow, I just knew it would be the last time I saw him. I left with a tear in my eye, as I have now as I write this. On November 8th, 2001 he was gone.

To honor him I wrote a book named, "The 20th Century Samurai." It tells his entire story and I honestly believe he was the greatest martial artist of the 20th Century.

May he rest in peace. Don Warrener

THE CANADIAN EXCEPTION

HANSHI PATRICK McCARTHY

While I had seen him many times before at tournaments, and Richard Kim's 9th Dan Hanshi seminars, I had never spoken to him. The little bit I did know about his character came from my dojo partner. Whether it was rivalry, jealousy, or fact, conservative Rick Marshall did not care for Patrick McCarthy.

It was easy to see why, as he was everything Marshall was not.

McCarthy was a vibrant peacock of a showman, full of confidence, and very talented. He also had what I can only describe as a photographic memory. If he saw something once, he could, not only retain it, but almost instantly perform it! This skill belied a far deeper ability and appreciation for the art of Karate Do than his façade pretended.

I was with Bateson's Karate School when I first saw him compete in Weapons and Kata competitions. McCarthy won a lot of tournaments. He was a top competitor on the west coast circuit and given his talent, he also seemed to have the ear of Sensei Kim. He was always asking questions. This irritated Marshall, since he had been given the title as the Butoku Kai Western Canadian Representative, and McCarthy was always *"eating his lunch"* so to speak. To me, and given Rick's influence, Pat seemed aloof and somewhat distant, so I gave him a wide berth.

In 1982, being new to the Butoku Kai Organization, I was cautious of the infighting that surrounded the leadership. When Richard Kim spoke, everyone listened, and when he was quiet, they seemed to elbow each other to be near him. I witnessed a lot of distrust and pettiness. It was the opposite for me, as I just wanted to stay under the radar. I was uncertain of the protocol when I was around the master, and as everyone seemed very uptight, I was happy to listen to Rick's consul and keep to myself.

Unfortunately, being on the sidelines doesn't get you very far. I was Rick's Dojo partner and he needed to me be visible. He told me that my Bateson Karate rank of Nidan (2nd Degree Black Belt) needed to be qualified by testing and grading for Sensei Kim. If I did well, it would help our Dojo and assist Rick to grow his status.

All competition is a matter of degree and comparison.

I expected there would be several people on the test with me, but when I arrived at the dojo there was only one other person grading. Pat McCarthy was warming up.

Once I got over the thought of being compared with him, I don't remember much about the grading other than my mother was there. Of the two memories that remain, I remember doing well, save for a couple of technical errors, and seeing McCarthy's poise. As Pat was testing for Yondan (4th Degree Black Belt), Richard Kim threw him a couple of curveballs and he took them without faltering.

His performance made a good impression on me. That impression lasted for over 30 years, as we hadn't spoken to each other even though we shared the grading floor. It was just a brief moment at the beginning of a long journey. Over the coming decades, I became so busy making my career that I barely noticed that Patrick McCarthy had left the west coast scene.

When, in 1984, I traveled east 3000 miles to begin my professional Karate career, McCarthy also went east - the Far East. Unsatisfied with his knowledge about Karate-do, he traveled to Japan and then through southeast Asia seeking the history and hidden truths behind the ancient art. Along the way, he learned the Japanese language and formally studied everything he could to enhance his knowledge. Perhaps, unlike others who had traveled a similar path, McCarthy's savvy took him beyond the ordinary. He was always questioning and looking for more out of what he was learning. He didn't want to simply know how something was done. He wanted to know why.

So widespread and fascinating were his studies that they resulted in the publication of many books and he became a best-selling Martial Arts author. He cross-referenced the information he had learned, from which he developed a unique perception and vision. While doing this, he began to formulate a system of understanding about many forgotten Karate insights. This would make him world-renowned. Patrick McCarthy rediscovered applications and techniques that had been lost in time for many generations.

Time has a way of circling back. In 2016, I noticed an internet post featuring a McCarthy Hanshi interview. I listened with amazement. The man I had known had now traveled the world and taken his training to the highest level possible. He left petty jealousies and small-minded people behind as his teaching picked up where his mentor, Richard Kim, had left off. I was fascinated by what he had to say and wanted to hear more, so I looked back 35 years and then reached out to him.

From his home in Australia a zoom call was arranged. After almost 40 years without a word, we spoke for over two hours. Hanshi was gracious and every bit the master teacher that his reputation had promised. His photographic memory and capacity for knowledge had also come full circle as his talent to question had become his ability to impart wisdom.

Looking at the depth of his work, I have come to think of him as the Canadian Exception. A widely recognized ambassador for the art, Patrick McCarthy, 9th Dan Hanshi, is now a treasured friend and mentor to CBK. He fittingly resides with his wife Yuriko in Naha, Okinawa - the ancient birthplace of Karate Do. There, he continues to oversee his worldwide organization [The International Ryukyu Karate Research Society], and to study, train, travel and teach to the world.

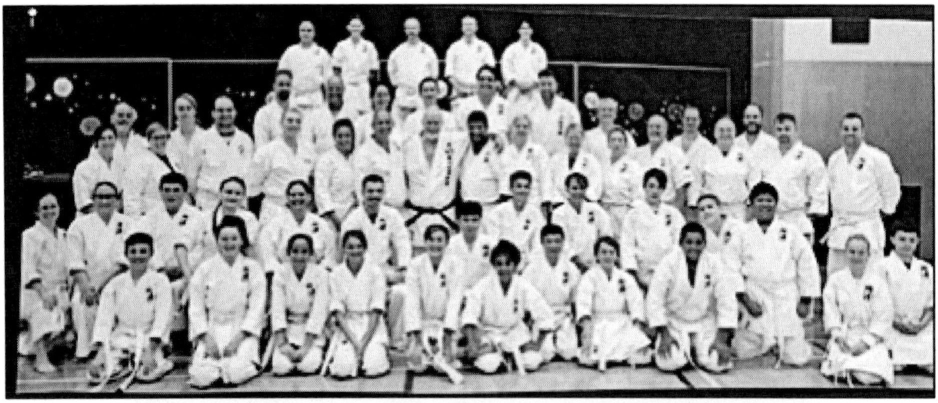

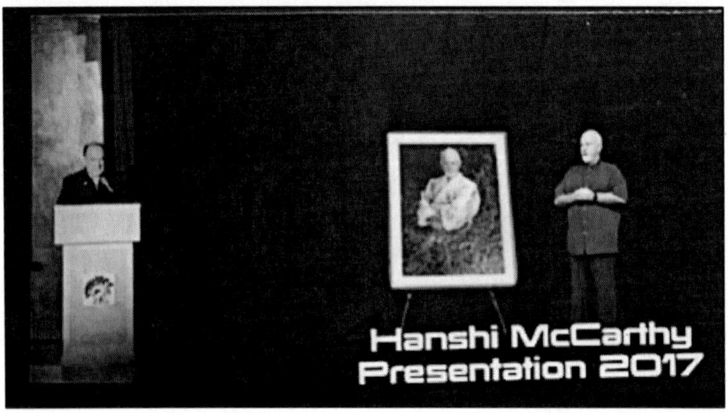

IN SEARCH OF?

BY PATRICK MCCARTHY

Jack Dempsey said, "*The best defense is a good offense.*" No one is sure if his idea came from something uttered earlier by George Washington, but such sage advice, nonetheless, has since been applied in many areas of life, including the fighting arts. That said, you can't defend against, "what you can't see!"

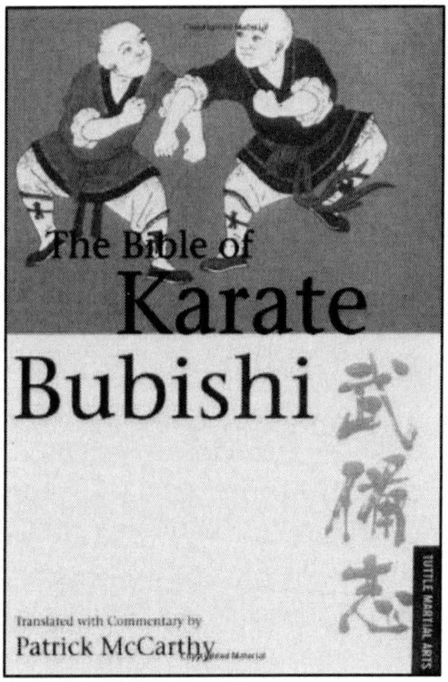

What I came to see, has become one of my deepest beliefs; that there are no styles ... unless you call teaching/learning methods styles! "*If forced to distinguish the differences between these sects, then I would have to say that it is only teaching methods that divide them.*" I believe that not everybody can do the same thing the same way to achieve the same outcomes... and an even deeper definition of this is that "*Even you, will not be able to continue to do the same thing the same way, across the spectrum of your life, to achieve the same outcomes, if only because of the* ravages of *age.*"

My name is Patrick McCarthy, 9th Dan Hanshi. I've spent my entire life traveling the world, researching, studying, training, and teaching martial arts. The following is a short, brief part of the story of my adventures and what I learned. With age, I am often asked how I began Koryu Uchinadi system. By the mid-1980s, I had spent nearly two decades vigorously learning various fighting arts. About fifteen of those years, I spent actively competing in a myriad of municipal, provincial, national, and international competitions. The last ten of those years were spent teaching in my own school. No longer satisfied with the confines of a modern tradition, and hungry to delve deeper into the original art, but unable to find it anywhere in the West, I considered the idea of stepping outside my comfort zone.

In the summer of 1985, I packed my bags and traveled to Okinawa, having no idea what I'd find. Over the next decade, my continued quest for learning became a remarkable journey of discovery throughout Japan, across the East China Sea to Taiwan, and beyond. Coming into contact with a myriad of fighting arts from as far north as the Forbidden City, and beyond the Great Wall to the Shaolin Monastery, to the south of the Yangtze in Fujian and Guangdong, and finally into the abyss of SE Asia.

Probably better described elsewhere, in a separate publication, the experiences I gained during that wonderful era of extensive travel, cross-training, and independent research, opened doors of learning that changed my entire perspective.

With academia knocking on my door in 1993, a College offer to transform my collective experiences into an accredited system of teaching to benefit instructors entering the fighting arts industry as an occupation, presented yet another unforeseen learning opportunity. Over the next few years, and with the support of colleagues in the Faculty of Education, I worked diligently to create a basis for instructor candidates to not just better understand how to learn, but a way in which to explain, analyze, describe and predict its process. A most enlightening learning experience, all on its own, I ultimately succeeded in creating a theory-based and outcome-orientated instructor's training program. That program would also become the basis of *Koryu Uchinadi* [古流沖縄手]; aka KU.

"The Needs of the Many Outweigh the Needs of the Few."

Despite what it's morphed into, I never actually conceived KU with the idea of it ever becoming, "*A Style.*" I was more than happy for it to remain a unique delivery method of empowering one's existing practices. The many enthusiasts I came into contact with during the first few years of introducing its practices through the seminars I delivered around the world, had all come from various fighting arts styles. I met with great success then, and, during the entire time, seminar participants kept asking me, "*What style was I teaching*?"

I typically described what I was teaching as a unique collection of old-school 2-person application practices that I had collectively amassed from my historical studies, a journey of research, and cross-training in China, SE Asia, and Japan. Still, such an explanation didn't seem to be enough for enthusiastic seminar participants, who were bent upon knowing more about this, "*UNIQUE STYLE.*" So, despite explaining the seemingly easy-to-understand process, it seemed to go unnoticed.

Knowing this history, it's easier to understand how and why KU had become so popular, so quickly. On the one hand, enthusiasts throughout the world were ready to embrace a more practical interpretation of a rule-bound tradition which had become so overly ritualized and dysfunctional. On the other hand, those who did not buy into this "*more innovative*" approach, to better understand the art [i.e.Kata], believed I was, "*appallingly disrespectful and a direct threat to a timeless tradition*."

It soon became evident that my desire to usher in a new way of examining the dysfunctional parts of this art was not being welcomed by all. Perhaps, however, this is a topic best left for another conversation... as the 1990s' anti-McCarthy/KU criticism was in the extreme, and ad hominem was the tool of choice, employed by my detractors, seeking to undermine my credibility; "*Associating with McCarthy will close many doors of opportunity in Okinawa*!" What we find most amusing these days, more than two decades later, is seeing those same detractors being congratulated now for teaching what they so harshly criticized me for. It's always easy to know the right thing to do AFTER someone else has already done it! Reminds me of the Russian joke, "*Their future is clear. It's their past that keeps changing*!"

I mention the distractors as a means of balancing my intent. I believe deeply in the study, history, and culture of this tradition. I'm inspired by how some of its pioneers had established a symbiosis with the art, so that their lives became as much a product of it, as did it become a product of their lives.

I entitled this piece, "*On The Shoulders of Giants*," to emphasize the value of, "*using the wisdom gained from the great thinkers who have come before us to make progress*." Wonderfully expressed, Newton's idea of discovering the truth by building on previous discoveries assures progress, and this is exactly why traditions must be preserved and studied. Walter Lippmann [1889-1974] makes the point clear, "*Men can know more than their ancestors did if they start with a knowledge of what their ancestors had already learned*." Nietzsche said, "*You have your way. I have my way. As for the right way, the correct way, and the only way, it does not exist*."

Therefore, forging your own way demands nothing less than finding a worthy mentor to help guide the way. A Japanese proverb reads; [千日の勤學より一時の名匠/*Sen'nichi no kingaku yori ichiji no meishou*] "*Better than a thousand days of diligent study is one day with a great teacher*."

Knowing when the time has come to turn the page and move on, is not always an easy decision. Nowhere is such a thing more difficult than during a journey, where the destination has not yet been reached. Believing that traditional meant authentic, and by extension, functional, I did not fully understand that the modern practice had become so overly ritualized that it no longer exampled the original art. At that point, the most intelligent choice made itself quite apparent. When I reflect upon that decision, and the many challenges it represented, I had no idea of what a fascinating journey lay ahead but only that genuine passion was fueling a quest for meaning ... this was the entry onto a pathway where KU was conceived.

Paraphrasing Funakoshi Gichin, "*Training is like boiling water, turn the heat off and the water gets cold...*" therefore, keeping the flame alight remains the learner's torch upon an endless journey down a pathway of discovery.

Wonderfully grateful even to my detractors, as the many stones were continually thrown at me, has resulted in not only being able to construct an impenetrable foundation but also valuing Plato's warning; "*One of the penalties for refusing to participate in politics is that you end up being governed by inferiors.*" My late instructor, Kinjo Hiroshi, told me, as a young man growing up in Okinawa, no one was more surprised than were his own teachers, family, and friends, that Karate ever became so popular, let alone evolve into an international phenomenon.

Additionally, and in spite of the wisdom handed down by Teijunsoku [程順則 1663-1734], few from Kinjo's era, or before, knew about, cared much for, and/or placed any emphasis upon the pursuit of its history and/or scholarly study. That said, Karate is, nonetheless, a microcosm of the culture from which it comes; i.e. a miniature representation of Zen simplicity and Japanese social values.

Therefore, it does make wonderful sense, that the more we study the art, the more we learn about its culture, people, and ultimately ourselves. Liking this to a pathway, it depends how far down we get before it becomes evident that the destination is not the goal, it is the Journey.

To close, I can't help but think of a quote by Douglas Adams [1952-2001]; "*I may not have gone where I intended to go, but I think I have ended up where I needed to be.*" I welcome you to stand on my shoulders.

The MOST ADVENTUROUS MAN I HAVE EVER KNOWN

JOHN CRAIG

I invited him to my home in the late fall of 1999, as the 20th century was about to become history. It was a timely opportunity as my special guest had information, among other things, about the coming turmoil of the new millennium. John Craig didn't need a big build up, but I gave it regardless, as I called him the most adventurous man I had ever met. The audience was made up of select group of somewhat nervous and excited CBK Black Belt students. As John took a breath before beginning, the collective was holding theirs with anticipation. He looked everyone squarely in the eye and said, *"Thank you for your kind invitation, but please forgive me if I misspeak or break a custom or two here - you see it is this first time I have been to this planet!"*

It was kind of like a Rod Serling intro to the TV show "*Twilight Zone!*" and John's discussion did not disappoint. The next few hours were full of adventure, mystery, and tales about his magical journeys. He presented, with his best Scottish brogue, *"a wee taste"* of his life and personality. It delighted and enlightened everyone present.

John Craig is a good friend who I admire greatly. I love hearing his insights, particularly when he puts on his Scottish swagger to emphasize a point. Of all the charismatic characters I have ever met, John Craig, aka Echan Deravy, is the most fearless, free spirit of them all. Like a modern-day William Wallace, the 12th-century warrior of Braveheart fame, he has dared and defied the odds throughout his life.

I first met him when, as a new immigrant to Canada, he registered his 3 children into my Victoria Karate Dojo. With his martial arts background and inquisitive nature, it didn't take long for us to become fast friends. What began as friendship quickly turned into an adventure, as we traveled to Hong Kong on an entrepreneurial quest. While the Chinese business attempt failed, our mutual respect has never faltered.

The week we spent in Hong Kong, while unsuccessful financially, was not wasted time. We shared stories and discovered that we were kindred spirits. I learned a lot about him and his incredible journeys.

Like me, John had left school and his Aberdeen Scotland home when he was 16 years old. While I drove 100 miles north on Vancouver Island to begin my life, he hitchhiked 8,546 miles south from Aberdeen to Cape Town, South Africa to start his. How you hitchhike across the Mediterranean Sea is beyond me - that must have been a pretty good trick! He told about traveling through some war-torn parts of Africa, many times sleeping in ditches as protection from militant militias that roamed the countryside. From Cape Town, he carried on through India and Thailand, finally arriving in Kyoto Japan hoping to become a Zen Monk. He did all this before his 20th birthday.

As a young man in Japan, his thoughts of becoming a monk faded as he studied oriental medicine. He became a Doctor of Acupuncture, a University Lecturer and an accomplished martial artist. His training elevated him to a 5th Dan in Kyudo (Zen Archery), and then into many aspects of Zen meditation and Japanese arts.

Along with his formal education, he developed an instinctual head for business by connecting his passions for language, culture and travel. For the next 20 years, with his family in tow, he began a dual life as father/husband, and world-traveling entrepreneur. His company, Japan Consultants, brokered Real Estate deals between Canada and Japan, and his adventure tours took Japanese Nationals around the world. He guided them to the Pyramids in Egypt and other sacred sites like Machu Picchu, Rosslyn Chapel, and the rain forests of the Amazon.

As a skilled teacher and lecturer, he developed courses in *"Remote Viewing"* (once a top-secret CIA technique) and spoke about many metaphysical phenomena he had witnessed. Along the way, he researched alternative theories about space travel, religions, and altered states of consciousness.

Craig has penned over 40 books in his adopted Japanese tongue, writing about the various subjects he has researched. As an accomplished author he became the most successful non-Japanese speaker in Japan. His language skills allowed him to interpret Japanese for Mikhail Gorbachev and he became a noted interviewer. His interviews connected him with the likes of

Deepak Chopra, Graham Hancock and Wade Davis, all while rubbing elbows with many of the best and brightest minds around the globe.

Additionally, he has two full-length feature film credits to his name that highlight his earthing and walking adventures. His latest film documents his 636 kilometers walk barefoot across Iceland. Yes barefoot! You read that correctly!

I say he is the most fearless man I have ever met, not just because of the ferocity of his nature or the depth of his martial skills, but rather for his ability to face the unknown. There is not a door he wouldn't knock on, a room he is afraid to enter, or a subject he is willing to ignore. He is a seeker.

I suspect, had he lived 500 years ago, he may well have been a swashbuckler of sorts – perhaps discovering America and the new world. Yet with all his bravado, he is a true man of the world, as he is one of the most simple and unaffected people I have ever met. John's depth, discipline, and compassion are almost as profound as his adventurous nature.

When I think of John, I remember him saying to me, *"Don't tell me what you think, Laddie. Tell me your heart!"* Like him, it's a simple but profound statement.

I'm also reminded of the Zen Koan that Sensei Kim taught. He said Enlightenment is – the Zen Miracle.

When hungry, I eat.

When thirsty, I drink.

When angered, I forgive.

Knowing John and being his friend for the past decades is one of the great fortunes of my life. I hope you have the opportunity to meet him one day.

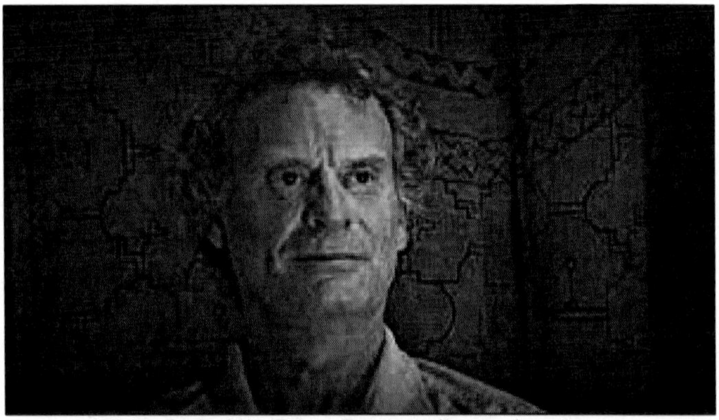

John Craig AKA Echan Deravy –director / producer
Earth Pilgrams and Why on Earth?

ONE ARROW, ONE LIFE

IN PRAISE OF MARTIAL ARTS
BY JOHN CRAIG

Steven Seagal is a big guy. And he has a presence, too. Back in the early nineteen eighties his aikido dojo in Osaka, Tenshin Dojo, contained a lot of my friends. My best buddy Pete, who I had taken to Japan from India in 1974, was his number one Uke at the time. That meant Steve thrashed him on the mats regularly. I would watch. One throw was so violent that Pete almost bit his tongue in half from the force. The randori (freestyle) was particularly exciting as Seagal floored multiple opponents coming from all angles as they all danced their way around the big man on the big tatami floor trying to tackle him.

Tackling martial arts and immersing myself in Japanese culture has been a huge part of my journey. A Scottish-born, lifelong adventurer/researcher, I am John Craig, also known in Japan as the writer and educator Echan Deravy. My feet have touched the tatami of many dojos, in many places.

Juso, where the dojo was located, just north of the main station, was a grubby area of Osaka, but it was close to my acupuncture college, so I took that opportunity to practice my new craft. I needed volunteers to stick needles in. I would treat the victims of Seagal's powerful throws; stiff necks, lower back pains, and swollen joints were commonplace. After classes, we would go out drinking, and Seagal would hold court. He had a big personality. He told tales of battles in the alleys with yakuza gangsters who came to test his skills and later, the plot outlines of his first movie. He, like Sylvestor Stallone before him, was writing a life-changing script for himself in what would become a breakout Hollywood movie. Over a cup of sake, the stories he told were all about his ideas for a future film called "Above the Law", or Nico.

Later I, as a 4th Dan Kyudo man, would teach Seagal the rudiments of Japanese archery. It was challenging, as he, at 6' 4" was so tall with a raised bow, that it was hard to face the makiwara straw bale without him spreading his legs far wider than they should have. I remember him slightly bent at the knees. His hands, like him, were also massive, so getting him to fit into a mitsugake archery glove was no easy task. He was a serious student - for a while at least. We were young then, both the same age, so I am guessing we were about thirty years old.

I distinctly remember staggering down an old shotengai arcade street with his students after drinking a bunch of warm sake. I decided to test them to see if they really could do anything with their aikido when it counts, so I sprung on one of the guys from behind. The answer came quickly; I had no idea how he hit and threw me, slamming into some metal shutters several yards away. I was a fast learner and Seagal was a damned good teacher.

One day we were sitting on an old sofa at the back of his dojo. Together we were watching his students' training when he said offhandedly, *"I'm tired of teaching."*

"Me too," I opined since I was a university lecturer in English. We were both tired and ready for a new adventure. Soon he would certainly be out of the teaching business. As would I. His fate lay in Hollywood, where he would achieve worldwide acclaim. Mine was as a doctor practicing in an acupuncture clinic in Kobe and then, with my growing family, off to a new life in Canada.

Of all the places in the world, the west coast of Canada, particularly Vancouver Island, was a dream of serenity compared to the crowded bustling big city life of Japan. Perfect for me, my wife, and our young children. Among my new experiences, in my new land, I found martial arts entering my life again. However, this time the dojo was not for me, I wanted my children to begin their education.

Bob Mueller is an easy-going and soft-spoken Canadian who embodies a different kind of martial arts teacher. There is never any show of power, though you know full well he has it. In that sense, he is very much of the tradition he teaches, since all Japanese martial artists I know are just the kindest, almost harmless-looking guys you could hope to meet.

I had walked into his newly opened dojo for kids in Victoria. Superkids Karate seemed like an odd name for a dojo, but it was welcoming and perfect for my needs. I had three small children in tow in 1989, the year I left Japan after my 15-year stint. There, I learned oriental medicine, zen, martial arts, and most importantly I learned the language. Becoming fluent in reading, writing, and speaking Japanese was the key to all of it. It transformed me.

The business-like dojo and friendly Bob took in my three kids. They never looked back. Martial arts became a part of their lives and still are. To this day I realize it was perhaps the most important decision about my kids' education I would ever make. And now my grandchildren are doing karate in Victoria - that should speak volumes to any reader who is serious about raising kids without martial arts in the curriculum.

Bob and I immediately clicked and are still good friends. I credit our shared passion for martial arts as being a fundamental reason for our decades-old connection. Though I would return to Japan, and not see Bob for many years, I always knew that he would remain a trusted and honest buddy. What else can you ask for? Trust has everything to do with the training every martial artist has to go through.

Throughout my youth, I had traveled and experienced a great deal of the world. In 1974 there were few Westerners in Japan. My journey across Asia had taken me to India to meet Pete. He had been meditating in a temple for three years, and I figured he needed a metaphorical kick up the arse to get him going. We were 22 years old, too young for enlightenment, and too old for school. I told him I had enough money to get us to Japan and he must come with me. That was how he ended up as Steven Seagal's Uke, and I experienced the big man firsthand. Today Pete is now a sixth dan sensei with seven grandchildren. Time, like the arrow, moves fast.

So, my first gentle hint to the reader is: Time waits for no man - if you are going to do martial arts, please be serious and commit yourselves, for life. Martial Arts is above all, a way of life and as such takes you through life to death. The lessons never end.

Those were heady days for the brave souls. We had made it to Japan with a keen desire to study tea ceremonies, Noh mask making, and every kind of martial art. Of course, the chief purpose for many, like me, who had read the beat poets like Alan Ginsberg and writers like Jack Kerouac and later Alan Watts, was to study and practice Zen. That was my aim at least. Kyoto at that time had become the cultural center of the world. We, the aspiring and motley crowd, got down to the serious business of adapting our spoiled Western minds to the idea of discipline, ethical fortitude, emotional control, and most importantly a strong sense of personal responsibility - all ideas that the sixties had pretty much blown to hell and back. This was the school of schools, and we knew it. Nay, we loved it.

My first karate teacher had been a mountain monk, or yamabushi, for decades before coming down from the hills to teach. A chain smoker, who would regularly smash his shins full force with baseball bats, he had knuckle dusters for knuckles that he would joke about with us. I would go home black and blue - the only white man in his dojo. Those were the days. And I was there.

After a decade coming and going from Canada to Japan as a businessman, I went back to Japan to complete the next stage of my education. Japan tends to demand a lifetime commitment, you see.

Of all my martial arts experiences, it was Japanese Archery that captivated me. Shodo, the art of calligraphy, led me to Kyudo, the way of the bow. As with everything in Japan, I needed an introduction to study ink brush calligraphy and through some good fortune had ended up at the Imperial Palace (of the emperor) police headquarters. The police were specially trained for guarding imperial assets, and though the emperor now resided in Tokyo, the Kyoto Imperial Palace had always been the most sacrosanct residence for the living deity for many generations. To be a palace policeman was a lifelong duty and all the men studied martial arts as well as other cultural pursuits.

My teacher took me through the steps of mixing ink with the slow rubbing of a hard black ink stick inside the mixing stone basin with water added. One day he told me about Kyudo. I was immediately smitten with the idea of having no opponent and yet still practice a traditional martial art - one that was a special favorite of the samurai. Thanks to the German philosophy professor Eugen Herrigel and his book Zen in the Art of Archery, Kyudo had developed the name Zen Archery in the West. In Japanese, it means simply "The Way of the Bow."

Interestingly the practice of seated meditation we call Zen is termed Zazen in Japanese. Sit Meditate in short. Unknown even to many Japanese, it has a counterpart called Ritsuzen or Standing Zen. I decided to fully immerse myself in Kyudo's Standing Zen; right from the first day, I was introduced to it at the Imperial Palace Kyudojo in central Kyoto. I was in my twenties then, and again, the only foreigner there. Most of the men were retired policemen, and the average age was easily sixty-plus on weekdays, but on the weekends, it was full of all age groups and types of people, male and female.

My first experience watching kyudo was unforgettable.

The dojo is set in front of a 28-meter long empty space. At one end there is a covered area full of banked earth on which are placed the five or six simple targets, about a foot in diameter.

Targets are placed at the level of the archer's feet and are so far away they look like a dollar coin in the archer's eyes. Gravity pulls the fast-moving arrow far enough down after release that the targets are set at the perfect height.

This day I watched my future first teacher, Ida Sensei, at practice in front of a densely packed straw bale held at six foot high: the makiwara. He was wearing the white training dogi and a black hakama, the pleated skirt that drops down to reveal white tabi socks. All Kyudoka must have this formal wear. With his seventh dan teacher rank, he would of course wear a full kimono at important events. He was a short, balding man with thick glasses who had retired as a policeman at about 65 years old. Slight of build, it was hard to imagine him as an archer.

"Observe this John san" he had said, as he stood in front of the practice makiwara. The bow sailed up over his chest and head, hoisted by both his arms gently until its seven-foot length could go no higher. Standing in front of him, I saw how he kept his right arm as high as possible, as his left arm swung the bow around until his thick glove holding the bowstring was just above his right ear. With consummate calm and grace, and with no sign of the effort it must take to pull the bow from that position I saw his right elbow move down and backward until the bowstring was even with his lips at full draw. Amazingly, there he remained at full draw for several seconds. A seemingly long time.

What happened next totally astonished me. An unforgettable sound rang out as his gloved hand moved backward with incredible speed. He had shot the practice arrow deep into the long straw bale with such natural poise that the bowstring literally sang with a loud, snap-like retort, a bit like a whip. At the same instant, I noticed something else. His grip on the huge bow, one-third up from its bottom leaving a majestic two-thirds of bent bow still above his hand, was so delicate that the bow spun around on release. This caused the bowstring to hit the back of his left forearm. I could barely comprehend what was going on, but that sound, a vibration that only a trained archer can produce, still rings in my ears.

It has been known in Japanese mythology for centuries as *"the sound that drives devils away."* It is sharp, clear, and as my years of training continued, it is the most sought-after prize that only perfect posture and relaxation can ever allow. The thumb and middle finger are the only points of contact with the bow, like holding an egg as I was taught, thus allowing it to spin around on release. But it takes a long time of practice before that happens too.

I hungered to learn and practiced with great desire. So much so, that it impeded my ability. When performing, we all find it hard to relax; however, relaxation is surely a key to all martial arts. I felt that I was in a dojo with ancient remnants, the last vestiges of the samurai. Then, they were mostly old men who had been through the war – men who deeply respected their emperor. Gentlemen to the core, they were also among the kindest group of men I had ever been blessed to be with. They shared their secrets of technique with me. As many years of training passed, my still youthful vigor and pride seemingly overwhelmed their secrets. It was a huge obstacle they could see, but I could not.

My intensity and desire to hit the target were exactly what was preventing it from happening. It was the damnedest thing! No matter how much I tried, how many hundreds of arrows I flew over that space, it was only the occasional fluke shot that would hit. This was what Ida sensei meant by saying the opponent is yourself!

One day I was so exasperated after a daily practice that I decided it was time to quit this stupid Ritsuzen pretension. I told myself I would go back to only sitting Zen. That afternoon, as I approached the full draw position or Kai, I had absolutely no desire left to hit the target. Defeated and tired, I was empty. I had decided this would be my last session, so what did it matter now? Then it happened! The sound of the first bowstring release was near perfect and was immediately followed by the satisfying thud of a clear hit. I loaded the second arrow, which was held by my little finger as I had shot on the first. I was not in the least excited by the hit. I was devoid of emotion. The second arrow lodged next to the first, just off of the center bull's eye. As I went to reload, I sensed the old teachers were watching me carefully, alone as a reflection, on the polished wooden floor. The same thing happened again and again until Ida sensei came bounding across the floor and grabbed me by the shoulders.

With a sense of great happiness mixed with a stern expression, he said, *"Remember this John san! Never forget this! Each arrow is like a whole life. You only get one arrow to shoot at a time! One arrow! One Life!"*

It's a vivid memory for that moment indeed. More importantly, it's a mantra about how to live life - one moment at a time. These days fewer and fewer people practice traditional Zen Archery in Japan. Bamboo bows and handcrafted bamboo arrows take a lot of maintenance, and yes, they are costly. But that is not the reason. The whole purpose of Kyudo is expressed by three simple words on the huge plaque at the entrance.

Truth. Goodness. Beauty.

Today, only the non-Japanese seem drawn to such prosaic and outdated ideas like that. Since I departed from the dojo, Kyudo has seen massive interest from the West and in particular Europe. Like Karate, it has moved across the world, as individuals find that martial arts probably have everything they could possibly want. If only they would devote themselves to discipline mind and body. If they could stay the course each arrow of training would reveal its value.

There is the paradox and there is the draw...

Bob Mueller is not Japanese. Neither am I. But we have both lived long lives built on Japanese martial arts foundations. And as such, so have his students and then their students. Down through centuries, it is always the same. What matters, lasts...

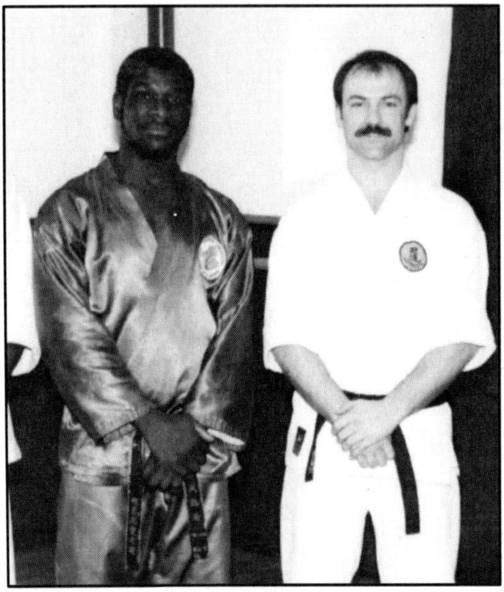

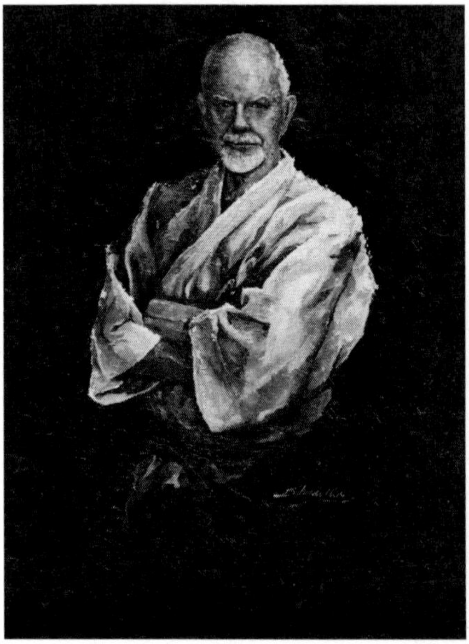

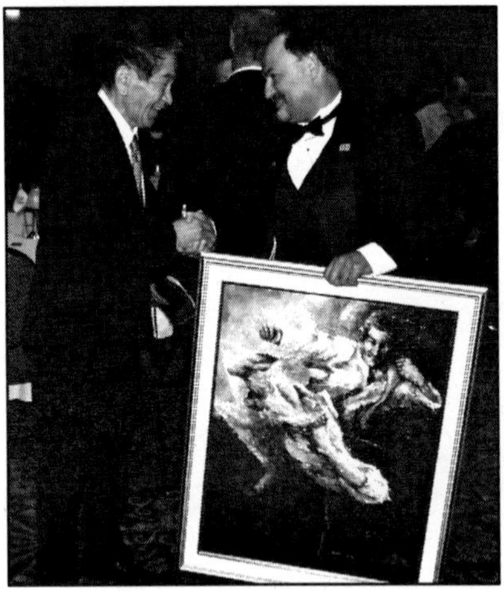

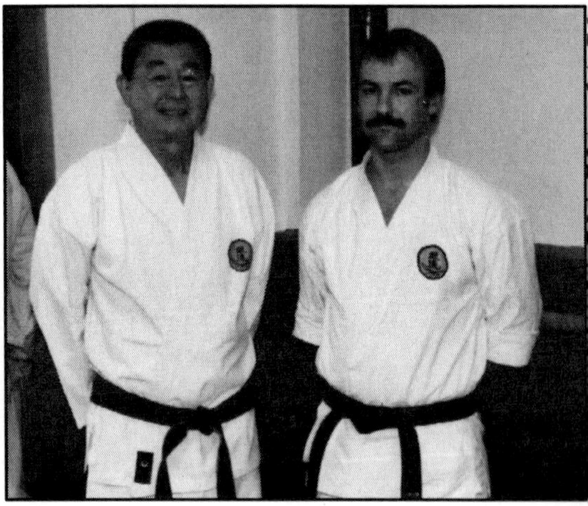

With Don Jacob 1987, Pat McCarthy Portrait 2017
With M. Tsuruoka 2014 Portrait, With Richard Kim 1986

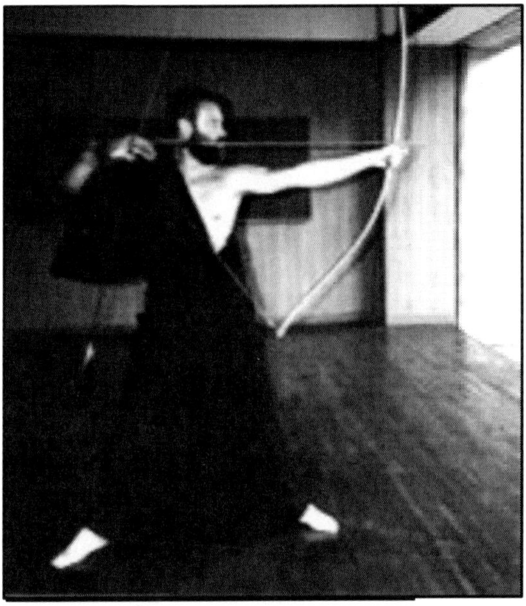

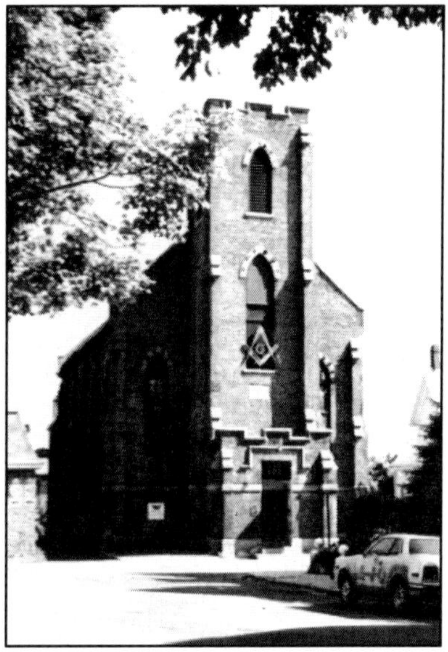

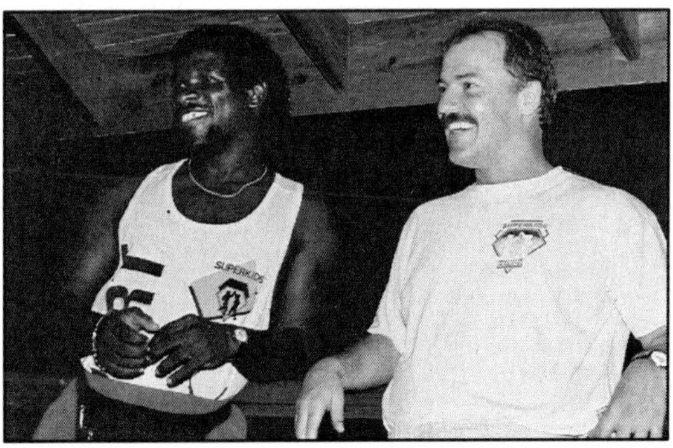

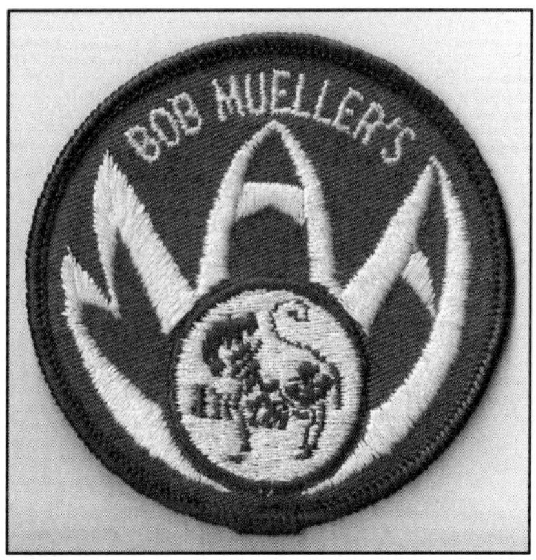

John Craig Kyudo 1980, Brockville Church Dojo
With Don Jacob Tobago 1988, Original BMMA Crest

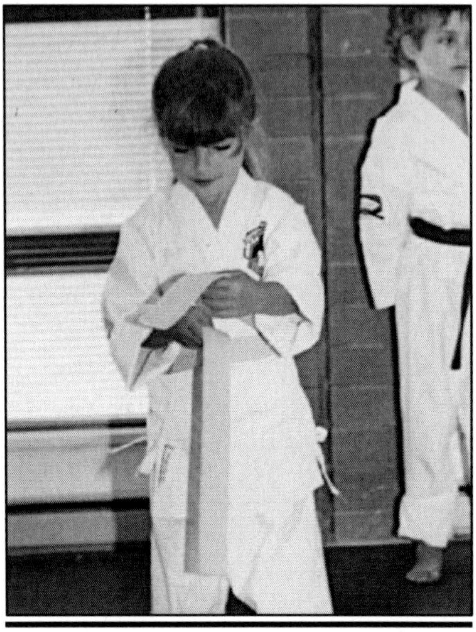

Brittany's Yellow Belt 1990
Leigh's first Competition 1986

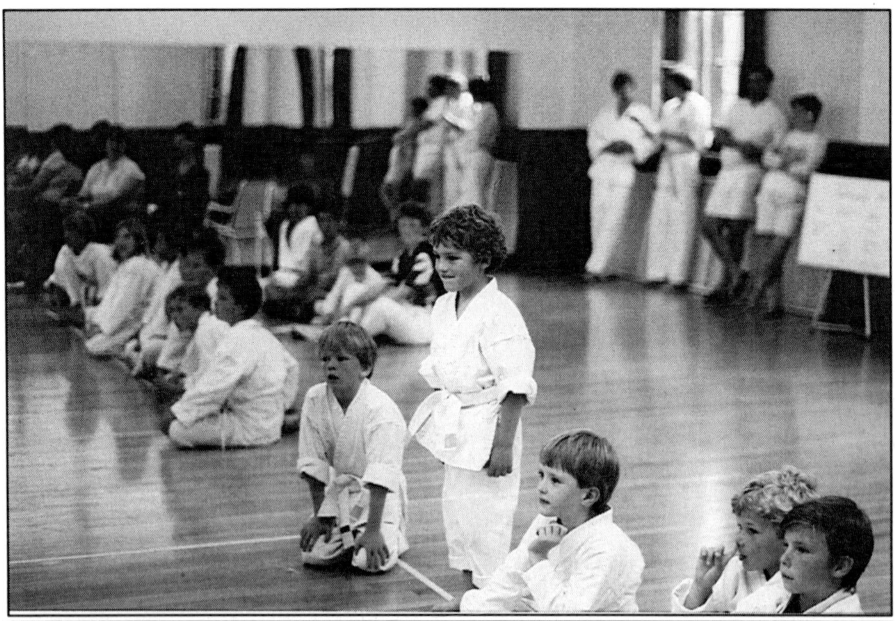

BOOK THREE

三

HAVE YOU HEARD A PERFECT NOTE?

SYNCHRONISTIC ZEN MOMENTS

"Have you ever had a perfect moment or heard a perfect note?" I asked at the beginning of my Keynote Address for the Chamber of Commerce Business Week Breakfast. As I struck an exquisite pinging note on the Tibetan Singing Bowl, the large audience hushed.

"I mean, have you ever had an experience where the perfection of that moment felt like the most beautiful sound you had ever heard? A perfect note is a vibration that you feel deep down in your belly that is felt in the depths of your soul!" I preached. *"Everything that we see, hear, and touch is a vibration, and when we align ourselves and are in tune with that vibration, it feels like perfection, and .... it is!"*

The study of traditional karate-do comes down to some very simple principles. Every movement is some form of expansion or contraction, and there are only three ways to create physical force. The basic elements are driving movement, rotation, and vibration. The act of creating a karate punch or kick is to apply two of the three basic elements and then finish it with "kime." This kime, or focus, is a technique known as the summation of joint-force and it can also create a zanshin moment. Zanshin literally means "remaining mind" or a sense of total awareness as you finish. Perhaps guitarist Jimi Hendrix might have said *"Scuse me when I kiss the sky"* as a way of describing the zanshin feeling of satori or enlightenment when you finish something exceptionally well.

Funakoshi Sensei, the father of modern karate, says it is the ideal of perfection – a perfect moment. What is interesting to me, as a martial artist, is why so many students and practitioners would perform techniques thousands of times, but never feel the vibration they make. That said, even with all my transformations, I too, have only experienced this vibration twice in my life.

The first was in the Spring of 1985. I was nearing 30 years of age and was close to the end of my first year at the Brockville dojo when I first heard a "perfect note". With a whirlwind of business activity and the idea of a new dojo in a church, the task of teaching and training was also omnipresent. Although I am not a fan of karate tournaments and such, I know it is good for students to experience the pressures of competition from time to time. So, when the opportunity to attend a local tournament, a "shiai," showed up, I took it. Smiths Falls is only about thirty miles from Brockville and a rival "Shotokan Karate" school from Kingston was sponsoring the event. I had yet to meet Paddy Savage, the Kingston Sensei, but I had talked to him on the phone several times. Like all promoters, he promised a big affair with great competition and notable competitors. Among his guests would be Jean Yves Theriault, the World Full Contact Karate Champion. The Champ, JYT, was legendary for his toughness and his knockout power. His career would record, in 76 professional fights, 69 wins with an amazing 61 KO's!

At the time, Danny Coles, Steve Stranges, and a newer student, Mike Sweeney, having attained orange and green belts, were among the top students in the dojo. Bob Noonan, Laura Fry, and Shelley Winters, along with white and yellow belt kids, Mike Croteau and Peter Townshend, would all try their skills at this, their second shiai. I put together about 40-50 students and, along with them, I intended to compete as well.

When we arrived at the tournament site, there were three large tables full of some of the most impressive trophies I had ever seen. The prizes were large, made of wood (rather than just plastic) and they made a huge statement. Paddy Savage said that he had gone all out to create a first-class event, and if the look of the trophies were any indication, this would be a great shiai! We watched and waited for the rest of the schools to appear, but as was typical of karate tournaments, they were slow and behind schedule. This was to be expected. Savage, looking at his watch and running almost an hour late, decided to start the competition. The problem was, he had expected well over 300 competitors and at this point, he had barely a hundred or so registered. Outside of a few stray teachers and a handful of random students, it was a head-to-head competition between his school and mine. Had we not attended, he would have had no one to compete with.

Like him, I was disappointed with the turnout, and I was equally concerned that my new school would be exposed too soon to such a direct comparison. A hometown advantage meant that many of the judges would be his Black Belt students, friends, and associates. As was my practice, I would not judge, as my job was to be there to help coach my students. We both practiced the same style of karate and, as he was far more established, I expected that this could be a tough day. Thus, in my pre-game speech to my students, I told them to focus on only themselves, do their best, and have fun.

What happened next shocked me. Each kata or forms division, starting with the kids through the adults, went head-to-head with his dojo against mine. The top three people were awarded the 1st, 2nd, and 3rd place trophies. Every single trophy began disappearing from the head table, where Savage and Theriault were seated, and was put into the hands of my students. As multiple divisions were being run at the same time, the transfer of the awards was dramatic. So much so, that we quickly acquired a table of our own and watched as the hardware went from his school to mine. When my final and most "advanced students", the green belts, accepted the top three places for their work, rather than relief, I began to feel a surprising sense of pressure. The only kata trophies that we did not win were the men's, and women's blue & brown belt divisions. I suspect this was only because we had not entered any brown belts!

The next portion of the tournament was the kumite or fighting divisions. Here we split the wins and losses about evenly. The Kingston group had shown up well for sparring. As the men's brown belt kumite competition ended, again without any of my students, it would be time for the Black Belt events. All the trophies at the head table, except the Black Belt and Tournament Grand Championship, were now gone. On the other side of the gym, we had been forced to set up a second table to accept all the awards that my students had won. Looking at my students and their accomplishments, I felt them also looking back at me. I felt the weight of the entire assembly wondering about me.

When you teach anything, and particularly anything physical, you must teach, not do. If your method is to simply demonstrate and show techniques by working along with your students, they won't learn much. While it is useful to show the effectiveness or the dynamics of doing something well, demonstrating is not teaching. Describing, adjusting, inspiring and cajoling, is teaching. Students learn by doing and by struggling to understand for themselves. When they can envision themselves achieving higher skills and abilities, they will effectively teach themselves and begin to perfect their understanding. To me, that is teaching. This means, for the most part, your students rarely see you do anything, and seldom see you under any pressure. I have also found, over the years, that all students think their teacher is great, regardless of how lousy or unskilled they may actually be.

For the past five years, with Butoku Kai, I had been stripped of any ego regarding my particular skills. In fact, even before then, as a student of Jimmy Mac, himself a fierce fighter and competitor, I knew what talent looked like. Jimmy Mac's other top student, Stan Peterec, would become a world champion and the amazing Mike Puckett and Sensei Linden Bateson were also top-notch martial artists. A self-evaluation of my talent would be that I was a competent journeyman grinder, or as Jimmy Mac would smile and say, *"a lumper."*

"Bobby, there are two types of fighters - technicians and lumpers, and both are equally dangerous. You and I are lumpers!" he would laugh as he taught. I made up for what I perceived as a lack of talent by simply out-working others. Over the years, I had won my share of trophies, particularly in kata, but in truth, I didn't care much for the game, or the gamesmanship, of the tournament scene. Even though I had competed in over 100 tournaments, the angst of this kind of performing brought out all kinds of emotions from performance fears to outright anger.

Now, while warming up and focusing on myself, I took notice of the competition so I might get a read on what I was up against. Admittedly, there were only a few competitors for the Black Belt kata, but the additional ninety expectant eyes of my students were all completely focused upon me. I felt their excitement. Jean Yves, Paddy Savage, his students, and all their supporters were also very curious to see a performance from this Brockville Sensei. Surely, if his students are that good, he must be something!

While I appeared calm, my nerves were raw and the pressure I felt was immense. I drew the final position, so I knew I would perform last in the kata competition. I watched the other competitors, but I did not see them. I noticed my nerves but did not feel them. And when my name was called, I stepped up. I would do my favorite kata, Arakaki Unsu, a simple, but exacting and beautiful form.

As I stepped onto the spot and into the spotlight, I announced myself, and time slowed down. Like in a real street fight, everything began to move in slow motion or as I would later learn directly from Richard Bandler, the Neural Linguistic Programming guru, I was actually manipulating time itself.

Power is rooted in the feet, developed in the legs, and delivered by the hips and as I began, I felt my entire body deliver. Every strand of every muscle in my legs and abdomen fired together. I could feel the clear vibration of power and the beauty of its perfection. It was an out-of-body experience, and by the time I reached the 180-degree jump near the end of the form, I jumped high and, if just for a moment, felt like I had touched the gods.

I landed precisely, with great posture, and I finished with a zanshin sensation like never before. The moment had been stunning and, although entirely exposed, it was also deeply personal. And then there was silence - a simple void, as the entire room caught its collective breath.

Had it been a dream? What had happened? Was it just my imagination? My mind raced from absolute ecstasy back to the norm. Had anyone else felt this? Had they even noticed? Abruptly, the crowd erupted with applause, drowning out the silence of the void. A standing ovation was the recognition that the audience had been right there with me.

Moments later, the Champ, Jean Yves Theriault, made his way to me, his eyes warm with respect. *"That was amazing!"* was all he said, as he shook my hand and left.

I would also win the weapons competition and place 2nd in kumite that afternoon, thus making me the Grand Black Belt Champion. My story, however, has nothing to do with trophies or winning and losing, rather just the simplicity of a perfect moment. Although I have had some good performances since, I have never again recreated the physical feeling of power and perfection as I did at that moment. Perhaps it was offered as a taste of what I could be if I put myself in places beyond my control.

Perfection is only created in the mind's eye. It is flawed to think that we can, in some way, own it or live in a perfect state. First, there is birth, and then there is life. It only takes a moment to be born, but it takes a lifetime to discover why. My life experiences have taught me that only through some acute pressure, realized by situations beyond our control, or by feelings of extreme love, can we find moments of perfection.

Perhaps my karate training - the expansion and contraction or simply the 'kime' - gave me the tools to feel that vibration and recognize its truth, if just once and only for a moment.

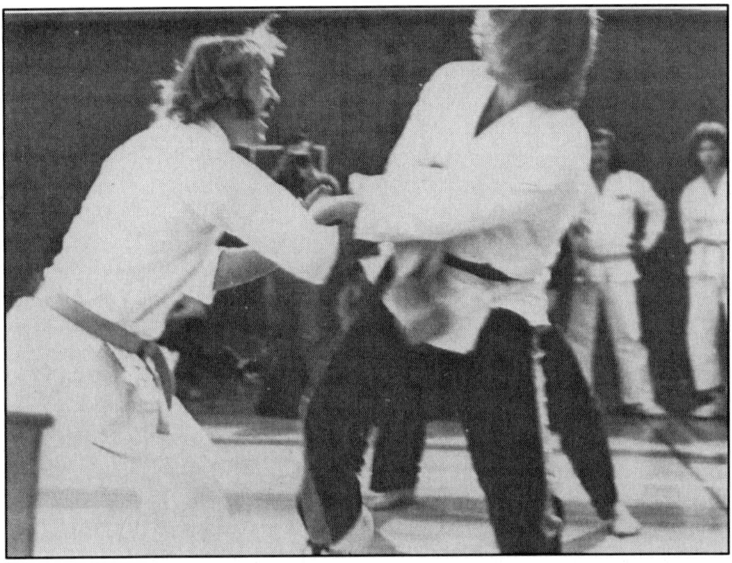

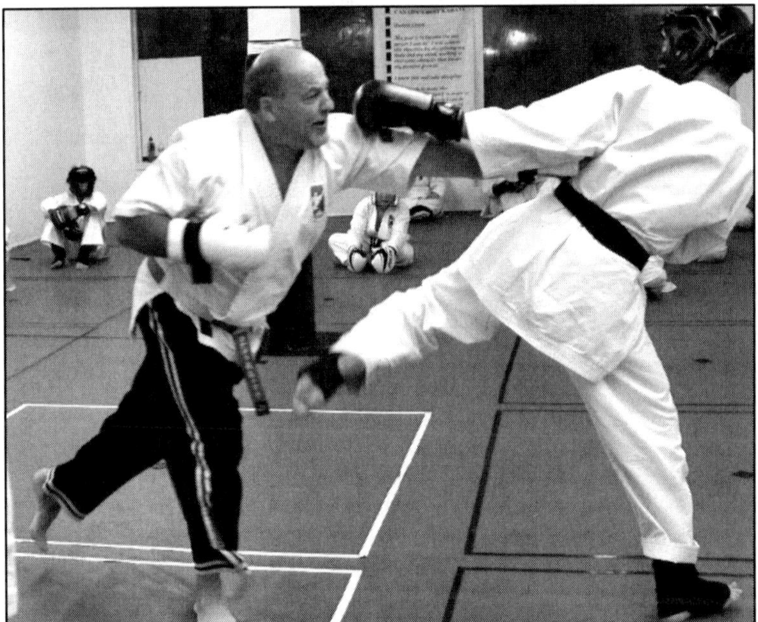

Kumite Fighting 1976 / 2019

THE FIRST CAUSE

STORIES OF THE ORIGINAL THREE

Taikyoku means "first cause" or the first step. *"In the beginner's mind there are many possibilities, but in the expert's there are few."* – Zen Master Shunryo Suzuki.

For me, learning how and when to knock the rough edges off of my students is part of my duties as the Sensei. The Dojo Creed is something that takes me back to the beginning of being a teacher. I have spoken of the school of hard knocks and how I had to learn the hard way. In that, many of my students have also followed in my footsteps.

At the Castle on George St, I taught the sons and daughters of many fathers. Like my Sensei, I took my responsibilities seriously and trained my students hard. The intent to transform others with my teaching was always on my mind. I had dozens of truly inspiring students, too many to mention, so I will allow them all to be represented by the first three. Danny Coles, Steve Stranges, and Mike Sweeney were the first of my students to achieve the rank of Black Belt in Leeds County. Stranges, fit and incredibly built, was about my age and in my mind, he had leadership written all over him. The other two were in their late teens. Coles was lightning fast, and Sweeney had a mind like a steel trap.

In the beginning, it was Steve who impressed me. He was hungry and, given his age, was almost ready to be a *"sempai"* right away. Steve Stranges was a physical specimen, with a strong build and a lot of athletic talent. I recognized his abilities immediately and began grooming him as a future assistant. Danny and he were part of the original eleven, but Mike, who had been away at college, joined the dojo some six months later. He scrambled to catch up.

Before I had come to Brockville, there had been others who had tried to teach karate on the local scene. The most recent dojo failure had Mike Sweeney, accomplish an orange belt, as its top student. When that dojo folded, Sweeney was left with a fire in his belly and a hole in his heart.

They weren't the three musketeers, but these three men were an interesting and diverse mix. Stranges was respected, Coles was admired, and Sweeney was disliked! Danny Coles was a gifted athlete with natural punching power and unnatural speed. He seemed like he could fly! As the youngest, Danny came from a tough family where some of his brothers were hardened criminals and they all could fight. That said, he did not indulge or go near trouble, as he wanted more out of life than what he had grown up with.

If Coles was determined, then Mike Sweeney was driven ... to the point of obsession. Like the others, Mike had also grown up the same kind of tough. The difference was Stranges and Coles were nice guys, and Sweeney, with a chip on his shoulder the size of Texas, was not. This, however, did not detour him, as he quickly regained his former karate rank and became a challenger for tops in the dojo. Being incredibly ballsy and needing a job, he showed me how I could hire him for free on a government grant. I must admit I was reluctant to hire him, regardless of his drive and obvious talent. At the time, like my students, I did not particularly care for him as a person.

On his first day on the job, I watched as he interacted poorly with some of my fitness clients. I took him aside saying, *"You cannot treat people the way you do. Not in my business. You are being an asshole! If you want to remain, you will have to change.*

"Furthermore," I continued angrily, *"I won't do you the service of firing you, but if I ever see you treat a customer badly again, I won't have you inside the building. I'll get you a shovel and send you outside to the parking lot. You can dig a hole in the morning and then fill it up in the afternoon - for the entire next six months!"*

Chin in his chest and truly remorseful, he first begged for another chance, *"Yes Sensei! You have my word."* Then, in a cocky way, he said, *"but ... I will be the best person you have ever hired! ... So much so, that when the government funding ends, you will have no choice but to hire me!"*

"Ya right," I said, as I rolled my eyes. "*Fat chance!"*

Six months later I hired Mike Sweeney full-time. Never in my life, before or since, have I seen anyone transform, and then outperform, like he did. He began to read and study books about how to become a better person and it worked. Every day, he was full of energy, ideas, and most importantly, confidence. As a full-time employee, he also trained and helped as a teaching assistant. With his steel trap of a mind, he absorbed every detail. Not only did he catch up to Coles and Stranges in rank and ability, but he also pushed them to be better.

Now rid of his bad attitude, there was nothing in his way. If he had the physical talent and body of Danny Coles, he would have been the greatest ever! Fortunately, he did not. (His ego at that time would have made him unbearable).

Mike, for all his gifts, was not a natural athlete. At best he was average. He wasn't very strong and although precise, he lacked the fast-twitch quickness of a premier athlete. There was nothing explosive about his physical technique, but his mind and will to compete made his body keep up with the others.

Although I was impressed and applauded his personal growth, the student body believed that this cocky guy didn't deserve to be among the best – at the top of the crowd. They didn't like that he had started late, and now was in a leadership role. He had surpassed them, with what seemed to be effortless ease.

As he applied to test for his brown belt, he would join Stranges and Coles, and together they would make the run to be the first in the dojo to earn their Black Belts. Despite the mood of the dojo against Sweeney, I knew he was worthy, but I also knew that the morale of the school was at stake. All eyes, looking at the coming month's grading, would be on both of us. I made up my mind that Mike Sweeney's Brown Belt test would be tough. One for the books.

As I worked my way through the testing, I took extra opportunities to tire Sweeney out. I started with the white belts and included him in everything. With every drill and kata, and as each belt would finish up, he would remain. He would be the last man standing. This was not unusual for this type of testing. Typically, once you were down to testing the highest rank, and since you had already seen them do everything many times during the evening, you would finish quickly. The advanced belts would then perform their kata and perhaps have a few rounds of sparring.

If they did well, you would call it a win and present the belts.

Mike, with his strong desire, showed he had all the technical ability to beat anyone on the test. Although he was fatigued, he still had plenty of gas in the tank. Now as he stood alone on the floor, standing in a deep kiba dachi – a horse stance - he readied himself with anticipation.

What happened next was beyond the physical. It was a real test of spirit. I put down my clipboard and approached him, as Mike Tyson might say, with *"bad intentions!"* Without warning I drove a front kick into his belly, ripping it just below his solar plexus.

He doubled over and, with his wind gone, I forced him to move without a break as I threw kicks and punches at him. I put him on the ground over and over. Non-stop katas, push-ups, and basic combinations ensued for the next twenty or so minutes. When we were done, I returned to the head table, sat down, and demanded more. When he finally collapsed in a heap of whimpering tears, he had momentary convulsions as he tried to recover from his total exhaustion. Not letting up, I demanded fifty more pushups. After about twenty he collapsed. Over and over, every few reps, he failed, but would not give in. With tears in his eyes and "goo" coming from various orifices in his body, he refused to quit!

No one cheered. No one said a word. I'm not sure if they even took a breath until it was over. Psychology states that when you feel a strong emotion like fear or sadness, as part of the empathetic response, you are imagining it happening to you. There would be no more talk, not even a whisper of backroom gossip regarding his worthiness. No one who saw the end of that grading, or the ones who heard about it, could imagine themselves doing what he had done! No one else was that mentally tough.

On that day, I had put my finger on the scale to balance the rewards earned by the price paid. Mike Sweeney, because of the inequality of his talent to outperform, proved he was more than equal to the demands of leadership.

I knew that to be accepted, and for the good of the morale of the dojo, I needed to, metaphorically, beat him like a dog. The difference is when the dog cowers, you hold back. I did not. I would never again do anything like that, as I never felt that I had to. At least not like that! I have never met anyone quite as bull-headed as Mike Sweeney, and perhaps he had never met anyone as determined as me. For a while, this became legend.

Sweeney, Coles, and Stranges would soon step up and, again, create a legend that something special was happening in my school. They made me and our Brockville dojo proud. July 1987 was the Shodan / 1st Degree Black Belt Grading. They had the chance to not only be my first Black Belts, but also be tested by O'Sensei Richard Kim. At that time, I required students to grade twice. First was at our home dojo and then for the Butoku Kai Organization. Students were judged by me for their Canadian Dojo Black Belts and also received international recognition by testing for Sensei Kim's Japanese Organization.

After earning their 1st Degree rank with me, we all traveled to O'Sensei's yearly training camp and Black Belt Grading. Five days, four sessions per day of Karate, Tai Chi, History, and Philosophy. Richard Kim, at 75 years old, was Black Belt Magazines Man of the Year in the 1973 and inducted into the Hall of Fame. He was an incredible man and the most unique Martial Arts teacher in the world.

This wasn't lost on my guys as they went all out to show their mettle to the old master. It was the final day of the week-long Butoku Kai summer camp and Black Belt Grading Day at the University of Guelph. Things were going well when. Mike Sweeney had joined Danny Coles and Steve Stranges three years before and together they were the first students to represent my dojo. For the past six months, they had entered the hardest phase of training – working from Brown to Black Belt.

It's surprising how many people get to the threshold of a big accomplishment, but never see it through. They get to the doorway but never enter or take that first step. Many times, something happens, either externally or internally, to get in their way.

These three represented themselves and my first step of Black Belt recognition. In a sense, we were all beginners. Like them, my entire dojo and I were all, as yet, untested. My students were testing to become legitimate practitioners of the art and my credibility was being tested as a karate teacher. Over the past five years, I had worked incredibly hard to learn and then teach Sensei Kim's more traditional training methods. So much so, that I had all but eliminated much of what I had learned from Bateson Karate and Jimmy Mac. Yes, what they had taught me was the biggest part of my skills and abilities, but I wanted more for my students.

So, I tried to teach karate, its philosophy, and techniques as Sensei Kim demonstrated it. The rub was, although the technical theories were sound, I didn't like what I saw. In my opinion, most of the Shorinji Ryu practitioners that practiced the same style of karate looked weak and moved poorly. I had initially ignored what my eyes showed me because my ears told me that Kim, with his credibility and philosophies, taught karate at the highest level. However, for me, what I saw didn't transfer to the end product.

Sometime around my second year of teaching, it occurred to me what the problem might be. Sensei Kim, for all his knowledge and experience, was a man of seventy years, and his students were copying what they saw. It was like the riddle of the mother crab that asked her children, *"Children, why do you walk so crooked?"* and they answered all together, *"I don't know momma, why do you?"* Perhaps it was that simple. His students emulated what the old man did, rather than applying what he said.

This thought occurred to me while watching Don Warrener's Goju Ryu students demonstrating their katas. Goju, while similar, was a completely different style to Richard Kim's Shorinji Ryu. When Warrener and his students took direction from Mr. Kim, they heard the message of the technique, but they followed their own criterion of what it should look and feel like.

This made sense to me, so I began again to teach what my body knew how to do. I added my expertise, as taught by Jimmy Mac, to the fundamentals that Richard Kim expounded on. The result, to my eye, was a strong, athletic style and a fundamentally correct method of basic applications. I saw my students performing their basics and their kata like the young and powerful men and women they were. My motivational teaching methods added to their individual talents and allowed them to explore and push their limits. I knew they were good.

Suddenly, a strong, loud voice broke the silence. "*Stop everything! Whose student is that?"* demanded Richard Kim.

All three grading rings stopped as everyone in the gym looked around to see who O'Sensei was talking about. Mr. Kim was seated at the table grading the 3rd and 4th Dans and myself, along with two others, were grading the brown and 1st-degree black belts. As I had the option, I had chosen to exclude myself from the ring where my students were being graded. Although I had kept them in the corner of my eye when I could, they were on their own. I wanted an impartial panel to place judgment. I was too close to them, and I wanted them to succeed as much, or more, than they did.

Like everyone else, I was looking around to see who Sensei Kim was focusing on. As I scanned the groups I saw Danny Coles, who had been stopped partway through his kata. Now standing at the top of his grading ring, he looked bewildered and was looking for an exit to sit back down.

I quickly realized that Kim, watching Coles, was speaking to me, so I half raised my hand, saying carefully, *"Sensei, he is my student."* Like the year before, in front of the church, I was unsure why I, and now Danny, were being centered out.

A rush of insecurities raced through my mind. Had he made a mistake? Was the protocol wrong? Had Sensei Kim noticed and was he pissed that I had adapted his teachings and changed the look?

Pointing at Danny Coles, he said, *"You! Start your kata again!"*

Dutifully, Coles returned to the starting mark, announcing his form *"Kushanku Dai"* and he began. Danny had speed, power, and presence, and his natural abilities did my teaching proud. He performed beautifully and, although he made a mistake and repeated a sequence twice, he finished strongly with poise and confidence. Kim had noticed. He noticed everything, and perhaps he had been noticing them all week. Coles, Stranges, and Sweeney had presented and performed their katas all week as well, but it was now that Sensei chose to speak.

"He is your student? And the other ones, too?" he demanded again. My answer confirmed his questioning concern. *"That guy is good! He passes right now!"* he announced, and everyone took notice.

Now that we all knew Sensei's thoughts, the rest of the teachers and students nodded their approval. I felt the relief of a job well done. He passed all three on the spot, but it was Danny's exceptional talent that gave Sensei Kim the opportunity he was looking for.

I later learned that O'Sensei had never done that before. His protocol was to read the essays, and then confirm, sometimes months later, the appointment of the new rank. I will never know what Mr. Kim saw that day or the message he wanted to send. I would like to think that he saw a favorable reflection of his teaching and he wanted his direct students to take notice. Perhaps it was as simple as *"those guys are good"* and perhaps there was a little more to the new guy - me - than was first expected.

Coles, Stranges, and Sweeney made a mark and at the same time set the bar high for others to follow, and many would. It had been our first cause. Our "beginner's mindset" showed the possibilities of what we all might be, but it was the expertise of our "first step" that opened the door for future accomplishments.

Collectively, our Taikyoku moment would give us all the confidence to step up, again and again.

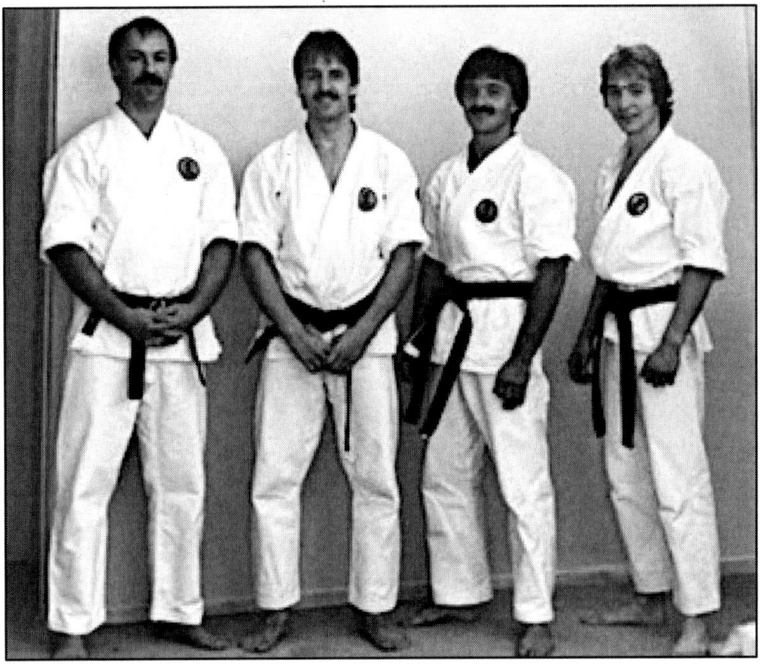

With the Original Three
Mike Sweeney, Steve Stranges & Dan Coles
Brockville Black Belt Grading July 9, 1988

IT HAPPENED BEFORE IT HAPPENED

MEANINGFUL DÉJÀ VU MOMENTS
BY STEVE STRANGES

In my family, I was the youngest with an older brother and two sisters. My father was a hard worker who sold cars for a living. He eventually became a Sales Manager, winning awards for Top Sales in his Region. My mother was an alcoholic and never worked outside of our home. This had a huge effect on all of us growing up, and as such, none of us went very far in school. Before graduating, I dropped out in grade twelve. I couldn't stand being at home any longer, so I decided to get out into the workforce. My Father and I were exceptionally close and I felt sorry for him for having to put up with the same problems that we did as kids. He deserved so much better, but I respected the way he stood by my Mother. He was my best friend, and I always wanted to make him proud!

At sixteen, I moved out and started my first job at the Black and Decker factory. I also played many sports, but Junior Hockey was a big deal for me. You see, at that time I was only about 125 lbs soaking wet. Today they call it Small Man Syndrome and as such, I always felt I had to prove myself by doing more. I overcompensated by outworking everyone else. Being the smallest guy on my team I played with heart, always determined to win without fearing my opponents. Junior Hockey is highly competitive, and every league has its share of on-ice bullies.

A guy in our league who was particularly bad was Doug LaForte. He was a big Indian guy we nicknamed, from a distance mind you, Fred Flintstone. LaForte was a bit of a cement head neanderthal, with tree trunks for legs and a body like a brick wall. He was nasty, hurting many people on and off the ice. Once, my brother got blindsided when Doug sucker-punched him, breaking his orbital eye socket. He didn't get a chance to defend himself and, as he was unprepared, he was badly injured. It made my blood boil! But LaForte was the kind of guy you wanted to avoid. While I had no fighting experience, if need be, I wasn't afraid to drop the gloves. Truth is, I would have liked to avenge my brother, but the opportunity or the defensive need never appeared for me. My defense was working out with weights, as the added strength was a size equalizer for me. I kept myself in top shape. But even though I was fit and strong, I always wanted to learn how to properly defend myself. I found the idea of martial arts fascinating and hoped that someday I'd get the chance to learn.

Looking at things in the rear-view mirror, I can see that fate kept introducing me to the person who would fulfill my self-defense desires. I worked hard and liked to have a good time on my time off. In Brockville, Ontario, circa 1977, my summer holidays were the same as everyone else's, as back then all the manufacturing plants shut down at the same time. This made the last week of July and the first week of August a party time! There were street parties and many night clubs created special events for the summer celebrations. One evening some friends and I attended an unusual event at a popular watering hole called the Skyline Disco Lounge.

Unexpectedly, the dance floor cleared, the lights came on, and two guys - a Black Belt and a Brown Belt took center stage to do a Karate Demonstration. Turns out they were waiters working at the Skyline for the summer, and while it was an odd place and time for this kind of show, it was well received. What wasn't odd was the impression it made on me. It was the first time I'd ever seen martial arts live, and I found it fascinating! I said to the guys I was with that if ever I get the chance to learn that "shit", I'm going for it! They all just looked at me, then took a swig of their beer, and said, "You are crazy, Stranges!!" This impromptu show was my first brush with the man who would change my life in the coming years.

When the 1980s began there was a lot of hype about Bruce Lee and Chuck Norris. But in Brockville, there were no Karate Schools or places offering instruction.

That changed when I heard of a guy teaching Karate in the Old Catholic Culture Building. I found out he was a Bouncer / Bartender at the Old Hotel Manitonna and Skyline Hotel. Bill O'Meara or Buster, as he was called at the bar, was the Sensei. Unfortunately, O'Meara was also an alcoholic, and given my past experiences, I kept my expectations low. Everything was erratic about this club, as many times the classes were taught by unqualified junior students. Even when Buster did teach there was little or no structure, and seemingly little thought was put into the classes. Adding insult to injury, he often reeked of booze and stale cigarettes or was recovering from a hangover. O'Meara's teaching was hit and miss. Eventually, the students got tired of being burnt from paying fees with no classes being taught by the Sensei. So much so, that the club folded after about 6 months.

It was a lousy experience and certainly wasn't how I had envisioned Karate to be taught.

While the club didn't last, Buster reminded me of a story I had heard about my old hockey nemesis Doug, "Fred Flintstone", LaForte. Until I attended O'Meara's classes, I had always assumed that Bill had been responsible for tuning up the town bully. But it wasn't him. O'Meara told of how Doug LaForte, drinking at Julie's Lounge, had gotten beaten up by some unknown Karate guy. Doug, like most bullies, was notorious in bars for challenging people in all kinds of ways. Routinely, to win beers, he frequented a rugged bar named the Cap N' Tap, where he would challenge Alberta pipeline workers to arm-wrestling contests. Strong "Fred" drank lots of free beer. No one could beat him arm wrestling, or in the back alley.

LaForte's bully mentality got an abrupt attitude adjustment on New Year's Eve 1979, when he provoked the wrong guy's wife at Julie's. Apparently, his unwanted presence showed up at a table where another hockey guy, Gary Wyatt, and his wife were entertaining a couple visiting from out west. LaForte began obnoxiously flirting with the wives while subsequently challenging the men. Wyatt, no slouch himself, was also the Skyline Hotel bar manager. As he was about to deal with Doug the other man leapt into action. Seconds later, LaForte's disrespectful tough guy attitude got him broken ribs and two rainbows for eyes. While it didn't make him any nicer, he did quit drinking for a year and bought a gym membership.

I still remember the day I found out that truth. How the fate of an urban legend had put me again in touch with my future Sensei. This fun fact was revealed at a Seniors Hockey League game years later, and it explained why tough guy LaForte, knowing who I trained Karate with, kept his distance from me. On the arena ice, they say: *"revenge is a dessert best served cold."* Fred Flintstone wanted no part of me, and it felt great.

Fate finally revealed itself in the spring of 1984, about a year after Buster O'Meara's club had failed. I was downtown when a friend told me some guy was walking up and down the main street handing out flyers. A Martial Arts School was opening next month in the basement of the old Eaton's Store. I asked around to find out who this person was and where they were from. There wasn't much information, except that he was from the West Coast and seemed to be legitimate. After a few days, I couldn't take the suspense any longer, so I went to check it out for myself. It was midafternoon on a sunny June day when I opened the door to the Dojo and peeked around to see what things looked like. I was impressed!

The place was clean and organized with Trophies, Certificates, and Weapons of the Arts. It had all the things that I had imagined a proper Dojo should have and be. At that moment a flame ignited inside me as I began to get excited. Over to the right was an office with the door slightly ajar. I looked behind the door and I saw a well-dressed man in a suit and tie, feet up on his desk, taking a nap. I kind of chuckled and knocked gently on the door. He awoke startled, half asleep, but still found a way to say, *"Well Hello"*. We both laughed and I thought to myself, maybe he was just meditating.

I'm not sure why it happened, but like a déjà vu moment, I knew that I had an instant connection with him. It was one of those feelings when you meet someone, and you just know they are going to somehow make an impact on your life. Bob Mueller was one of those people. We sat and talked as he laid out his program and what I could expect. He said he had a five-year plan, which told me he seemed committed. That was good enough for me, and I was in for the long haul! I never looked back. I put everything else on the sidelines and began training almost every day at the Dojo.

From the very first class that Sensei Mueller taught, he had a way of explaining the techniques and demonstrating them that intensified my desire to train. You felt his passion and couldn't miss his intensity. I remember he finished one class saying, *"What we did here tonight won't sink in until later. Don't be discouraged if you didn't get it right away - just trust the technique we practiced, and its importance will occur to you later."*

I thought it was odd, until later that night. What he had taught suddenly made sense and what had seemed complicated now seemed simple as to how it worked. This was a different way of being taught than my first experience with O'Meara. That's when it occurred to me. Mueller had not only been the karate guy from out west who taught Doug LaForte a lesson, but he was one of the waiters doing the demonstration at the Skyline Hotel. It had been him and his teacher, Jim MacDonald, who had first inspired my desire! Life is often strange and there are no coincidences!

Sensei Mueller taught all kinds of things. It was obvious that he had been classically trained and was morally the kind of man that it is easy to follow. He taught us self-control, respect for others, and to be disciplined in everything we do. Under no circumstances was any of the fighting we learned to be used outside the Dojo except for self-defense. Bad behavior and bad attitudes would get you expelled immediately. In my mind, and to many others in our class, this was the difference in what a good Sensei was as compared to a bad one.

After a few months of training, classes got bigger, and nobody was quitting. Word had got around that his school was reputable, and it was here to stay. Sensei saw how things were progressing and looked for an opportunity to expand. We were running out of space because of the large class sizes, when a huge building came up for sale. He found a way to purchase the Old Shrine Hall, a former Episcopal Church on Court House Avenue. This was an even bigger commitment, and it showed the people of Brockville, as well as his students, that he was here for the long haul. Things just kept getting bigger and better. We all chipped in and helped with major renovations to this place. It was heaven for me, as the downstairs was renovated into a fully equipped gym which quickly became a force in the local fitness community. It was like we were family, all very close, learning and helping each other. He was always coaching us, inspiring everyone to grow physically and mentally. It was a real learning experience; one I will never forget.

When I look back at what I have learned from all this, I can say that we are all born into life with no training manual. What we do with our lives is entirely up to each of us. There is no right or wrong, only do or do not. Many of us are afraid to take a chance of doing something for the fear of failing. But if we don't take a chance in life, we will never know our potential or what we will become. I truly believe there is much we can accomplish in our lives, but unfortunately most individuals lack the confidence to take that chance.

What Sensei taught me was to have the confidence to take that chance. Some of the greatest ideas are probably still out there because people are afraid to fail. Failure, if you don't allow it to define you, is a bully you can overcome. The truth is: failure builds character and if we see it the right way, we will learn from failure. Martial Arts helped give me the confidence to try things that others struggle with. We can't be afraid of making mistakes in life, as, when we make them, we grow from them.

Martial Arts is more than learning how to defend yourself in an encounter on the street. It's learning how to defend yourself in the everyday battles of life. Dealing with your job, home life, stress, finances, and relationships is all learning how to fight for yourself. It's being able to cope with your problems and also help others who struggle with the same things. Karate helped me to build a strong family and guide my kids to grow into strong individuals. It's fair to say that I wish my Dad could have had the same kind of help with my Mom.

I will always remember a class where Sensei said to all of us *"Look into the Mirror, is what you see - really what you see?"* How do I see myself now when I look into a mirror? I see a person who will never give up. How, when an opportunity presents itself, I strive to help others who struggle with their lives. It's the person I have become, and my Karate helped me develop this attitude. I am proud to be one of Sensei Mueller's first three Black Belt Students in Brockville. It's an honor that no one can ever take from me.

For me, the Spirit of Karate remains strong, and when I need a little extra motivation, I always go back to my roots. I like to remember how fate put me in touch with the people, places and things that became my destiny. If there is ever a day where I'm losing focus or desire, I go back to my training and reboot ... so to speak.

It never fails me!

LESSONS OF A LIFELONG LEARNER

BY MIKE SWEENEY

The razor-sharp blade flashed dangerously close to my left eye, stopping inches away only because my right forearm intercepted that of the attacker. That wasn't the end of it though. No sooner had the forward motion of the blade been arrested, it changed course to slash low, passing mere inches from my midsection, again, only missing because I guided the attacking arm clear with the back of my forearm. Over and over the motions were repeated, and because the practice blade had, this time, been replaced with an actual live edge, I dared not let my attention falter.

The drive home from our training session was quieter than normal. More often than not, the conversation between the two of us, my Sensei and I, flowed freely but on that occasion, even though we had just completed a productive workout and had also enjoyed an interesting meal in the city's Chinatown – interesting because there were a few too many unidentifiable ingredients for our liking – our communication was subdued. This was no doubt because we were both aware that, at least for some time to come, the last of our weekly excursions to Ottawa had come and gone. And so, the miles ticked by in relative silence with each of us lost in our own thoughts.

During the several months prior to that day, we had been booking Friday afternoons off – I was at that point working for my Sensei at the dojo – investing the time to travel to the Nation's capital to study Filipino Martial Arts, stick and knife fighting, with Bob Carver, a friend who owned an academy there. Making those trips was an idea proposed by my instructor and employer, Bob Mueller, and one that I immediately jumped at after having it presented to me. In reflecting back, his suggestion that we make the effort to learn something new, and the training that followed, had a profound impact on my martial arts career and I dare say, influenced the tide of my life in general.

Martial Artists are seldom lacking in confidence. In fact, having confidence, including a belief that the system students have chosen to invest their blood, sweat, and tears into will protect them, to see them through adversity, is almost a necessity if they are going to persevere with the hardships of training. Unfortunately, after a period of time, that confidence, however otherwise valuable, can sometimes result in students shutting themselves off from learning new things, developing a belief that they have "it" all figured out. To back up those assumptions, or to prevent them from being shattered outright, advanced students, and even more tragically, some instructors, occasionally begin to shelter themselves, to only train with those who practice similarly. This is an unfortunate outcome and one that only serves to eliminate the possibility of growth.

At that time in my life – admittedly, even though I had a few years of training behind me, I was very much a beginner – I felt that my martial arts instructor did have it all figured out. He was successful in every way that I wanted to emulate. If I didn't harbor that belief, it would have been unlikely that I would have invested 5-6 days per week to study with him. With that in mind, the act of my Sensei committing to travel to study with someone else, to put on the proverbial white belt of a beginner, challenging himself by trying something completely different, with one of his students, me, there to witness it all, was an example that struck deep within my psyche. If he could be a beginner again, of course I could. It was the birth of a concept that would ultimately define how I often choose to describe myself: that being, a lifelong learner. That phrase, lifelong learner, is one that figures prominently on my resume.

If I was to stop this story here, there is a risk that some readers might assume that I'm referring to martial arts in isolation. That couldn't be further from the truth. Countless times in the 30+ years that followed that day, I have found myself adorned with a white belt. Yes, in one case, it was an actual belt, one tied around my Brazilian Jiu-jitsu gi. I donned that while running a successful martial arts school and I wore it proudly alongside my karate students. At many other times though, they were virtual belts: the white belt of a sailor, a snowboarder, a yacht captain, a long-distance cycle tourer, a writer! Each time starting a new activity, when I was attempting to acquire some new skill or knowledge, I was faced with the misgivings of a typical beginner, oftentimes second-guessing myself. Why should I put myself through this struggle? Why not stick with what I'm familiar with? These are things that, I imagine, we've all said to ourselves from time to time even though, from the outside, it's easy to see that those questions are far from empowering. What allows me to answer those queries successfully, or better yet, ask improved questions, is the habit that I first began to establish in the dojo all those years ago, and a lesson that I had driven home to me sometime later at a martial arts camp.

The annual Butokukai camp held at Guelph University was a week-long event, a gathering of numerous martial arts schools and one that would ultimately conclude for us, my training partners, Dan Coles and Steven Stranges, and I, testing for our Black Belts under the watchful eye of O'Sensei Richard Kim. Strangely though, it is not that exam that stands out most prominently in my memories. It was earlier in the week when a couple of broken bricks taught me the power of having belief in oneself, of having confidence in my abilities.

The path from our dorm room to the university cafeteria led us all past a low brick wall which, due to the pile of bricks beside it, we had concluded had just recently been repaired. As a lark, my friend Dan and I set a brick up on the wall and attempted to break it in half with our bare hands. Contrary to what you might have seen in other martial arts demonstrations, in this battle of brick vs. fist, the brick came out victorious, leaving each of us with nothing more to show for our efforts than a throbbing hand. Not easily dismayed though, we made several more attempts but no matter how hard we smashed our hands into them, the bricks failed to yield. It was only after trying to trick my friend that the pattern would be broken.

One day, on our way back from the cafeteria, I found myself arriving at that wall a few hundred meters ahead of my friend. It was then that I noticed on top of the pile, the pieces from a brick that had already been broken in two. Quickly, I concocted a plan for what I thought might be a fun trick and holding the two pieces together so that they looked like one solid brick, I first raised them overhead so that Dan could see them, and then set them down on the wall and struck them sharply with my fist. When I subsequently raised the two pieces overhead and yelled victoriously, Dan came running up, shocked at what he imagined had happened. When he deduced that I had been able to break a brick, something that multiple times over we had failed at, he confidently stated, "If you can do it, so can I." And so he did... within seconds, he had broken one of the solid bricks! Of course, I was shocked, because I had only just pretended to do it but after witnessing his success, I shouted "I was just kidding but if you can do it, so can I." You may be able to guess what happened next... I, too, was able to break the brick. It was like Bannister's 4-minute mile. All we both needed was the belief that if someone else could do a thing, we could follow suit.

Without a doubt, learning new things, especially those that require change, can be scary. It might give you butterflies, not unlike the feelings I experienced all those years ago when that sharp blade darted precariously close to my face. That said, you've probably heard some form of the quote "growth begins at the edge of your comfort zone." If there is a lesson to be learned within the hallowed halls of a dojo, or for that matter, in a boxing ring, or on wrestling mats, it is that learning, and by necessity, maintaining the heart and mind of a beginner, is a requisite for growth. Whether that learning includes trying to perfect a new technique, studying a new training method, or immersing yourself in a new art altogether, embrace the learning process.

Don't stop there though. Study that new-to-you language. Pick up that new instrument. Take that course. Be a lifelong learner. Your karate and your life will only improve because of it.

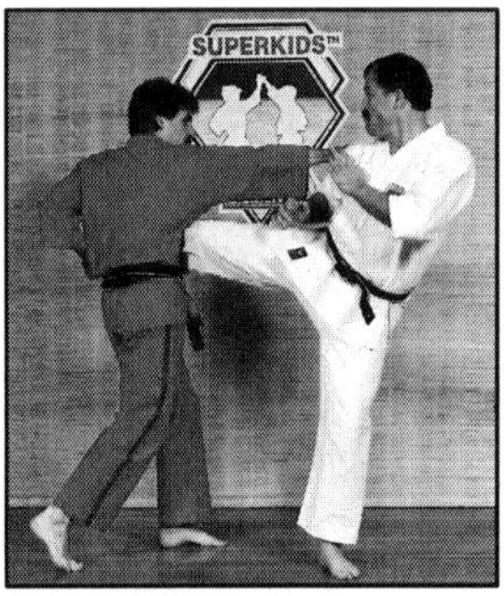

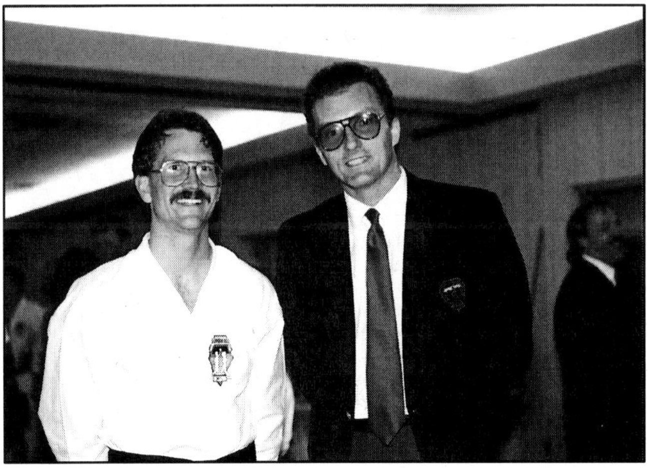

With Mike Sweeney 1988
Dan Holland (1st Victoria Black Belt) with Bob N

FROM KARATE TO KICKBOXING

AN ODYSSEY OF RESPECT
BY DAN COLES

It was in the late afternoon on a gray 1988 February day when a man in his mid-twenties climbed the old church stairs to the third floor of the dojo. He was in Brockville for his Ottawa based job to take a training course. Obviously fit, he was looking for a place to train for a few weeks until his business course was complete.

"What style of Karate do you practice?" I asked

He smiled and explained, "I don't practice Karate exactly." His eyes told me that he guessed that I was a bit confused as to why he had come to a Karate school.

"I'm with Jean Yves Theriault, the World Champion Kickboxer from Ottawa Ontario. Mr. Theriault suggested I find Sensei Dan Coles and check out your dojo while I'm here in Brockville." He continued, *"I realize you teach a traditional style here, but what I am hoping is that I could pay a drop-in fee or something like that so I can do a little bag work and shadow boxing. I need to stay sharp."*

I was intrigued about why he needed to be sharp and somewhat unsure about him. To buy a little time and investigate his motives, I offered to take him on a tour of the facility. Our 12,000 sq ft dojo and gym was impressive to say the least and it always provided the opportunity for some good conversation. We walked and talked as I got a clear picture of who he was and more importantly if he was legit. This was necessary, as I don't just let anyone use the dojo without first checking them out.

After I grilled him for about 10 minutes, I had a good feel for him. Jack Renault had trained for a couple of years, had 3 kickboxing bouts under him, and had another coming up. He couldn't afford a 2-week layoff, not if he expected to enter the ring.

I was about to tell him that we didn't do 'drop-ins', but my blood was boiling with excitement. All I could think of was *"I want to spar with this guy"*.

Instead, I found myself telling him that I saw Jean Yves Theriault years ago on television defending his world title. I guess I had been about 13 years old and after seeing him knock out his opponent - I wanted to learn Karate! Seeing Mr. Theriault was my first inspiration to become a martial artist. Jack nodded approvingly, saying that was a "pretty cool" story.

We became fast friends. He was respectful of my traditions, and I knew he would be good inside the school. That said, with my due diligence completed, I asked if he needed a sparring partner? If so, I had no problem with him coming up to use the bags, as we could do a little training together.

At this time, I had a little boxing experience and played around with some kickboxing. My interest in full contact training was the reason I had the heavy bags. You see, at that time the dojo had very few shields and impact equipment.

Jack mentioned that he had 3 bouts, so I asked what his record was for wins and losses. Three wins, and yes, Jean Yves Theriault as his trainer. This told me that I just might learn something. When it came to sparring and fighting I was always eager to test myself, as well as learn from more experienced competitors. I was also confident that with my 15 or so Karate tournaments, and boxing skills I would fare quite well. Perhaps I could show him a thing or two.

Here is where my life changed with regards to live combat in martial arts. I was pretty good, I thought. I had decent skills and I was fast, thus I could normally deal with different styles and approaches. Jack was a few inches taller, but about 10lbs lighter than me. Frankly, he looked a bit thin. He dressed in long pants and a t-shirt, so I decided to wear my karate-gi pants and a t-shirt as well. We put 16oz boxing gloves on our hands and, for added safety, a sparring helmet. We loosened up, stretched, touched gloves, and started moving around.

As the Sensei, and out of courtesy, I took the lead as the teacher. He was in my dojo, so it was proper that I should make the first move. Using my speed, I delivered a reverse punch to his center. He adjusted but did nothing more than shift slightly back. Then I attacked again, this time with a lead-leg round kick which landed on his arm. He had a good defense and was well protected with very few openings. No problem I thought - I'll just keep getting him with quick shots. I'll get in and get out. With that idea, I went inside again with another reverse punch to the body. As I landed my punch, he shifted and countered swiftly. He had measured my attack the first time and now he accurately responded. Bang, bang, bang!!

He told me later that his counter combination was left hook, straight right, left hook, lead-leg front kick to my body.

Out on my feet, I was swimming and had no clue what had just happened. My brain was on fire, and with glassy eyes, I could barely see him.

He knew immediately that I was in trouble and asked if I was OK. We took a break and talked about what he had hit me with. It was something I had never experienced before. One punch, yes, during point matches - but nothing like that. He asked if I wanted to keep going and I said definitely, but now I would be the student - not the teacher.

During the next 4 rounds he taught me several things. I absorbed them all. The new basics taught me that my feet were too wide, and I bounced too much. I needed to shift my feet without bouncing, then keep my hands higher with my arms like a shield in front of me. What little boxing I had done at age 16 helped a bit, but my Karate training's spirit, intensity, and timing helped a great deal. By round five I was landing some techniques and I started to feel good again. Fighting is fighting, but you need to know the game you are in if you want to succeed!

It was a day that I will never forget. I had all the basic skills, but when the bombs started landing, I went into shock. I had no idea how to take a punch or recover from one. Jack came back twice more to train and spar. I maximized his coaching and changed my path regarding sparring. I went on to convince fellow Black Belts, Bob Noonan and Bob McNeil, to do some "kickboxing" training with me. They, like me, got passionate about the contact, and we all added kickboxing to our training regime.

I still competed in point tournaments and found I was even more successful - except for a few DQ's for excessive contact. I am very pleased that I decided to invite Jack into the Dojo and give me my initial lesson. Even though it was hard to swallow, I say thanks, Jack.

For me, it was the missing piece to my martial arts puzzle. None of this would have been possible without the help of so many people. Every Sunday all my sparring partners would make time to do this extra training as we bruised and battered each other.

Still, it took a decade of dojo kickboxing before I decided it was time to put up or shut up. At the time I was actively teaching some kickboxing in my classes, but I wanted to do more. Ethically, I reasoned that I couldn't teach real kickboxing if I hadn't had at least one competitive bout. It was 1999, and I was 33 years old when I first stepped inside the ring to test my skills in a real setting. At that age most fighters are retiring, but for me, I hadn't even gotten started.

That all changed when I called Conrad Blas, the owner and promoter of Tri Star gym in Montreal. They had a well-known club with a tremendous 90% win record in their competitive bouts. I told Conrad about my Karate, the various tournament experiences, and my desire to have a fight in the ring. He was a world champion in Kickboxing and Muay Thai, so he wasn't impressed by any of my Karate stories. Regardless, I told him it was time for me to glove up and get it done. He happened to have a show scheduled in six weeks and was open to having me on the card. He asked about my age, weight and if I had any kickboxing or boxing bouts. I reminded him of my Karate background and the dozen or so tournaments that I attended.

Conrad responded, *"So you're a beginner. Frankly Dan, the Karate experience, I'm sorry to say, is worthless in the ring. I'll let you know if I can get you a match."* Then he cut the conversation off and that was that.

Given the tenor of our talk I was surprised when, a couple days later, he called back with the name of my opponent. Marco Brossard was 6ft tall and 160lbs, with one fight and one win. He was a beginner like me, but he also happened to be a student of Tri Star gym. Truthfully, it felt like a set-up, perhaps to prove that Karate guys have no place in the ring. Set up or not, I wanted it and I'd just have to take whatever they served up. Then I threw myself into training.

The six weeks went fast, and now it was fight day. I arrived in Montreal just before weigh-ins. Robert Panatan, the Commissioner of the Quebec Amateur Kickboxing, did the registrations, asking me the usual questions and then about my experience. With a smile he stated knowingly, *"No experience, just how green are you?"*

Directly, I answered *"Not too green - I have a Black Belt in Karate with about 20 tournaments under my belt."* With a chuckle he asked, *"Did you win any trophies."* Now the other men at registration table laughed, and I realized I was their little joke.

He then loudly proclaimed *"OK Karate man – you're as green as it gets, but you're certified to fight - bout number 5 – good luck."*

I had four fights before mine to prepare myself and to let go of the insulting sting these guys had laid on me. They made it clear that they had little respect for Karate fighters. When I met my opponent, I found out why they were chuckling. Marco Brossard is tall, lean and well-muscled. His coach, Conrad Blas, came up to me saying with a smile, *"Remember to keep your hands up – I'd like to see this go the distance. Marco's first bout ended with a TKO in the first round and I'd like him to get a little more work in this fight!"*

I didn't like the intimidation game he was playing so I looked him in eye saying, *"Don't worry, I came to fight."* But in my mind, I was wondering what is it with these guys and Karate fighters? The answer came when I watched the second fight of the night. Two older teens stepped into the ring; one wore Thai shorts while the other was wearing what looked to be track shorts without pockets. The young man with the Thai shorts was from a Muay Thai club and the other from a Karate school. Sixty seconds later the Karate kid was on the floor. He didn't stand a chance, as he was trying to point-fight a kickboxer. With his hands down, he was bouncing up and down trying to move in and land single points. Looking at his style and ability, I wondered if this kid had any proper training at all. The Thai boxer ate him up, ending the fight with a powerful kick to the body. Now I knew why there were so many smirks and chuckles – the Karate fighters didn't typically win.

The next fights flashed by and suddenly I found myself in the red corner with my name being announced. I felt the fear and the nerves, as my guts twisted with anticipation. This was it; this is what I asked for – God help me!

My opponent looked calm. Later I found out that I also appeared calm and composed, but it didn't feel like that on the inside. I felt all my energy drain and my legs felt like jelly as I stepped into the ring. I kept thinking about the Karate kid in bout # 2. Was that going to be me? Is this guy going to rain hell down on me? I knew he was going to be talented as he was part of a winning team with a winning record. With the referee giving instructions we were as close as we had been all day. I know he expected to put the Karate guy away quickly. Truthfully, no athlete wants the fight to go the distance and hopes to get it over as fast as possible.

Something happened in my brain during the pre-fight stare down. The jitters faded, as calmness overcame me, then my energy surged, and my adrenaline pumped. I looked him in the eye and heard myself say, *"Let's have fun and put on a great show."*

His face and his confidence changed. Just for a moment, he cracked. I think I stole a bit of his thunder and now he had to rethink his strategy. Perhaps I might not be what he thought I was and now it was his turn to have doubts. He hadn't noticed until now that I was 160lbs of muscle and Karate or not, I might just have something.

We were sent back to our corners. My nerves were calm, and mind focused like I was in a state of grace or something the Japanese call "mushin" – a no mind mental state. I no longer heard the crowd, as the referee pointed to each of us – *"You ready, you ready?"*

I smiled and said *"Absolutely"*, Marco said yes, but then he looked back at his corner-men with a certain dismay. Time stood still for second or two when I heard *"Fight"*.

My hands were high and tight, shifting and moving first left, then right, looking to measure the distance on a much taller opponent. This was not the typical "Karate" fighter they were all expecting. I forced him to attack first as I closed in. I figured he was going to throw a lead front kick to my face or a jab. I was ready for either when the left jab came. With lightning speed, I countered with a straight right to his body. I heard the crowd gasp at the sound my glove made on his body. The perfect reverse punch "gyakuzuki" hit home. He countered by firing a few techniques, but my timing and distance kept me out of range. Once again, I set him up and moved into scoring another big "gyakuzuki" to the body followed it with a left hook, right cross and a lead round kick to the body.

Over the next few rounds he fought back, catching me with a number of techniques but nothing that bothered me. I had him in trouble several times with some well-timed punches, and while forcing him into the corners I hit him repeatedly with uppercuts.

When the smoke cleared, we had gone the distance, and my hand was raised as the clear winner. I had done it – survived my first kickboxing match - and with success! After the fight Marco asked me how many kickboxing bouts I had, as he had thought it was my first? I told him, *"Yes, you're right, I'm a karate fighter and that was my first kickboxing fight in a ring."* When I returned to the dressing room the two Kickboxing commissioners were waiting for me. For the next five to ten minutes, they proceeded to interrogate me. They did not believe that was my first bout. They believed I was at the very least a seasoned boxer, as it was my boxing skills that won the day. I explained that my Karate training had taught me timing and distance because when you have only one technique to get a point it has to be a good one.

I believe it was the absolute focus (kime) when landing my techniques that won me that bout. I told them that I combined the strengths of Karate with those of kickboxing. After a few minutes they believed me, and from that moment on I became a favorite in their fight circuit. Of course, I had to learn the 'ins and outs' of ring fighting, but fighting is fighting. If you are well trained, be it Karate or Kickboxing, and you can adapt, you can compete. It was my hard-style Karate edge that made the difference in that bout and the many more that followed.

As time went on, I lived my dream of competing as a Kickboxer and competing in the ring under the guidance of the man I had watched at age 13. Jean Yves took me on as one of his fighters and coached me in many of my fights. I excelled and competed in 25 bouts, winning a Canadian Title, and then competing for Team Canada in Greece before turning pro and winning my three fights in the USA.

As I stated, fighting is fighting, and training is training. If you have a good teacher and you are willing to learn then the rest is up to you. I'm grateful for my Karate and for the guidance Sensei Mueller gave, often inspiring me to keep going when I was having some troubles. He may not remember that, due to financial concerns, I almost quit karate training a couple of times. He even gave me work at his house - painting and fixing holes in the walls - to pay for my membership as I finished college.

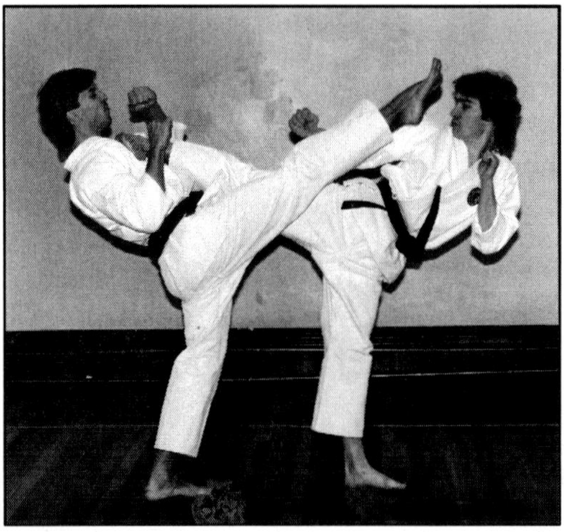

When things are meant to be, things find a way to work out. Many hands make light work. Without his words and belief in me, I never would have lived my dream. Today, I operate three dojos and teach a kickboxing curriculum-based with belt upgrades and traditional values. Like my Karate, everything - all training - begins and ends with courtesy. It's everything you would find in a traditional karate school plus the philosophy component.

It's how and what I learned. Regardless of the style of fighting or competition, if you don't value yourself and respect your opponent you won't go very far. It's the missing link in most "Kickboxing Clubs" and sadly in many Karate programs. Regardless of what style you train in: if you find a great teacher who believes in you, you can go far!

ENGINNEERING A WINNER

SCOTT BULLARD

The competitors stepped into the ring, one garbed in purple and gold, the other in traditional white. Friends, they had come halfway around the world to fight each other. It was just another strange part of a strange two-week trip that brought Trinidad & Tobago's Purple Dragon Team and Team Canada's Best Karate to a World Championship Karate Tournament in Australia.

Regardless of the circumstances, Canada's Scott Bullard was toe-to-toe against arguably Trinidad's top competitor Ludwin Jacob. Both men were about the same size and weight with strong, wiry bodies. Jacob was a seasoned international competitor with dozens of major wins and Bullard, in his first international tournament, had experience in many local Ontario events. I'd say they were friends due to the long-standing twinning friendship shared by Don Jacob and myself. Had this been the tournament finals, it would have been wonderful to compete head-to-head with our friends, but as this was the first round of the eliminations, it was very disappointing. Both Professor and I had gone to the judges asking that CBK not face Purple Dragon during the eliminations, but it couldn't be helped, as there weren't enough other competitors.

Surprisingly, despite coming from the other side of the world, Purple Dragon and CBK had brought the largest teams. The promoter, Sam Gervasi, had failed to garner any local Australian support for this Championship Tournament. As such, what should have attracted about 1000 competitors had only registered 76 participants. There was nothing world-class, outside of the Australian Minister of Sport attending along with a letter from the Prime Minister, about Gervasi's event. The 38 competitors from Trinidad and Canada were the only worthy teams there. We accepted this fact as being beyond our control and thus, we made the best of it.

Sitting with Don Jacob I was nervous about Scott fighting Ludwin. I had seen Professor's cousin compete many times before, and he was an amazing fighter and performer. On the other hand, I knew that Scott, as the Sensei of CBK Ontario, was a very good teacher, tremendous Karate technician, and athlete, but as his mentor, I didn't see him as a fighter.

Looking back at our long relationship, I guess you could say I was always nervous for Scott. While he was one of the smartest men I knew, there was always something about his good-guy demeanor that made me think he was over his head in whatever he was attempting to do. It had started a decade before when he first opened his Karate School in Woodbridge Ontario. I was always coaching him on how to make his students better and ways to improve his business. He took the advice to heart and did well, but for me, because he was modest and humble, I had the feeling that he always needed more. After what seemed to be years of struggling, he announced that he had decided to move his existing school to a new location. It was about 10 miles away, was twice the size and more than double the rent! Frankly, I was horrified! When Scott wanted my opinion about his plans I implored - no, I begged him - not to do it!

"Scott," I told him, *"I think this is a bad idea, it's way too risky! Look, you have a good thing going here, nice group of students and you're making an OK living – I think you should just renew your lease and be satisfied, be happy."* I could usually talk Scott into doing things, if I applied myself and some logic; after all, he had graduated from Queens University with Honors in Chemical Engineering. That's right: Chemical @#$% Engineering – this guy lived and breathed logic! It was his main diet. However, no matter what I said he just quietly made his case by saying, *"If I go to this new area, I will be able to dominate the market there and I can grow the school. I think the bigger rent is worth the risk."*

All I could think was - maybe if it was me doing it, yes that would make sense, but for Scott, it's just too risky. Regardless, as Brian Tracy says, *"A man changed against his will, is of the same opinion still".* Scott wanted to try, and he had high hopes about what he could do. The fact is, he, in his quiet way, didn't just think he could do it - he knew he could.

Within a year of re-opening at his new location, Scott had the largest and most successful Canada's Best Karate school in our group. With an annual membership reaching over 500 students at its peak, he had more than doubled his dojo in every way. I was incredibly proud of him and happy that he had kicked my doubts about his ability in the butt!

Perhaps I should have remembered that story as the Australian center referee called *"Hajime!"* to begin the 5-point non-contact, winner take all match. Jacob in purple and gold began in a side fighting, tight sword-type motion as he measured Bullard's, in traditional white, style and ability. Bullard set himself strongly and as Jacob was thinking, Scott moved in with a foot sweep and quick right hand that landed flush on the side of Ludwin's head. One point Bullard! Just as quickly the next clash saw Sensei Scott fake with a hand attack and land a picture-perfect mawashi geri (roundhouse kick) once again to Ludwin Jacob's head. Two points Bullard, zero Jacob!

An astonished Professor Don Jacob looked at me saying, *"Alright man, let's see what happens!"* then clenched his fist, as he became a cheerleader for his top man. Almost on cue, Sensei Ludwin attacked with a hard back-fist to the face, one that bloodied Bullard. A clear foul as hard contact usually requires either an immediate disqualification or point reduction against the offending competitor. Instead, the judges awarded Ludwin Jacob a point, while Scott got some medical attention. During the next few clashes, the score went back and forth as the Purple Dragon fighter pulled out all stops to dominate and take the lead in the fight. From the stands, Professor encouraged while I gritted my teeth as Scott, although having lost the element of surprise, kept the fight even with his determination and impeccable technical execution. Now tied at 4 points to 4 each, it was a great match that ended with Sensei Jacob finding the win with his go-to backfist technique. Jacob won the match, but Bullard scored the psychological win that told everyone there that CBK was a contender and we belonged.

Scott Bullard's first-round example of ability and toughness set the tone for every CBK / Purple Dragon match to follow during the tournament. As friends, we fought each other hard and made an otherwise forgettable tournament a worthwhile experience for all those who had made the long trip to compete.

For me, it was just another chapter in my long experiences with Sensei Scott Bullard. Confidence is the product of competence. His training, drive, and quiet mastery have made him a lifelong winner on every stage he has taken.

As with any of my many sons, my concerns and fears about their abilities were just that, they were mine. You would think that after all this time I would understand that our CBK love of the underdog and championing success by overcoming obstacles is part of our DNA. In the case of Scott Bullard, I never have to worry that he will succeed, as his logical analysis and ability to engineer a win never fails. But, like any good mentor, my illogical worries keep me cheering hard for his success.

A KARATE STORY

FROM SUPERKIDS TO CBK
BY SCOTT BULLARD

"Life is what happens to you while you're making other plans."

I didn't plan to become a karate *sensei*; I was supposed to become a chemical engineer. Like most events that shape our lives, there was really no way I could have predicted or influenced the outcome. I could only react in the moment based on the principles I held most deeply.

And I wouldn't have wanted it to turn out any other way.

"*You should do this; you'd be good at it.*"

I had stopped by the dojo in the afternoon to pick up a pair of shin guards that I would need for the next sparring class. Only an Orange Belt at the time, karate was still pretty new to me and I was enjoying all the aspects of training that I was experiencing.

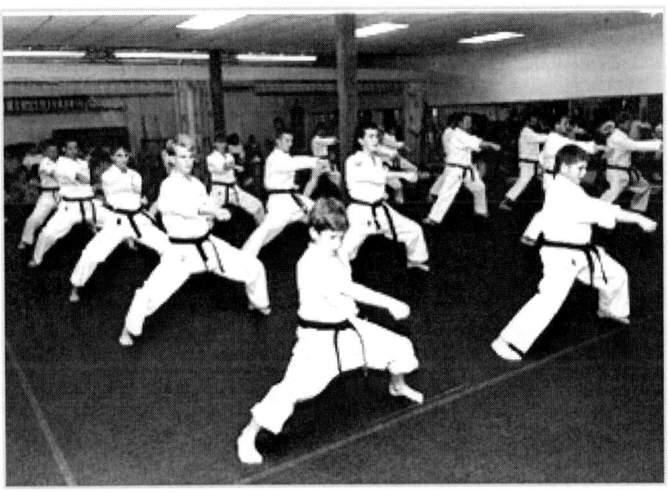

No one was at the dojo other than Sensei – that's Sensei Bob Mueller, my first martial arts sensei and the only person I really think of as "my" sensei – so he was helping me out at the pro-shop.

That's when he dropped a little bomb on me. We were talking about karate and he said that he thought I would be good at teaching karate - had I ever thought about it as a career?

I was a bit taken back. I am a shy person by nature, although I work hard at overcoming that, and didn't really know how much Sensei noticed me in class.

For him to come out and say he thought I could be a karate sensei like him, well – I was surprised, and at the same time proud of the compliment. Little did I know that Sensei had this conversation with a lot of students! But I still take it as a compliment.

I politely thanked him, but I had already planned to go to university to become a Chemical Engineer.

That sounds great, he said - good luck!

After that, I took my sparring gear and left the dojo to head for work. I don't know if Sensei remembers that day, but it's one that had planted a germ of an idea in the back of my mind, not blooming until many years later.

One thing you should know about me: I'm an all-or-nothing type of person. No half measures, no "let's do this for a little while and see how it goes". Perhaps that was part of the alure of the martial arts.

As Gichin Funakoshi said: "Even if it must be ten million foes, I go!"

1990 was a milestone year for me; within one month of graduating from Queen's University with an Honours Degree in Chemical Engineering, I had earned my 1st Degree Black Belt in karate. With papers – and belt – in hand I drove away from small town Ontario to make my mark in the big city: Toronto.

Starting my new adult life was at once exciting and discouraging. I was living on my own, with plenty of school friends close by to introduce me to the busy Toronto scene; yet at times, I felt quite alone and suffered from this loneliness.

I had also continued my karate training at a club located on Danforth Avenue in Toronto's Greektown. This club was filled with friendly people who shared my love of the art, and was taught by top level instructors, but something was missing. It didn't have that atmosphere of family that I enjoyed before.

After a year of training, I started making excuses not to go to class: it was late, I was tired from work, there was too much traffic. Eventually I took an honest look at myself and admitted the truth: I just didn't want to go any more. I looked around for another club but didn't find what I was looking for.

I did what earlier that year I couldn't have imagine was possible: I quit karate.

While I was not happy about my decision, I knew it was what I needed to do at the time. What I didn't realize was how it was going to happen next.

About a month after I quit training, I received a phone call out of the blue from Mr. Harold Warden. He and Mr. Wally Slocki were the owners of the Superkids Karate franchise, and they were opening up a "head office" Superkids Karate dojo; he wondered if I was interested in coming by to see what they were doing.Their new location was only 20 minutes from where I was renting a house with some friends. I don't believe in fate or karma but there were definitely some strong coincidences taking place!

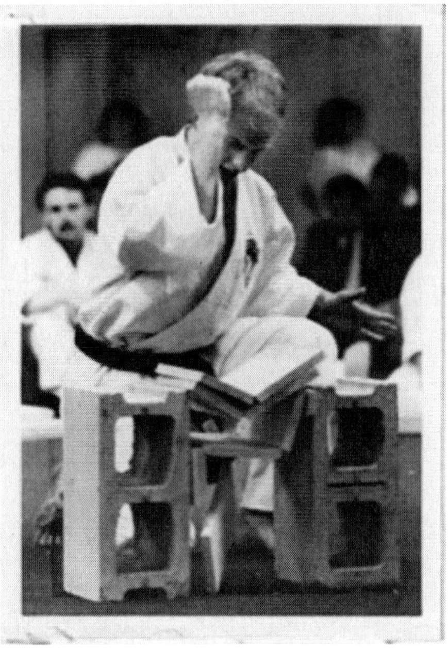

I met Warden and Slocki at their dojo, which was under construction and scheduled to open in a few weeks. And what a dojo it was going to be! A grand entrance with stone flooring, a waterfall in the reception area, TV monitoring of the dojo, wall-to-wall padded flooring - this place was going to be grand! You have to remember this was in 1992 when most karate schools had stinky sweat-stained carpet on the floor and holes in the wall from people falling into them after an especially heated sparring match. A nice club would have hardwood floors reminiscent of a tradition Japanese dojo but those were rare.

After giving me the tour, Warden and Slocki said they were looking for instructors to help out and asked if I would be interested. I'm sure the speed at which I said yes gave then a hint that I was looking for something more than just a pastime.

This began a routine that consumed my non-working hours: every day after work I would drive 45 minutes from East of Oshawa where I worked directly to the dojo to assist in all the classes for the evening, then stay after class for about 30-40 minutes to work on my own training, many times under the tutelage of Slocki, before heading home to bed exhausted but happy.

Eventually another ritual was added on to this schedule: Warden would take me out for dinner after the evening was over, where he would give me a master class in business and marketing. I would rush home after these "classes" and make notes in a diary of sorts on all that I had learned from these two modern martial arts masters.

Weekends were of course a chance to break the routine and get away from everyday pressures, so naturally I went to the dojo to teach and train some more. I had finally found the "home" I was searching for.

It was after about a year of being the "sempai" at the dojo that I had my epiphany.

As I was enjoying my time at the dojo, I was becoming increasingly disappointed with my working life. I enjoyed being an engineer but the company that hired me out of university was a large employer, with tens of thousands of employees across Ontario. Increasingly I was feeling like a small cog in a very large machine, and I knew that I wanted to be able to make more of an impact on the world.

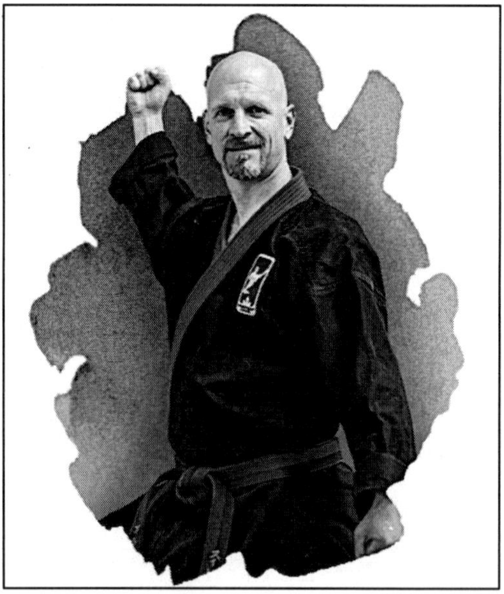

Which lead me to the day where, standing in the parking lot outside of work, I was struck with such an intense "truth" that I couldn't contain it anymore - I had to yell it for the world to hear.

"I hate my job!!"

There was something liberating, maybe even cathartic, about admitting this not only to myself, but to the world at large and not caring who heard me. Because once I had admitted the truth, I instantly knew what I needed to do.

I raced to the dojo and sat down with Warden and Slocki. What do I need to do to open up a Superkids Karate school, I asked, because I was prepared to do whatever it took to own my own dojo.

Within a few months of having that conversation I had quit my job and begun working full-time for Warden and Slocki at their dojo. One year later I took the biggest leap of faith in my life and opened my first dojo!

As my life was progressing down this new path, I often thought back to that innocuous conversation with Sensei. Did he know something I didn't know, even back then?

2021 marks the 35th anniversary of the first day I stepped into a karate dojo. Like most influential moments in our lives, I had no idea how that one innocent action would lead my life in directions I could never have imagined.

When I became a sensei and opened my first dojo, I was pretty confident that I had the skills to succeed: good athletics, world-class coaching and mentoring, a proven business plan and a willingness to do whatever it took to create my vision of what a karate dojo should be.

There was just one thing I felt I was lacking: I didn't have any good stories to tell.

Early on in my karate training, it was impressed on me that one of the traits of a great sensei was the ability to tell a story. If you've ever had the privilege to be in a class taught by Sensei Mueller then you know why I felt this way.

But how could I ever be a great sensei when I had no stories to tell? Nothing exciting ever happened to me; I'm not a world champion competitor, I've never been in a bar fight or defended myself or a loved-one from a mugger.

So I chose to follow that age-old wisdom: fake it 'til you make it!

I told stories about the people who I had trained with and respected. Some of these were told to me by the subjects themselves, others were events I actually witnessed.

As I grew my student base and become more comfortable with the role of "sensei", I came to realize that it's not the stories of our lives that are the important detail – it's the lessons we learn from them.

That's why martial arts training can bring such profound changes to so many people's lives: we can all find lessons in the stories we live and, through the search for these truths, become the fullest expression of ourselves.

And that's a story we can all be proud to tell!

LOOKING FOR THE KING

And Finding Karate

Looking at his large storage locker I was shocked at the length, depth, and breadth of his collection. It was as obsessive and as all-consuming as I had ever seen. Saying that, I consider myself an expert about all-consuming obsessive behavior – you could say I wrote the book on it! I had won a TV Emmy Award years before for my obsessive journey called "Finding Your Butkus." The book chronicled my life's story of a passionate journey into hero madness. But this guy, and his Elvis Presley fascination, he was over the top. He is a collector of the highest degree.

Sensei Ed Comeau, a Karate student dating back to my Brockville/Kingston days is now a thoughtful, yet dynamic martial arts leader. He's one that I always liked but now, knowing his life's work, I hold him in the highest regard for his ethics and honor. While I knew he was always highly ethical, I also knew that as a younger man he was very emotional and given to impulsive decisions. And not always good ones. While I don't know for sure, perhaps it was the ideals of self-control that first drew him to his Karate training many years ago. What I do know is, whatever he was looking for he found it.

Elvis aside, he is the epitome of what a good Sensei is and does. Outside of fa ew chance encounters, I lost track of him for several decades until he emerged with many of his students at a seminar I was teaching in 2009. I was surprised to see him and very impressed with the caliber of people he was training. When he presented me with a gift and an invitation to his Dojo, I was intrigued. I made a point of accepting the invitation on my next visit to Ontario.

What I found was perhaps the most traditional Karate Dojo that I had seen in many years. Clean and organized, his students were all as gracious as their teacher. Honestly, it was like going back in time, and seeing my own work in action. Like all good leaders, he took the lessons of his past, then sorted out what worked for him and what didn't. What interested me was that while he treasured his beginner's days, he moved past where he had been to develop his own ways. After analyzing his experiences, he did, in many ways, the exact opposite. To his credit, he took an extremely negative experience with a bad organization, then along with partner Dan Wilson, developed a Dojo and system to be admired. I am such an admirer. His focus was to develop his Budo mindset and as such, he made classic Japanese Karate and its traditions to be his touchstone.

If there is one thing or trait in people I admire above all else, it is the tenacity to act. Too many individuals suffer from paralysis through analysis when they become leaders. The details of what you do are very important if you plan to succeed over a long time, but in my experience, it is always the person who takes action that gets results. A lion doesn't dream of hunting, a lion hunts!

Sensei Comeau is a lion. Since that first day I have visited him regularly discovering his many leadership talents along with his storage locker. As to Elvis Presley, I enjoy and share Sensei Comeau's passion for iconic personalities. I would have to say that his impressive collection surpasses my own Butkus memorabilia, but of course, he didn't get any international awards for it. Thus, in the obsessive fascination department that would make me still "the King."

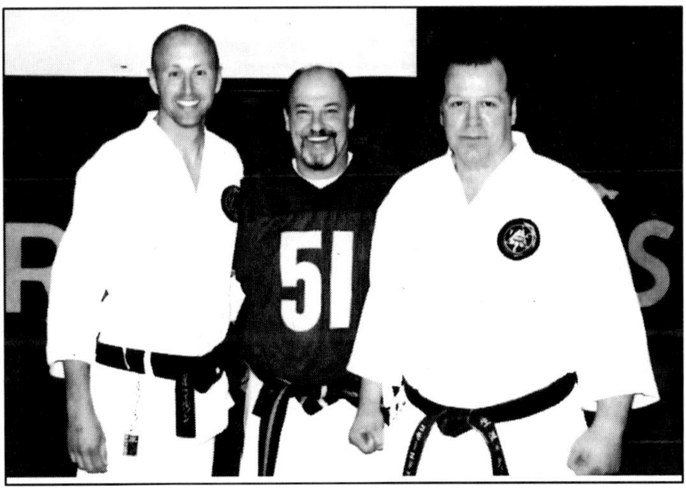

With Dan Wilson & Ed Comeau of Team Canada Black Belt Institute

DISCOVERING KINGSTON KARATE

By Edward Comeau

'Window Shopping' through the Frontenac Mall in the late 1980's was nothing to be overly excited about. It had always been one of those lackluster shopping arenas between the downtown City core and the ongoing expansion of the Kingston, Ontario Township.

This day was different though. Stepping into the mall in early May of 1988, just shy of my 22nd Birthday, I had no idea that my life would change forever from that day on.

I could see down a distant walking aisle, the immediate visual of two impressive *Samurai* Swords (*Katana* and *Wakasashi*). They were majestically displayed on a proper weapons rack, centered on a draped banquet table. Their eye-catching appeal successfully accomplished its task, as its magnetic energy immediately drew me to the display table. The sign read:

"FREE DRAW: 1st Prize, WIN A SAMURAI SWORD"

"2nd Prize: 2 FREE KARATE LESSONS"

Like most testosterone-driven, young adult males enthralled with the resurgence of Martial Art films, I loved many of the mainstream theatrical releases. At that time *"The Karate Kid", "Teenage Mutant Ninja Turtles", "Above The Law", "BloodSport", "Best of the Best" and "Perfect Weapon"* impressed me the most. These films created a calling and the hope that I would someday learn Martial Arts. The movies had heroic power, as they were full of self-control and justice. Add to that the appeal they held for the ladies – I found my opportunity staring at me in the form of two *Samurai* Swords. It was just so damned cool!

The man minding the table, with blond feathery hair and a stylish '80's mullet, greeted me with a noticeably bold, confident, and distinctive radio announcers'-type voice.

The young Black Belt, *Sempai* Daniel Coles from Brockville Ontario, would soon become my first *Karate* Instructor. I disappointedly did not win the Swords (like I thought I really wanted), but luckily I did win those 2 Free *Karate* Lessons (that I really needed).

This first step on my journey reminded me of my earliest memories of wanting to pursue *Karate*. At the age of 5, pointing to a sign on Bagot Street in downtown Kingston, I told my mother, "*I want to do that!*" The sign read *"TSURUOKA KARATE SCHOOL"*. I don't even know if I truly knew what *'that'* even was at that age, but I knew I wanted it!! Yet, it took filling out a simple ballot, 16 years later, to finally get up the nerve and find the opportunity to walk into a legitimate *Dojo* (Training Hall / *'The Place of The Way'*).

The marketing ploy definitely worked!

Although born and raised in Canada's first Capital City, I was unaware that a basement existed at the Frontenac Mall, and that a *Shotokan Karate* School was operating there. The *Dojo* had a spacious training area with an adjacent secondary warm-up floor space, divided by see-through roll-down split-bamboo screens. The floor was a thin red-black industrial carpet over the cement base. Concrete isn't very forgiving for joint-impact and when performing physical exercises barefooted it was neither safe, nor hygienic either. Two of the walls were covered with mirrors and the front one had a formal presentation on it, called the *'Shomen'*. Soon I would grow familiar with its portraits of Karate legends: *DAI SENSEI: GICHIN FUNAKOSHI* and *O'SENSEI, RICHARD KIM*. They have remained with me for the rest of my life.

The environment had all the makings of (at least in my mind, heart and desire) what a proper, traditional *Karate Dojo* was supposed to be like.

Those Private Lessons forever changed the trajectory of my existence. Almost 33 years later, I can still recall several of the items taught during those first two Private Sessions.

It did not take me any time at all to decide whether to continue with regular classes after the Promotional Prize. I wanted this badly - and I really wanted that great looking white outfit!! The *karate-gi* fulfilled a childhood dream to have a *'Superhero'* uniform.

"I READ COMIC BOOKS AND I WAS THE HERO IN THE COMIC BOOK.
I SAW MOVIES AND I WAS THE HERO OF THE MOVIE"

Although perhaps a bit *'misguided'* in my initial motivations, my passion and enthusiasm for *Karate* goes back to my life-long research and fandom of the entertainer, Elvis Aron

Presley. Unfortunately, over the years since he *'Left the Building'*, the Traditional Martial Community has mocked Presley's authenticity as a Martial Artist. Most have never fully comprehended his true accomplishment, and the influence he had on *Karate* in North America.

Before Elvis, there had only been 2 note-worthy depictions of Martial Arts in American Film: 1945: James Cagney in "Blood on the Sun", and 1955: Spencer Tracy in "Bad Day at Black Rock", making Presley one of the early Pioneers to promote Martial Arts in American Cinema, seven years before Bruce Lee.

As an impressionable only child from a broken family, Elvis provided me with the positive male role model that every young boy needs. He was the ideal *'Superhero'* for my fantasy. Regardless of how many times I had seen them before, Presley Movies from the '50's and '60's, were always *'must-see'* TV events during my formative years. There was nothing not to like about Elvis! He was cool and dashing in every way, always getting all the girls, and heroically winning every fight. I recall from the age of 6, I wanted to be like Elvis.

Later in his career, Elvis reinvented himself somewhat unintentionally with *Karate*. Two Feature Film Concert Documentaries showed Presley and his natural athletic expression of *Karate* technique when he returned to live performances for real audiences after a 9-year movie absence. In the early 1970's (a primitive stage in the development and comprehension of Martial Arts in Western Society), millions of fans got to see actual demonstration of *Karate*, show-cased in an exciting, dramatic fashion. Elvis wore a series of elaborate, stunning costumes originally inspired from his traditional *Karate Gi*. Later, with the inclusion of capes he completed the visual image of a legitimate *'Superhero'* for this wide-eyed, impressionable young future *Karate-Ka*.

Elvis spent 19 years exploring the *Karate* Systems of *Shotokan*, *Chito-Ryu*, American *Kenpo* and *Pasaryu*, finally being awarded an 8th-Dan Black Belt. Sadly, this accomplishment happened less than a year before his untimely passing on August 16, 1977.

Eleven years after he passed, I put on my first *Karate Gi*, feeling a little more connected to my hero. It was exhilarating, magical and mystical, and yet, all so natural. It was meant to be.

However, my potential super powers were tested when I first attempted to tie my white belt. The *Obi* (*Karate* Belt), took more practice than I was prepared for. If it were not for the kindness and sweet nature of a petite, dear lady I might still be working on getting it right! She spotted me, a total stranger, on the other side of the floor, struggling to get ready and came to my rescue. Without her help my first formal class would have been a thousand times more awkward.

With no introduction, *"Here..."* said Ms. Denise LaFrance, motioning her outstretched arms to retrieve the belt from my clumsy hands. *"It goes like this"* as she took over. Then, carefully hugging me from behind, she began the intricate tying procedure. I did my respectful best to pretend that I wasn't enjoying the process. From then on, Denise would forever become one of my *Budo*-Sisters. I was honored to follow her into training and over the next two years we were able to test for our Black Belts side by side, along with our other two *Budo*-Siblings, Jennifer and Michael Roffey. The four of us had grown together to become our own *Dojo* Family.

The *Dojo* training was energetic, and the atmosphere was positive, very positive! I found the content fascinating and the camaraderie infectious. I was hooked. Absolutely. Completely. Whole-heartedly.

I also learned that the Kingston location was under new management with Dan Coles. Apparently, the Instructor before him, operating under a different business name, did some questionable fund-raising events. With the false pretense of having terminal cancer, he raised money for diagnosis, and treatment in the U.S.A. When he was ousted as a fraud, that previous Instructor grabbed whatever remaining money he could and "*ran for the hills.*" He unscrupulously left his Student Body dumbfounded without explanation, leadership, or what they should do next.

When one door closes ...

In walked Sensei Robert Mueller - a successful *Karate Sensei* with a great track record. His Brockville *Dojo* had a strong reputation and, as he was less than an hour away, he and his group of Instructors would come to *'save the day'!*

Sensei Mueller always impressed and intimidated me. He was a handsome mustachioed, athletically fit, no-nonsense *Karate*-Man, who was about a decade my senior. Part of his arsenal was to cleverly disarm you with a friendly smile and an infectious chuckle. But I knew, from the very first time I received a *Migi-Gyakuzuki* (Right Reverse Punch) that the charm had a backbone. While sparring, his strike had deceptively found a path through my feeble guard, reverberating in my spine as it penetrated some 4 inches into my upper chest. Mueller-*Sensei*, while being a skilled *Karate-Ka* simply referred to himself as a

"Lumper" - meaning a man who loved the basics. A great smile yes, but the basic fact was, this was a man not to be messed with and one I did not want to displease....EVER!

Having just graduated his 1st-Generation of Black Belts a few months before, Mueller-*Sensei* proposed a plan to create the 2nd *"B.M.M.A. Academy"* in Kingston and rescue the students who had been ripped off by the former Instructor. To do this, he enlisted two of his top Students to teach and manage the satellite School.

First Dan Coles made the drive from Brockville every day to teach, but within a few months, circumstances made his daily commute impossible. Initially this caused a concern, and the membership braced for a change. Learning Martial Arts is a very personal connection-type experience between the Teacher and Student. What made it extra difficult was that the Kingstonians had to face losing a great new Teacher once again.

Enter Sempai Michael Sweeney. Equally talented and committed, he was perfect for such a tough task. Confident, bold, and focused, he had an exceptionally strong character - with a splash of arrogance. If he experienced any feelings of self-doubt, or weakness, it never showed. He pushed forward regardless of any resistance and would not accept failure, not by him, or for that matter anyone else. His *Karate* training had served his nature well, always forging his ability to persevere. Without realizing it at the time, watching him persevere and succeed would forever be an inspiration to me. As such, I committed myself to training as much to honor my teachers as a way to serve myself.

Sweeney got me to believe in myself and ultimately become what I had always dreamed of being: to be my own hero! Along with my 3 *Budo*-Siblings, I became one of his 1st generation Black Belts. It is still one of my proudest accomplishments.

My future road was not without speed bumps and a few potholes. However, after 30+ years and several successful *Dojo*s later, 22 of which, as an Independent Owner-Operator, of *Team Canada Black Belt Institute - The Heritage Dojo*, I represent my teachers through my actions. I believe I have done them proud. It is also my firm belief that what you do and who assists you, particularly in the beginning, is paramount in becoming successful. For me, my youthful fascination with Elvis provided the dreams of what I might be but tying that belt around my first uniform showed me what I could be. After that, it was my effort and determination to become what I would be.

To this day, even though I have chosen a more traditional route in my training and study of *Karate-Do*, I still love Elvis. I owe great debts of gratitude for my life in *Karate* to my many Teachers, Mentors and Heroes – from the Rock and Roll Icon himself, to the aforementioned Coles, Sweeney and Mueller-*Sensei*, to Kenneth B. Tallack - *Shihan*, Wally Slocki - Sensei, brothers Daniel K. Wilson – *Shihan,* and John Wilson - *Sensei*, Takemasa Okuyama - *Kancho*, Patrick MacCarthy - *Hanshi* and Cezar Bortkowski - *Hanshi*.

Once, Mueller-*Sensei* said that I was a lot like him: a *"Lumper with Spirit!"* It may be the nicest compliment anyone has ever given me.

OSU

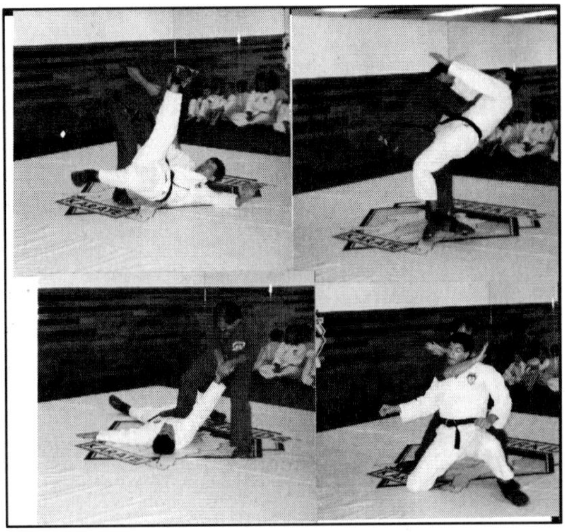

First Victoria Demonstration 1989

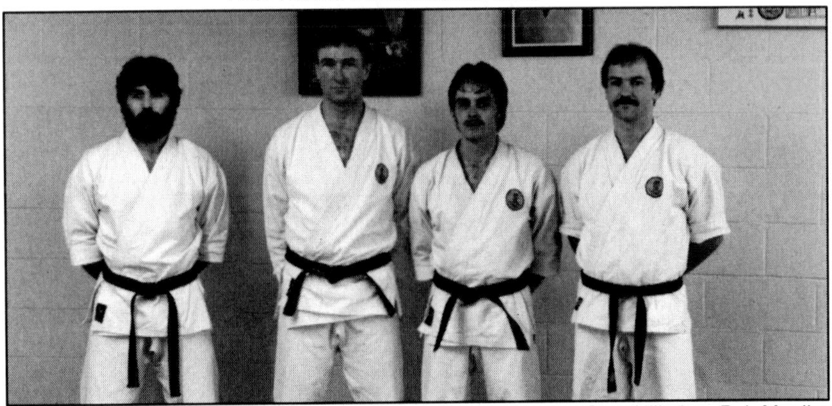

First Parksville Black Belt Test 1981 Kieran Baldwin, Rick Marshall, Glen Hillsden, Bob Mueller

HEROES, CHARACTERS and CHARLATANS

INTERACTIONS WITH MARTIAL ARTS PERSONALITIES

Sensei Richard Kim was at the far end of the table, seated next to Don Warrener and Rick Marshall. It was a typical group of senior Butoku Kai Instructors who had assembled for the evening meal and subsequent Sensei Kim lecture. After 10 years of participating in Kim's inner circle, I was used to the long days of the Karate Camp training, lectures, and private round table discussions. When Mr. Kim was on tour, he would teach his entourage many lessons in what he always referred to as the "Socratic method." It meant we, the various heads of the Provincial Karate Schools, would travel with him from city to city listening to his prepared stories and lectures over and over.

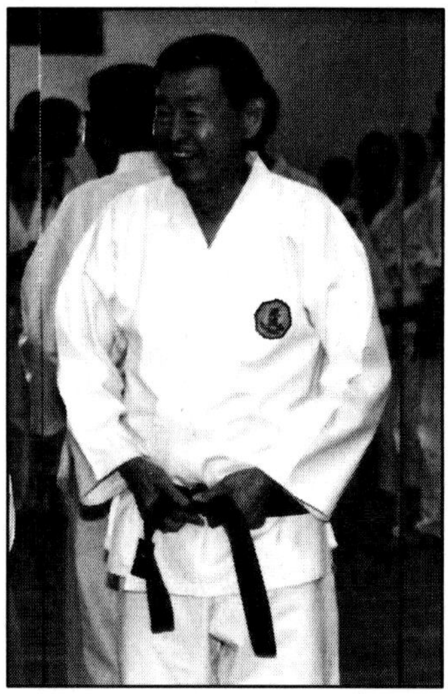

Each day there would be new local people join us at the table so he would repeat his lessons for them. The net effect was, by the end of his tour the inner circle had heard the various lessons a dozen or so times. He held court every day and often he was the only person speaking at the table. Once, we had a 7:00 AM breakfast in a hotel restaurant, and sat listening long enough that we ordered lunch before leaving our seats later that afternoon! Repetition is part of the martial way – mind, body and endurance, thus Kim's Socratic method was just another part of our traditional Karate training.

This would be my last tour as, having established myself as the top Superkids Karate Franchisee, a conflict was brewing with Kim's Bukoku Kai representatives and me. They, specifically Rick Marshall, wanted me to choose between organizations, as they didn't like any split allegiances. For me, there was already a clear separation, as Superkids Karate was a national business organization with a clear platform of how to promote and teach Karate to children. On the other side, the Butoku Kai was an international organization that offered membership and classical training through Richard Kim.

There was no conflict in my mind, but it's the kind of inner politics that makes up most Martial Arts Organizations. What it really came down to was a personal conflict between old friends: Western Butoku Kai Representative Rick Marshall and Superkids Karate's Harold Warden. I had already chosen the Superkids Group, as I now headed up 6 Franchises, and as I had a binding legal contract, I had to stay with them. Besides doing what I must do, it was also the correct decision for my family and my future.

I guess you could say it was the "last supper" when Warrener asked Sensei Kim about my Superkids Karate boss, Harold Warden. Don threw out a baited question to Kim, *"Sensei, I can't understand why Harold is trying to take business away from me? I have known Warden for over 20 years, and I've seen him start many things, but he never finishes - something always goes wrong with that guy!"*

Sensei knowingly took the bait as he answered with a short discussion about people who had dark auras. No matter what they do, or how much momentary success they might enjoy, their dark aura would always lead them back to failure. While he didn't know him personally, O'Sensei Kim said he had known about Warden for many years, and he stated that Harold Warden was a person with a dark aura. He was someone you should avoid.

It was an uncomfortable moment that was about to get downright "squirm in your seat" edgy!

The next instant came without warning as Richard Kim yelled, *"Harold Warden!"* then looking directly at me he pointed his finger saying, *"Harold Warden is a salesman, a clever monkey - he will pluck your eyes out and sell them back to you as grapes! Believe me - he is bad news"*

I can't say I remember much past that statement, other than I accepted Sensei's opinion and moved on. Later that month I wrote him thanking him for my time with the Bukoku Kai and what I had learned from him.

In reflection, I know that leaving was the correct thing to do, as Superkids was the future, and I had gone about as far as I could with Sensei Kim. Interestingly, shortly after this moment, several controversial reports came to light stating that Mr. Kim may not be as authentic as his legend made him out to be. Again, this was Karate politics and the ever-changing game of life. It's like the ocean's tide coming in and going out, where you must decide for yourself where you stand and what is right and what is wrong.

For me, Mr. Kim was a consummate Sensei or master teacher – one I enjoyed and learned a great deal from. Sensei Kim taught, through his example, how to be a leader of men. I have never seen another person of his equal. To quote one of Richard Kim's lectures, he stated, *"There is no such thing as good or bad – the fight between Heaven and the Hell exists only in the heart of man. True judgment is not external - it is internal."*

He continued by talking about negative energy, *"In nature there is no such thing as a straight line – all natural energy is circular. Man created the straight line, the arrow and the bullet are man-made to shoot straight. In the orient we call this energy "the sha-chi", the negative energy. The only way to combat negative energy is with the natural cycle or circle. When the man-made sha comes towards you, it can be reversed by the circle and sent back where it originates from. If you notice, many oriental homes have a feng shui mirror on the front door – this basically the means if the devil comes to their door and sees himself – the negative energy in the mirror scares him off. That's what I am talking about!"*

If that is true, then, without judgment, I have held a mirror up to my various martial arts experiences. I offer some straight facts and circular opinions about some of the martial arts heroes, characters, and charlatans I have met.

Harold Warden taught me how to be successful in business. His insights and mechanical methods of sales psychology, methodology, and the integrity of how to teach children inspired me to be better in every way. What I learned from him allowed me to expand my influence from local to national. Confidence comes from competence, and Warden could teach just about anyone how to a make a living teaching the martial arts. Unfortunately, his dark side also had a litigious nature where he tied people up in contracts, many times unfairly, and then sued them.

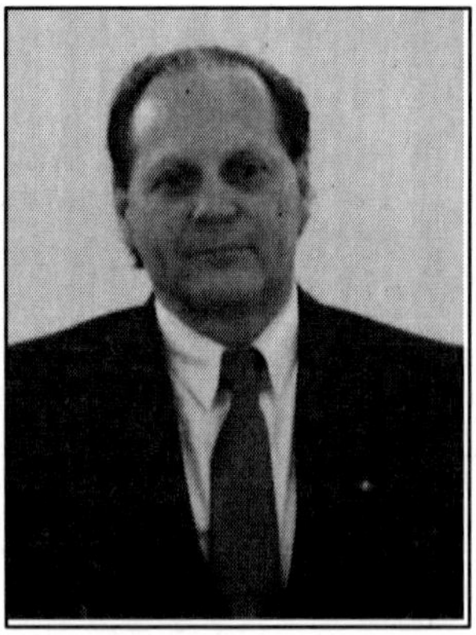

Harold also associated with some real scoundrels, and as his passion was making money, he often made bad decisions. I can say unequivocally that the few regrets I have about my career came by supporting some of Warden's ideas. It's a fact that when I trust someone, I trust fully, and when

I supported Superkids Karate I gave them 100% loyalty. In the end, after paying Harold Warden royalties amounting to many hundreds of thousands of dollars (yes, you read that correctly) for almost 20 years – he tried to sue me and my son, Leigh. When I took it to my lawyer, he laughed, noting that Harold was living in the Philippines and the lawsuit was bogus. He told me to ignore the writ and that was the last I heard of Warden. Sensei Kim was ultimately correct: Harold Warden's sha chi energy and aura ultimately attracted darkness and failure. I'd say he burned every bridge he ever crossed.

Wally Slocki was acknowledged by a 1970 Karate Illustrated Magazine as the Canadian Exception – the only Canadian of his era who could compete with the top Americans. He was also known as *"the bad boy of Canadian Karate"* - a charismatic rogue if you will. Wally Slocki was one of the great competitors of that time and in the class of Karate legends like Chuck Norris, Joe Lewis, Bill Wallace, and Mike Stone. The first time I met Wally was long after his competitive career was over. It happened in 1985 when I walked up a dingy flight of stairs to a 2nd-floor Gym where Slocki trained fighters. It was one of the dirtiest places I had ever been. The Yonge St. Gym smelled like an old hockey bag, with equipment and garbage strewn everywhere. I had seen this kind of place before, but given whose gym this was, it made a lasting impression on me. I didn't like or respect it. Slocki, on the other hand, seemed respectable. He was friendly and initially easy to talk to. He was also a salesman.

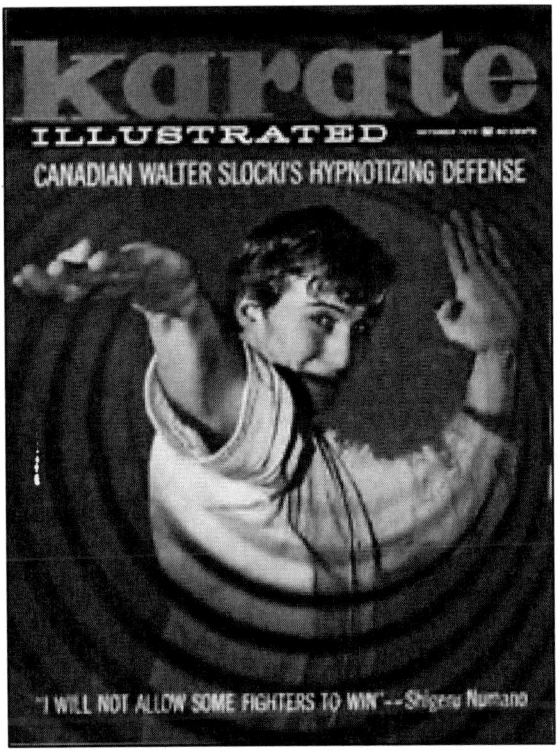

At that time Harold Warden and he had created Superkids Karate from this dump of a dojo. While I found the disarray horrifying, I accepted Harold's explanation that it was where Slocki had been, not where he was going.

Wally Slocki, sometimes called the Wayne Gretzky of Canadian Karate, had allegedly gotten caught up in a Karate Club scam during the early 1970s. Under his banner, he and his partners opened dozens of schools in the Toronto area and then went bankrupt. A lot of people lost a lot of money. Harold said that Wally was innocent and had been duped by a group of unethical businessmen, who took the money and left an innocent Slocki holding the bag. Thus, the result was Wally's smelly gym and his un-professional manner. Warden's plan would rehabilitate Slocki's tarnished image, then use his exceptional physical skill to attract new franchisees and through Superkids Karate restore his good name. It was a great concept, and an even better idea, but like the Zen Tale about the Scorpion – it didn't end well.

The Zen story goes like this:

A scorpion is standing on one side of a river when he asks a frog to help him by putting him on his back so he might cross by swimming to the other side. The frog states he is afraid that if he carries the scorpion he'll get stung.

The scorpion reassures the frog that he will not sting, as he cannot swim and needs the frog to cross the water. The frog agrees and they set off together. Halfway across the river, the scorpion without warning suddenly stings the frog - killing him. As the frog is dying he asks the scorpion, "Why, why did you sting me? Now you will drown when I die!" The scorpion's answer, *"I stung you because I'm a scorpion, it's my nature"*

Within 10 years, between Warden's dark aura and Slocki's nature, the Superkids Karate group, although initially very successful, was doomed to failure.

When they fought over the money and the influence, they not only created failure for themselves, but for their supporters, which included me and my students. They effectively stung the people who supported them. It is said that every cloud has silver lining and from this betrayal came the making of Canada's Best Karate.

What was Wally Slocki like as a man? I can't say I knew him very well, as he liked to be mysterious and aloof. What I can say is he acted, and dressed, like a character out of a Marty Scorsese's *"Goodfellows"* movie. Slocki, high on his ability, was also disrespectful of any of the "old guard" Karate authorities. He constantly made fun of traditionalist ideas and the Japanese culture itself. He'd ask, *"Are you still Osu-ing and Goosing?"* It was his way of asking if I was still bowing and scrapping to teachers like Richard Kim - one who Slocki nicknamed Kim-Booties, because of the black ninja tabi shoes he wore. Wally's favorite thing was to ask leading questions to see if he could trip people up or catch them lying. It was unpleasant, and I found it somewhat obnoxious. I'd say he was as distrusting a person as I have ever met.

Being from the west coast, I never personally saw him fight but by the way he moved, you knew he was good - really good. His way of striking was downright incredible, but it didn't transfer to his teaching. I'm quite sure he was a very good coach, one on one, but as a Sensei leading a class, he had very little charisma, or for that matter, much content. Truthfully, he was one of the most boring instructors I have ever witnessed.

Many people still praise his abilities and persona, but in my opinion, it is most likely politics and apple-polishing, as Wally Slocki, is now an old man who tries to rewrite his history. He seeks to be an all-knowing aged Karate Master, but to me he is just another talented fighter who added very little value outside of the competition ring.

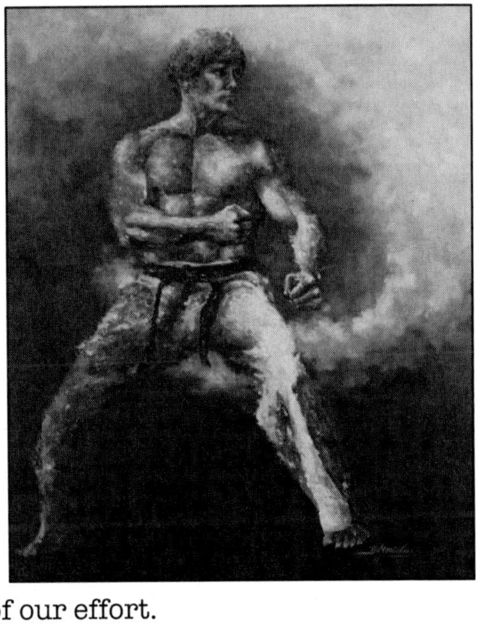

Joe Lewis fought Wally Slocki in 1970 in Toronto, Ontario, breaking his nose during an exhibition full contact match. It was a foul. Lewis is known as the father of American Full Contact Karate / Kickboxing. While I never met him, I did have the opportunity to create a work of art for him as a fundraiser to help pay for medical bills. I was commissioned by John Graden to do the art piece as a joint effort in the U.S.A. Lewis, then in his late sixties, was dying of brain cancer and was appreciative of our effort.

As I had no personal experience with him, I cannot comment regarding his character other than to say he had a reputation for being rude. My teacher, Jim Mac Donald, did have some interaction and knowledge about Lewis. Jimmy Mac, in a typical Scottish flair, told me that he would have loved to fight Lewis. He said, *"I would like nothing better than to give that prick a shot in the mouth!* Then added, *"I don't like the man - and yes, Lewis would probably beat me up, but it would be worth it - to just get a lick in."*

From other accounts I have heard, Joe Lewis often disrespected and trashed people while doing the seminars he taught. I think it is probably a fair assessment of his nature and ego that he could be mean spirited and aggressive. That said, through my efforts with John Graden, who was an admirer and student of Joe's, I wound up with a relatively balanced opinion of him.

Ed Parker was the guest of honor at the 1977 M.A.R.S. (Martial Arts Rating System) National Finals in Cleveland Ohio. Jimmy Mac and I, fresh from a big victory at the Seattle, WA M.A.R.S. qualifying round, now represented the Pacific Northwest. He had competed as a Black Belt and I, in the Brown Belt division. Jim did well the week before, but Seattle had been particularly good for me. I had taken to the evening stage in the finals, winning 1st in Kata and finishing 2nd place in fighting. I was on fire that day and was now full of confidence as we crossed the country to the nationals.

Maybe it was the 2500-mile drive, or just the fun of our road trip, but I turned in a flat performance in Cleveland. Just as I was about to do my prize-winning kata from the week before I caught the center judge's eye, and it rattled me. For a second, I couldn't remember the first step of the form! The judge saw my hesitation and gave me a zero. It was fair, as I knew my gaff and so did he. To say the least, scoring was much tougher then - no participation ribbons in those days. Fighting was much better for me, and I won several matches in a large division of competitors. I did well until I ran into a black guy built like a Sherman Tank. His left leg front kick blasted through my defense, virtually kicking my ass around the ring. It was as humbling a defeat as I ever experienced in the Karate ring.

Jim, on the other hand, placed 3rd with his Sai Kata in the Weapons Finals and had an amazing fight with the #1 rated fighter in Cleveland, James *"Cookie Monster"* Cook. MacDonald was always fearless, especially when his opponent had a big reputation. The center referee was Ed Parker himself, and I believe that added to Jim's determination. His hard reverse punches were fast and aggressive. Most likely *"Cookie"* had taken this match lightly, as he had never seen this west coast fighter before. Jimmy Mac bull rushed him, cut off fighting angles and swept him to the ground, repeatedly tearing James Cook's uniform and upending his day. It was actually a very close fight that went into overtime where Cook eked out a 3 - 2 win. But for everyone who saw the fight, including James Cook, knew it had been a good old fashion ass-whipping by MacDonald.

The evening finals brought Ed Parker, the father of American Kempo, to the center stage to do a short demonstration. Parker was a legend and almost a myth. He is credited as one the first American professional Karate teachers in the 1950s and he became a household name by teaching rock and roll icon Elvis Presley and movie stars like Steve McQueen. He was also highly educated, with a university degree in Psychology and Sociology. Parker penned this famous quote and then used it as his dojo creed.

"I come to you with only Karate, Empty Hands. I have no weapons, but should I be forced to defend myself, my principles or my honor, should it be a matter of life or death, of right or wrong, then here are my weapons, Karate, my Empty Hands."

Jim had seen some top Canadians like Wally Slocki demonstrate, but I had never seen any one of this caliber before. I was very excited to see what this great man could do.

Ed Parker, a 9th degree Black Belt, was in his late forties when we saw him. He had a bit of a belly, but a very strong stage presence. Taking the center ring with him were two *ukes* (assistants). Everyone wore Kempo Black uniforms and had Black Belts with a lot of rank stripes on them. I accessed his two assistant students to have a couple of distinctive features - they had 6th or 7th Degree Black Belts and were big guys with even bigger bellies. The men were a few years younger than Parker and were what I would call mid-western corn fed good ol' boys. I'd say they were 260 - 280lbs each. I don't say this to be harsh, but the fact is I was surprised, as these out of shape karateka seemed unusual to me. After a few brief bows, Parker demonstrated his American Kempo techniques.

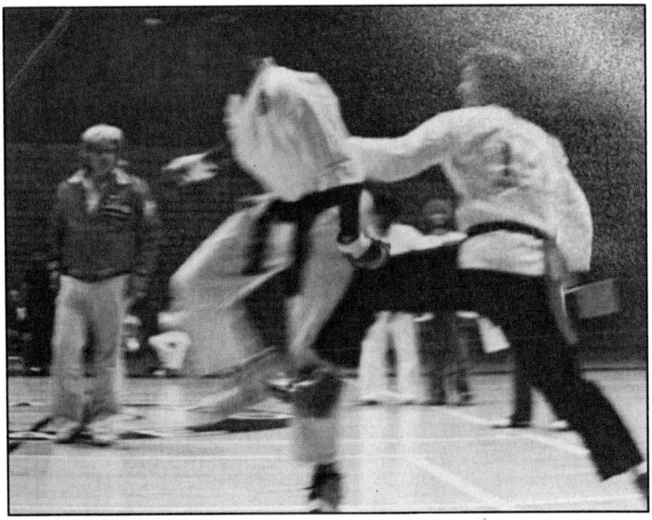

My jaw dropped as I looked over at Jimmy Mac for confirmation of what I had just seen. Mac Donald looked back, rolled his eyes, and uttered *"Jesus."* I guess he had seen that same thing I did.

For the next 5 minutes or so, we witnessed what I must say is just about the worst crap imaginable. Our background of straight line, hard style Shotokan Karate had not prepared us for what I can only call this kind of BS. I do not believe, even now as a worldly and tolerant martial artist, that I am being unfair when I say: this was the silliest stuff I have ever seen.

The technique was: the attacker steps in with a punch or kick – Parker would block and counter with a quick slap, followed by a foot sweep taking the man to the ground and then, like any angry house wife, slap the man 30 - 50 times. This slapping technique would start at the point of attack, and then proceed to strike all over his opponent. The man on the ground would writhe in pain like a fish caught on a hook, as he accepted this pitter-patter slapping defense. Incredible. At first, I thought is must be a joke of some sort. It was not.

To qualify this statement, I can say that later in my career I saw Professor Don Jacob use slapping motions in an exacting and very destructive way. I also had a Chinese stylist train at my dojo. He used incredibly powerful Kali like slapping strikes instead of punches. In both these cases these techniques were impressive and effective. American Kempo was not.

Unfortunately, Ed Parker's demonstration did not pass the smell test. His Karate lacked credibility to my eye, or for that matter to most of the assembled audience in Cleveland. We heard a lot of astonished whispering from the crowd. I believe it is this kind of teaching and demonstrations that created phony practitioners like George Dillman and various bogus martial artists that came on the scene in later years.

Regardless, Ed Parker's contribution to Karate history, with some well-crafted words and perhaps a legitimate past, is well documented. I do not discredit that. But what I witnessed in Cleveland was disturbingly bad and made me very grateful for the Karate training I had received from MacDonald and Bateson.

Rick Marshall was an unusual man in my history, and to CBK's eventual creation. It was his personality that was unusual for a Karate man, as he was a pure introvert. While he could have a fierce look and was undeniably a hardened, streetwise fighter from Hamilton, he was always clean-shaven and quiet. I never under-estimated his determination or his ability. Rick underscored his Goju Ryu Karate style with his massive ham-hock like hands, combined with his powerful forearm strength. His Karate, while simple, was very impressive and as he became my partner in Parksville's Shima Karate School, I learned to appreciate his quiet management style.

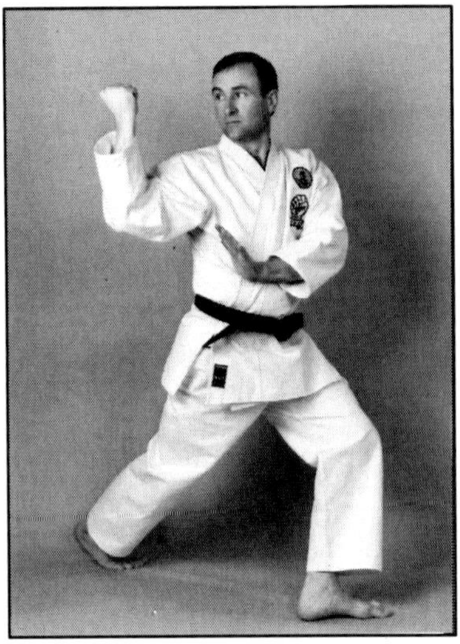

Marshall's influence brought me many talented teachers like Sensei Kim and Don Warrener. His influence took my local view of Karate training to an international understanding; that if I took on these new teachers I could participate at a higher level. Rick allowed me to grow while he learned from me – it was a fair exchange, one that benefited both of us. I credit him as being the catalyst that allowed me to make the jump from carpenter/builder to Professional Karate Sensei.

I have always believed that you should credit a person, not just for how they helped you, but when they did it. Rick Marshall showed me a world of possibilities at the right time and in a way that truly helped me create a vision for my future. In 1983 he accepted my resignation as a partner in Shima Karate, and although he didn't purchase my shares in the company, his blessing to move on allowed me to become successful.

Superfoot, and the Jet. While taking a 1976 holiday trip to Los Angeles, California I saw Bill Wallace and Benny Urquidez fight in the ring. They were individually defending their PKA (Professional Karate Association) World Titles. Wallace was the Middleweight Champion and Urquidez the Lightweight Champ. Bill Wallace, the headliner, had famously the fastest feet in the world, and hence his moniker as Superfoot. Benny "the Jet" Urquidez was unknown to me in 1976, and I was blown away by his ability. I was a Karate Blue Belt at the time, and Full Contact Karate was only about two years old. Both fights were tremendous! In those days all the top fighters had come from a traditional background, with lots of point fighting competition under their belt – so to speak. It made their abilities very clean, and exciting as compared to the UFC-type muggings of today.

Bill Wallace is known around the world as an incredible guy and tremendous teacher. Again, I have not personally met him but without exception, everyone I know who has met him agrees he is as good as his name. He's a super guy - funny, and personable. As to Superfoot's longevity, he was able to fight an exhibition match (against Wally Slocki, no less) in 2019 at the age of 73. Wallace's feet were still remarkably superfast."

Benny Urquidez is unquestionably the greatest Full Contact Fighter of all time. I personally saw him fight three times during his 62 wins (57 by knockout) undefeated career. What I witnessed was the most incredible display of skill, power, and toughness I have ever seen. The guy was magic in the ring, as he could perform techniques that most people couldn't do on a bag or in the gym, yet he did them live and against some of the best fighters in the world.

I saw him fight the Japanese Champion, Yutaka Koshikawa, in Vancouver BC in 1982. It was a give and take fight, where both men had equal determination, toughness, and ability. Late in the 8th round, Benny struck Yutaka first a hard spin back-fist to the temple then immediately reversed himself, striking with a spin kick that landed flush to Koshikawa's belly. The shot dropped him instantly. To the Japanese Champion's credit, although badly injured, he got up quickly. Benny looked at him as if to say *"Really?"* – then executed the exact same technique again. I was seated directly beside the red corner post, and when the second spin kick struck - I saw Koshikawa's back ribs virtually explode. It was like his ribs had been momentarily removed from his body. He didn't get up this time.

Benny "the Jet" was a classy fighter and a respectful man. Once again, Jimmy Mac experienced the champ firsthand. Urquidez held a seminar, teaching about 60 Black Belts the next day after the fight. I regret that I had not been smart enough to register for this class myself. Regardless, Jim told of sparring with Benny, as the Jet fought everyone in attendance who wanted to have the experience.

"I'm a traditionalist," said MacDonald as he entered the ring with the Champ. Benny said nothing, just smiled and nodded, and then went a round, allowing Jim a few openings, while landing a couple of light shots himself. When the round ended, Benny patted Jimmy Mac on the back saying, *"Nothing wrong with tradition."*

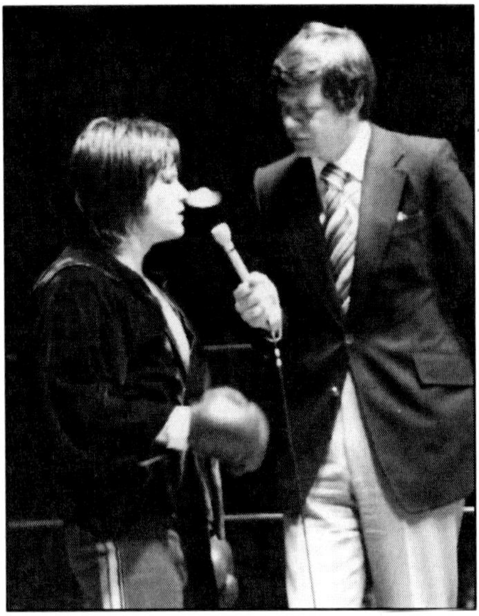

Urquidez, as a lightweight (135lbs), would fight anyone regardless of size or weight. Others in the seminar, who tried to land a hard shot, or were disrespectful, were all treated the same. It didn't matter to him about your size, belt, or standing in the community. If you messed with Benny, he knocked you out. Like Wallace, everyone who talks about Benny speaks with reverence regarding his ability and demeanor. They are both class acts.

Dan Inosanto. As a result of training in stick fighting with Bob Carver in Ottawa, I met Bruce Lee's no #1 student, Danny Inosanto. In 1988 Bob Carver brought him to Ottawa several times to teach his brand of Phillipino Kali and related self-defense techniques. Inosanto, once a paratrooper in the 101st Airborne, was well versed in all things martial arts. His fame, as it related to Bruce Lee, was only outdone by his overall skill and knowledge. I found him to be a consummate professional and, next to Don Jacob, his curriculum was the most extensive I have witnessed. Teaching Kali and Filipino Martial Arts he, then about 60 years old, was a specimen of fitness and a true gentleman. Personally, I found the vastness of his system overwhelming, but it was my good fortune to have my own #1 student Mike Sweeney with me. Sweeney, with his amazing mind, was able to remember and catalog much of what we were taught, and then re-teach it to me later! It is good to have great students and it was fun to train with a living legend.

Paddy Savage tops the list as the biggest rogue and #1 charlatan in my experience. After my school won his tournament in 1985, the Kingston native spent a considerable amount of time trying to be my friend. I'm usually open to new people, but there was something off about him and his Karate. He made me cautious. Like me, he was establishing himself in the eastern Ontario region, as he was creating a bunch of smaller type schools in outlying areas. I don't know where he learned his Karate but, given his student's wooden movements and unusual Shotokan katas, my best guess is; he learned it from a book! Savage was a big, stocky man with sheets of power-lifter-type muscle that contrasted with his soft eyes, and he had a gift of the gab. Given his somewhat hard looks, he was a charmer and got his way with people by having a fierce look and a soft touch.

For whatever reason, I kept clear of him, except to participate in mutually beneficial events and tournaments. A few years later I found out why my "spidey-sense" had gone off whenever I was around him.

Paddy Savage was an interloper and a con man. He called me one afternoon telling me he was sick, and abruptly had to leave town. Savage had cancer and as such, it softened my stance about him enough for me to listen to his request. He wanted me to take over his lease space, and potentially his student base at the Kingston Frontenac Mall and he needed it done now. After checking his story and the potential obligations I would encounter; I deemed it safe and an extremely good opportunity. I took the deal.

As his former students carefully checked me and my staff out, we began to hear the true story. Paddy had two families – one in Kingston and one in Tennessee. He was also a serial womanizer. I doubt there was a female student he hadn't hit on. The coup de grâce was: for over a year he had been raising money through donations from his students and the community to fund some experimental cancer treatment in the U.S.A. - Tennessee to be exact. He then used the cancer money to buy martial arts equipment in the U.S. and smuggle it across the border back to Canada. Yes, you are correct – Paddy Savage did not have cancer. I suspect he is still running somewhere and from someone.

Bob Noonan. Along with Laura Fry and a dozen or so others, Bob Noonan was part of the 2nd wave of Black Belts in Brockville, Ontario. Of all my students, Bob was among the quietest and most patient student I have ever known. That said, his work ethic to train everyday nonstop at weightlifting and Karate made him a close runner up to the original three. I called Noonan a man of Zen as he took in the simple pleasures of life - he was as devoted and dedicated student as I have seen. **Martin Nicholson** from the Parksville days, like Noonan, was among the first generation of Black Belts at the Shima Karate Dojo. Unlike

Bob, he took the basic training he received from Rick Marshall and I and he went international. He aligned himself with traditional Okinawan training by travelling to Japan and Okinawa to find the kind of training and leadership that would enable him to grow as a martial artist. Nicholson created his own Dojo which as of this writing, he still operates. I admire people who use their past training effectively and improve themselves. Personally, I believe it is the highest compliment a teacher can receive! I mention Bob and Martin as I feel they represent the kind of martial artist that doesn't like to take the spotlight but has the ability to run with the top guys - someone who competes with himself and is always an example of how to be and how to act. Noonan taught at and kept the essence of the Thousand Islands Brockville Karate School going with his teaching and integrity. It's as admirable an accomplishment as he is.

Kieran Baldwin. Perhaps the kindest and humblest Karate man I have ever had the pleasure to know or work with, Kieran Baldwin, fresh from London England, first showed up in Parksville when I was a brown belt. He himself was a freshly minted Black Belt with a pure hard style JKA Shotokan pedigree. His teacher had been a direct student of the legendary Keinosuke (Tiger) Enoeda and Baldwin was every bit a product of his teachers.

That said, Karate was a hobby for him, as he was the Head Chef at the Island Hall Hotel, and he didn't have much evening time for training. To keep up his fitness and his Karate skills, he trained religiously in his garage at home. His focus: kata and pushups! In those days we would routinely have fitness challenges like how many sit-ups you could do in 3 minutes, or the number of push-ups in 1 minute. An average person could do 30 - 40 push-ups and if you were extra fit perhaps you could get to 60 – 80 reps in sixty seconds. Personally, at the top of my class, I could do 70ish push-ups. Kieran, on a rare night off from the kitchen, attended a class where we finished the training off with a push up challenge. It was something I will never forget, as Sensei Baldwin set a mark that no one has ever approached before or since. Stopwatch in hand, I counted out 122 real push-ups! The man was a piston-like machine! That's better than 2 push-ups per second!

Many have tried, but no one has ever bested that mark. Years later, Kieran Baldwin became a full time Karate teacher for me at the Victoria Dojos and one of my most trusted friends. Wherever he has ever gone, in whatever field he has worked, he has always been a valued asset.

Stan Peterec. Arguably the best pure fighter MacDonald and Bateson ever produced was Stan "Steamer" Peterec. The reason was simply while they taught him Karate, they didn't need to teach him how to fight. He was a natural. Left-handed, and left footed, Stan had knock out power, flexibility and a toughness born of his Port Alberni upbringing. Peterec was a powerhouse. He was my junior when we trained together under Jim MacDonald, but I knew from sparring with him in the dojo, he had superior talent for fighting.

Routinely when we went to tournaments, I would win the Kata and he the Kumite. Peterec also had a great sense of humor and was fun to be with – that is until he had a few drinks. Personally, I rarely had any trouble in bars or the like. Friendly and somewhat easy going, I often wondered to myself why I never got into any altercations? Stan Peterec taught me the answer.

One evening on the dance floor at a house party - a fight suddenly broke out. While dancing, Peterec purposefully leaned his shoulder into an innocent fellow dancer – when the guy turned around to see who had struck him, Stan pummeled him without warning, knocking the poor guy unconscious. Everyone in the room, including me, saw the truth of it, and given the unfairness of *"the fight"*, a near riot ensued. As I had brought Peterec to the house party, I made it my duty to get him out. Holding a door against the mob, I ushered him and then myself to a get-away. Unfortunately, this was not a one-off event for Stan as I witnessed Peterec start and finish many fights – some in the ring, and many outside of it.

He went on to win two World Kickboxing titles. He tells many funny stories and, while I have always respected his ability, I have little respect for his attitude. Like Wally Slocki, I don't blame or even dislike Peterec for his actions, as he is what he is. Many times in life you have to deal with people you distrust, and once you shake hands with them – you count your fingers to see if they are still all there. When I'm around Stan I know to enjoy his stories and humor, but to also take them with an educated grain of salt. When my boys have fought for and with him, I said yes, go learn from him as he is one of the best, but be careful.

Mike Puckett. Of the old school Bateson Karate School Black Belts, there is no finer athlete or skilled Karate technician than Mike Puckett. I would also say that, like Kieran Baldwin, Sensei Puckett was as hard working and humble a martial artist as you could hope to meet.

For me, Mike falls into a group of people, along with **Sukwinder Manhas, Frank Clayton** and **Mike Bernardo,** who were top competitors and first-rate Senseis. Manhas in Port Alberni has operated an excellent part time program for decades and has consistently taught a competitive brand of sport Karate where his students have excelled. Vancouver's Clayton, like me, a Butoku Kai alumni, took a similar route as myself with multiple schools and for years has made a name for himself as a leader in the BC Karate scene. I always respected Bernardo, a world champion Kobudo competitor from London, Ontario, for his quiet determination to be the best. While these people have only been dojo acquaintances, their tenacity to create good work and good martial arts students is something that I have always noticed and admired.

I see Mike Puckett as a combination of these guys, as he excelled as a competitor, teacher and dojo owner. Sensei Lindon Bateson called him his right arm and molded him to be a Kata and point sparring Kumite champion, as well as a PKA Top 10 rated Kickboxing fighter. Mike had it all. When Bateson's Karate School failed in 1984, Mike Puckett picked up the pieces and created his own legacy dojo in Sidney, B.C. He trained and taught full time for over 30 years, creating a model of how to be a professional - both on the dojo floor and in his business relationships. If Mike Puckett said he would do something – his word is all you needed, as he was good for it.

Jimmy Mac admired him like a younger brother, and while my CBK schools took a similar but different path, we always enjoyed a good relationship with Leslie Noble and Mike Puckett of Puckett's Noble House of Karate.

Roy Vollinger. One of the most influential people in my life, who was not a martial artist, was Roy Vollinger: the "Coach". What does a BC Lions Orange Helmet Inductee football coach, who never stepped a foot inside a Dojo, have to do with our Karate School?

When the Pro Football Hall of Fame is considering nominees for induction into the hall they ask one simple question, *"Can you tell the story of the NFL without telling this man's story?"* I cannot tell the CBK story without discussing this important man.

Coach Vollinger would have been in his mid-twenties when I first met him in 1969. While I only knew him a little when I was a teenage kid, his influence on me has lasted a lifetime. Square jawed, handsome and gregarious, Vollinger, at 6'5" tall, was a big man with an even bigger personality. While he could be intimidating on the football practice field, his heart was so big that all you ever felt was his love. That is, after he kicked your ass. Sounds like a true Sensei to me.

As an adult, I would see him occasionally during a chance encounter in a store or on the street. He'd size me up with a smile and a knowing look. Recognizing me, he'd say, *"Bobby, looks like you could still play - well, maybe one play!"* then roar with laughter. In his later years I regularly reconnected with him, sharing a few meals with him and his wife Lynda. I would call his home occasionally with a smile and in a big voice I'd ask, *"Is this the Coach!?"* The gravelly voice I heard on the other end of the phone always smiled back and laughed, *"You got him!"*

The Coach was the first man I knew outside of my family that took an interest in me and inspired me to dream. It's always someone outside of your parents that gets more out of you than

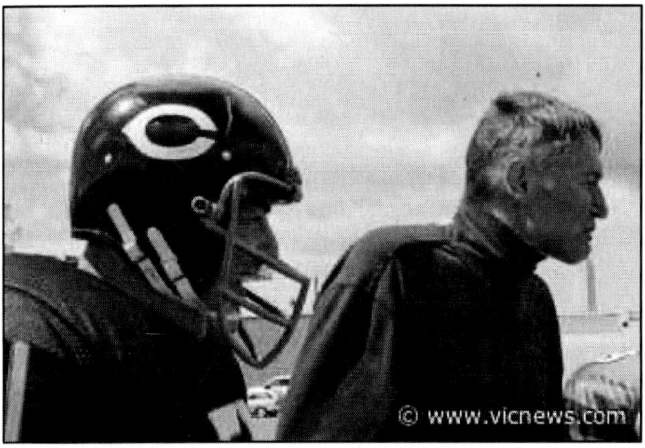

you knew you had. For me, Roy Vollinger was that man. His demanding encouragement expected your very best effort each and every time you took the field. The reward for your best effort was a wink, a nod, a laugh or a story from the coach. There was no better feeling than receiving his praise.

Vollinger, while not a father himself, did everything for his boys. If you were on his team, he not only recruited you, but he found jobs, gave recommendations to colleges and was constantly on the lookout to help you in some way. If you would do the work, he'd work with you. However, if you were lazy or whined, he was about as subtle as a car crash. But the truth is I don't remember anyone being lazy or complaining. Most likely those ones didn't make his team.

It's the toughest teachers, the ones who demand and command, that you remember the most. Past the personal effect he had on me, he also got results. Of the five seasons I played Bantam and Jr. Bantam with Saanich Hornets Football, we only lost one game ever and won the league championship each year. Why? The answer was simple. Coach Vollinger didn't just coach boys, he trained men. He saw football as a zero-sum game – either you do it or you don't. Winning was the natural reward for doing good work. Roy was like our very own Vancouver Island Vince Lombardi of the famous1960s Green Bay Packers. To quote a Lombardi player, NFL Hall of Famer Jerry Kramer, *"Lombardi was fair, he treated everyone equally and the same – he treated us all like dogs!"*

Coach Vollinger was like that. Almost from the first practice he worked us hard with old school discipline and expectations. Some of my team-mates grumbled a little, but no one complained. For the most part the only complaints I remember came from the parents. Often, they showed up at the end of a scheduled 2-hour practice only to see the field lights come on as the Coach added more grass drills or wind sprints for an extra half an hour. However, they accepted it as the price to be a winner. The coach kept everyone on their toes with his unbridled enthusiasm and indomitable spirit.

It was hard, and he was hard, but it made us winners and, more importantly, built our confidence. I loved it because I loved him. Actually, I loved the idea of playing football so much that I rode my old loose chain bicycle to and from practice. At 12 years old, in full pads, with my helmet held on the crossbars (in those days why would you wear a helmet on your head!) I'd make the 5-mile trek from my home near the Work Point Barracks in Esquimalt to Glanford Field in Saanich. Getting to the three practice sessions per week took about 30 minutes each way. Eventually my parents saw the wisdom in driving me when some other families offered to share the ride duties.

Yes, in 1969, it was a different time when, even as a kid, if you wanted something there was usually some extra work or responsibility attached to it. I feel that it helped me in many ways. While I didn't see it at the time I played football, I now understand how it prepared me to be the kind of Sensei I became later on in life - a Sensei full of kick-ass love. Perhaps this explains why the Dojo demands so much of our Black Belt Candidates.

Unfortunately, we lost the Coach in 2020 as he died unexpectedly at the age of 77. Personally, it's hard to lose a wonderful mentor, and globally it's sad to lose such a good man with lots of good years left in him. That, however, is the way of life, as you never know how long you have to enjoy and appreciate those you love. I'm just glad that I was fortunate enough to enjoy his laugh and joy for as long as I did.

Mark Yarnell. Have you ever met someone who was the best of the best? I mean in any field, when they were measured against the top people they were head and shoulders above the rest. Mark Yarnell was that kind of guy. Yarnell was to speaking and inspiring people like Dick Butkus was to tackling, Wayne Gretzky was to scoring, and Bruce Lee was to Kung Fu. There was no finer man in the word of MLM business and educating people about how they could live and be successful.

I first heard of Yarnell in the early 1990s when a friend got me involved in a trendy business opportunity. Seeking to be good at what I was learning, I purchased some audio tapes that featured the life and teachings of Mark Yarnell. Mr. Yarnell, a minister by trade, spoke with an American twang, born of his Missouri upbringing and his Texas lifestyle. With a quick mind and sharp wit, he became a world-famous celebrity speaker. His story told about his rise in the 1980s when he'd lived a classic "rags to riches" story.

Yarnell told about sitting on a street corner with his 5-year old daughter, Amy, the day their Church was foreclosed on and his car was repo'd. Flat broke and busted, he picked himself up, dusted himself off, and went from being a bankrupt Texas preacher in a small Texas oil town to becoming a multi-millionaire within a few years. He became a legend in that industry.

After earning a fortune with a company called Nuskin International, he became a best-selling author, a philanthropist and a professional speaker. His story is the kind that fuels dreams and his passion for life inspires anyone who has ever heard him speak. Norman Vincent Peel, author of "The Power of Positive Thinking", called him one of the most powerful orators in America and he was the only MLM professional to be a contributing editor to Success Magazine.

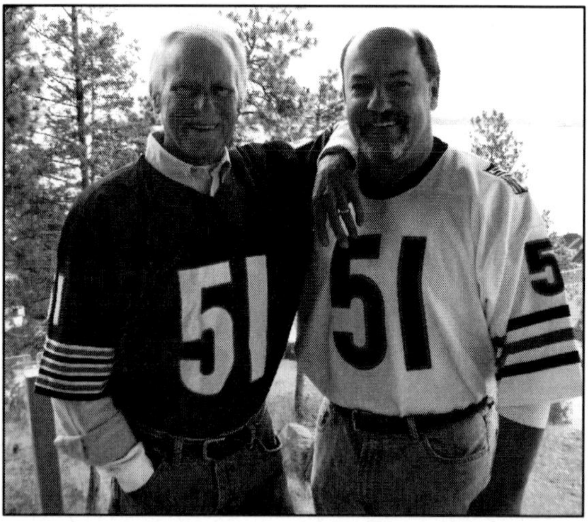

Through Mark's tapes I learned everything imaginable about this kind of business, but more importantly I learned real skills that applied to every part of my life. While I did not become a MLM wiz or millionaire, I did learn a lot about myself and found a way to apply it to my martial arts. Martial arts? Yes, just like the ideals of the ancient Samurai Warriors, Yarnell taught about facing your fears, doing the work, and believing in yourself. I admired Mark's tenacity and he became a kind of business hero for me.

One of the many secrets I learned early in my career was that if I could find a great teacher, in any field, I knew I could benefit by bringing their teachings into my world. Even if it was only through audiotapes. Fate is a funny thing and the Law of Attraction is an interesting concept, as what happened next is what Mr. Yarnell would call a fortuitous intersection.

A friend, Valerie Bates, formally Mrs. Ron Perkio, re-married and moved to Victoria with her new husband, Mark Yarnell. The year was 2000 - the turn of the century - when our Karate Team was invited to a World Championship Competition in Australia. As a result, our school was actively looking for fund raising ideas when a student brought in an idea about a company called Excel Communications. Land-line phones were still very expensive in those days, so if people were willing to move their service from Telus to Excel they could save some money and we, as a fund raiser, would receive a signing bonus as a reward. The program was a tremendous success and with the support of our student body we earned about $10,000 for our team travel.

Just as we were wrapping things up for our trip I received a phone call, *"Hi Bob, this Mark Yarnell. I heard about you and what you were doing with Excel. I'm wondering if I could find out some more - could I buy you lunch sometime?"*

As I got off the phone I thought to myself *"Wow, Mark Yarnell? OMG. The world's greatest MLM expert wants to join Excel and help us make a million dollars to go to Australia – holy crap! I didn't see that one coming."* ... And it didn't!

I did, however, have lunch with Mark. His generous nature and inspiring ways told me how he admired the martial arts and the work I was doing with kids. He, himself, had a background as an amateur boxer, but he jokingly said that he discovered his nose was better suited in the Network Marketing ring! Having a personal hero take you to lunch and feed you compliments was certainly a thrill, but Mark was even better than that. He became a good and trusted friend, helping us in many ways by attending Dojo events, offering his advice and mentorship. In fact, with his high energy and dynamic personality, he reminded me a great deal of my Sensei, Jimmy Mac. Regrettably, like Jim before him, Mark died too young in 2015 due to smoking.

I had the opportunity to see him speak live many times, and I still admire his abilities to this day. To witness someone who is the best of the best in their profession is inspiring but having them as a friend is magical. Mark's skill of invoking an emotional connection with an audience is the best I have ever seen. Many people remember Mark Yarnell for abilities and intellect, but for those who knew him well, he's eternally respected for his compassion and heart. Due to my own talent and drive, I had the opportunity to meet with many of my heroes, and Mark could hang with any of them – he was that good. He was a rare talent, world class in every way and a humble friend.

Robin Webb. When preparing to create his portrait, Patrick McCarthy and I were talking via Skype from Australia. During the discussion about the proposed art, we were exchanging views on past personal experiences when he asked if I had any other projects just now. Yes, I did – as I recently had agreed to help a fellow named Robin Webb on a movie project. I asked, *"Do you know Robin?"*

McCarthy responded knowingly, *"Ahh yes, the legendary Mr. Webb – that's a name I've not heard for a long time ..."* As he paused, I told him how an opportunity with Robin had fallen my way. Robin Webb was a local boxing and kickboxing referee who had a fabulous international past! He, at 68 years old, was about 10 years my senior.

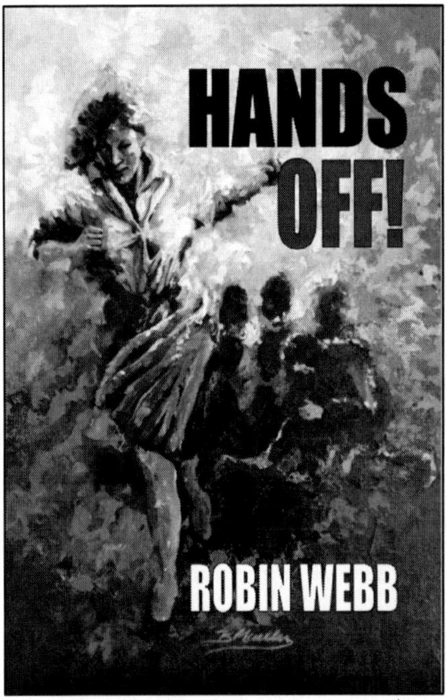

Webb was once the British Amateur Heavyweight Champion, who had held 22 National Boxing titles. Better than that, in 1963, when Cassius Clay went to Britain to fight Henry Cooper, Robin was selected to be his sparring partner. He spent a week with the man who became the most important fighter of the 20th Century, the iconic Muhammad Ali. Legendary indeed! After his boxing career ended, Webb became a Hollywood stuntman, actor and later a movie producer. Robin had an incredible number of awards, accolades, associates and wild stories of training members of the British SAS. His tales of being connected to the Rothchild legacy and secret SAS missions rounded out Webb's *"Soldier of Fortune"* image. Everything he said appeared verifiable and was on display in plain sight. The package also came with a winning smile, a can-do attitude and bubbly personality. When my son, Leigh, introduced us, we had an instant connection that some might say was a "bromance!"

Why Robin was courting me was a bit of a mystery. He qualified the interest by saying he knew my reputation, the Emmy Award, and respected what I had done with my career. As a referee, he was also impressed by the quality and integrity he saw when my sons had been in the ring with him. I took him at face value. Robin was kind, and caring, but he also held a secret – he was a con.

It was McCarthy's hesitation on the phone call that had me ask for more. Pat continued, *"I probably shouldn't tell you, but I got stung by Robin years ago when he promoted the Benny "The Jet" Urquidez fights in Vancouver."* Apparently, there had been a mix up with the money owed to Benny and Pat McCarthy somehow wound up in the middle of it - holding an empty bag. While it was eventually settled, there was a lot of uncomfortable finger-pointing going on.

"All I can say is I'd be careful if I were you" McCarthy's warned. It was good advice. As time passed, it turned out there were many stories of people, particularly women, "investing" in various projects with Robin Webb. None were out-right theft or criminal in nature, but all were suspicious and suggested a nefarious pattern. It's true that there is no crime in selling dreams, but when taken to the extreme, it can be unethical. In hindsight, Robin's rap appears like a stereotypical Hollywood B-movie producer on the hustle. The fact is, all the best lies are always told with about 75% truth, and they come wrapped in pretty packages. The problem arises when you open the package and it turns out to be an empty box.

The resulting effect is both the mark and the con then share a mutual disbelief. When the con is well crafted, both parties can point a finger towards a straw man, one who has been set up to take the fall. Robin engaged a lot of potentially viable connections, always with grandiose ideas, but they never seemed to work out. It's the classic work of a "flim-flam man" or grifter.

A famous quote from Harvey Mackay sums it up, *"When a man with experience meets a man with money, the man with experience gets the money and the man with the money gets the experience!"*

Thanks to Hanshi McCarthy, and the fact I didn't have any money at the time to invest, I did not suffer financially. I did, however, work for free on several his "projects", lent him grocery money from time to time, and wasted three years of my life. I must remember when dealing with charlatans to adhere to Robin Webb's program and make it a "Hands Off" relationship!

To sum up this brief presentation about some of the famous and infamous people I have met during my Karate career, I can say these people all taught me invaluable lessons. Additionally, even the rogues had an element of the hero in either their nature or in their attraction. Talented people are often given extra temptations in life, ones that test both their ability and their integrity.

I can verify that I have been tested numerous times and while tempted, influenced or bromanced towards the dark side, my "True North Dojo" demeanor helped me avoid falling and failing. Thankfully, given my many experiences with some characters and charlatans, I didn't have to purchase my eyeballs back as grapes!

BOOK FOUR

四

STAGING A DOJO

THE ROYAL THEATER

The Royal Theater is the largest and oldest theater on Vancouver Island. On December 21, 2019, the combined CBK Dojos of Vancouver Island took the Royal Theater stage for the second time. It was Sensei Leigh's idea to take our Karate Christmas Concert to the grand theater again. This would be the 25th Anniversary of what I have called "the perfect note" – the most perfect moment of my life. Leigh and I had felt it then, and we hoped to repeat the magic once more.

Perhaps you are scratching your head just now, and wondering about what a Karate Concert, the Royal Theater, or Christmas is to Karate? What does this have to do with punching and kicking? Admittedly it is unusual and perhaps that was the attraction in the beginning. What began as a pretty vanilla Karate demonstration turned into a full-fledged theater show, complete with lights, music, comedy, and action. Our show has staged Broadway-like demonstrations to Phantom of The Opera, Lion King, and James Bond, as well as fun comedy bits and amazing martial arts.

It is unique. Thirty-five years later our dojo has taken some wonderful stages and had thousands of students show their talents.

As far back as my second year in Brockville, my dojo created and began holding *"Karate Christmas Concerts."* Since we dealt with a lot of children, it seemed natural to want to show them off to their parents and celebrate the holidays. The event was both great fun and good for business. What I started in the 1980s, Leigh embraced and developed during the 2000s. His abilities have made our show into something very special.

But it was the Royal Theater show of 1994 that rings most in our memory. That night, the make-up and the make-believe created a vibration so impactful that I can still feel it if I close my eyes and listen to the music. It is fitting therefore to tell you about *"perfect note"* and its importance.

I ask you, what was the best moment of your life?

While the birth of my children, getting married, or receiving some windfall or accolade were times of great joy, they did not elicit what I would come to know as a perfect moment. To understand the concept of the perfect note, you must imagine someone waking you up from a dead sleep, shaking you, and demanding to know, *"What was the greatest moment of your life?"* Should you take on this question, without time to think or give a politically correct answer, you may be surprised at what your unconscious mind will tell you. I know I was.

Memories of times in my life when I cried without control are few - a phone call telling me that Jimmy Mac had died, a suppressed memory of my father throwing away my comic book collection without telling me, the thought of not being present for the death of my dog, Pete. These were simple moments full of real pain, all without thought – just the raw emotion of truth.

More enjoyable moments usually began with a question.

"What if we could do our Christmas show at the Royal Theater?" I asked Leigh, my twelve-year-old son, and his karate sempai, Mike Croteau. *"That would be something!"* we all agreed.

As he was approaching puberty, Leigh, a brown belt, was acutely aware of how I felt about Sempai Croteau, because he felt the same. Croteau was the big brother that Leigh, the eldest, didn't have. He was also the main teacher for all the kid's classes at the dojo, and he was simply the best young karate man that I had ever directly taught.

Mike had come to me as a shy eight-year-old, and by the time he achieved his Black Belt at the age of fourteen, he was the best on the grading. He was even better than the older and stronger adults. In my opinion, he did everything he was taught, including many, many things that I could not do well myself, and he perfected them. In my eyes, his style, his lines, and his persona were flawless.

After I left Brockville in 1989 and opened my new school back in Victoria, I told him that I wanted him to teach for me. The day after he graduated high school, he kissed his parent's good-bye and flew out to Victoria to become the center of my dojo. His energy and great character made him a treasure for all the students. Although young, his talent quickly allowed him to grow and to thrive as the unofficial leader and the hero of the dojo. He was deeply loved and appreciated by everyone who knew him, especially Leigh, who saw him as his hero. I treated him like a son, perhaps even better.

The Royal Theater was a big deal, as we would need to sell over a thousand tickets just to break even. But the thrill of creating a real show, on a real stage, was just too tempting to pass up. We would perform our representation of "The Phantom of the Opera" to powerfully open the show and close with a special presentation that I was keeping secret. During the two-hour show, we would feature the entire student body, over 250 kids and adults on stage, for their moment in the bright lights. The show had comedy, cute kids' skits, and our versions of Broadway shows. The whole event was labor-intensive, but it was great fun.

Stepping into this great venue was amazing. We now had real professionals lighting the stage and an incredible sound system. The accompanying technicians would run the music and stage us properly, just like they would for any other "professional" show. I felt like the famous music producer, Phil Spector, as I orchestrated my own *"Wall of Sound"*. Before the show, while doing the afternoon run-through, it was as if Steven Spielberg had occupied my body. I had students hitting their marks and taking my direction. I had a feeling that this evening would be something special.

During a late afternoon break, I took the lighting and sound men aside, telling them about a special presentation I had planned. I gave them my secret music, with instructions to lay it under my voice when I began my final speech. This evening I would award the rank and title of "Sensei" to three men. The first two, Kieran Baldwin and Peter Lindsay, were elder Black Belt statesmen and would be rewarded for their years of service to me and the dojo. The last award would be for sheer teaching talent, and to recognize the love and respect that a young man had created through his brilliance.

The doors opened at 7:00 pm sharp and over fourteen hundred people filled the main floor, overflowing into the upper balcony. The show was amazing, and the response was everything that I had hoped for. It had been almost ten years since I had first experienced the vibration of a perfect note. It had come to me then, as a highly physical event. Its potential had been created when a synchronistic series of needs, desires, and challenges, for a moment, occupied the same space of time.

Time itself had been altered and rearranged the first time I had felt the perfect moment as a means to relieve the build-up of overwhelming stress and pressure. Love, music, and a thousand heartbeats would be the catalyst to create this coming vibration.

As I began to reveal my secret ceremony, the audience applauded a well-deserved acknowledgment for Baldwin and Lindsay. It all made sense. They had, collectively, over fifty years of combined experience and they were great practitioners of the art. As they stood in acknowledgment, I allowed some time for the applause. As the clapping subsided, the sound expert waited for me to speak. The spotlight narrowed in on me, but when I opened my mouth to speak, nothing came out.

I had prepared and rehearsed my speech, but I could not seem to find the words. Then, as I found the first few thoughts, I heard the seemly sweetest and most haunting music ever written. I had chosen a bittersweet theme from the *"Lion King"* movie. Although I deemed it fitting and appropriate when the music began, it was like I had never heard the notes before. The sad, sweet sounds of a flute became the strings and horns of an entire orchestra. When I found the words, they were unrehearsed. It was something that Jimmy Mac, who was in the audience, had written for me years earlier.

"If I never did anything, or accomplished anything else in life, I would know that ..." my voice was cracking up and my eyes welled with tears. The music was now in full flight as the fourteen hundred joined me in a spontaneous expression of love.

They knew what I was going to say, and they knew who I was going to say it about, but they had to hear me say it. Their vibration compelled the words and the music to become one!

"I would know that I had," and again I stumbled, but now the heartbeats and music helped and encouraged me. The sound was so powerful! With the tears flowing and now fully present, I joined the music, *"I will know that I had some small part in your success. Ladies and gentlemen, Mike Croteau, the rank of Sensei of the dojo."*

Wearing my black tuxedo with a red scarf, I turned and saw Mike, shoulders slumped, with his hand up to his brow, vibrating and weeping. As I walked towards him with the presentation, the music segued into the accompanying song. The Royal Theater, along with the assembled mass, gasped with anticipation. When the song began, again from the Lion King, the lyrics brought the house down.

"Can You Feel the Love Tonight" filled the air, and they, the collective, sighed with joy and released their love down to the stage. Like the pride in the Lion Kingdom, the people moved towards the stage spontaneously creating a receiving line of respect, to thank me, and to acknowledge the new king.

Although I had planned the timing and directed the feel, the spontaneous love and the perfect pitch of the music created a vibration I still feel today.

To this day, if you wake me up from my dead sleep and ask me, *"What was your greatest moment?"*

The Royal Theater 1994.
It is still indescribable, and it was perfect!

Update: The Royal Theater 2019
it was indescribable and,
25 years after the first, it too was perfect.

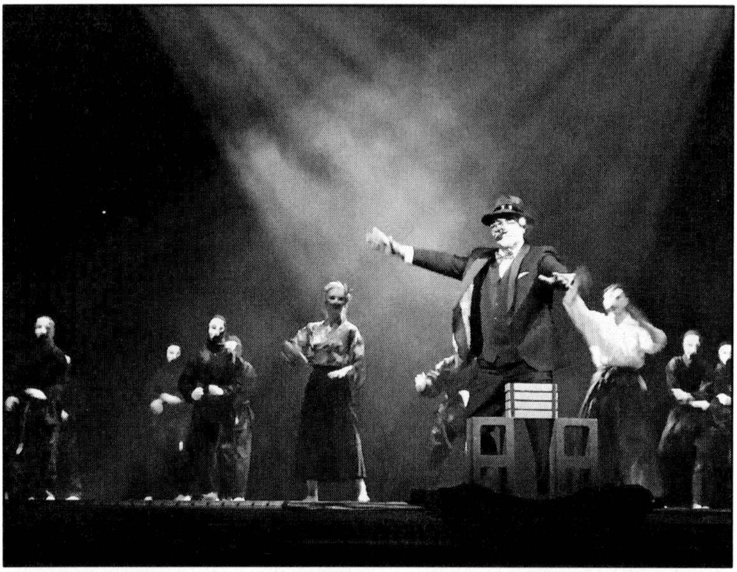

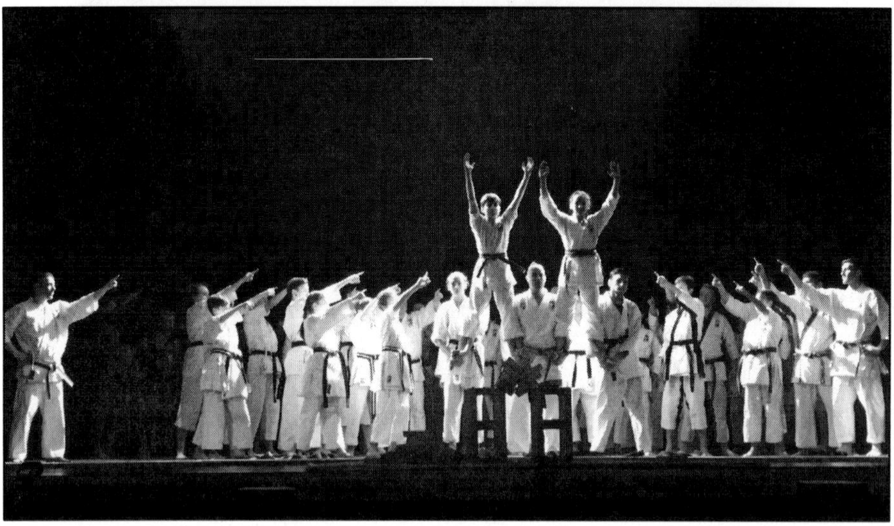

Performances of the Phantom of the Opera
and The Lion King

THE TRUTH CRUSHED TO THE EARTH

SHALL RISE AGAIN - THE 2nd ACT

"Let him do it. He can. Trust me. He can. Let the kid do it!" implored Warden. It was a lot to ask, especially now when the weight was so great. How could this be true? If I couldn't get it done, how could the kid do what I could not?

In Greek mythology, a phoenix is a long-lived bird that is cyclically regenerated or reborn. Associated with the sun, a phoenix obtains new life by arising from the ashes of its predecessor.

If my teenage son was a phoenix, I was a once proud eagle turned ostrich, as I had laid a big egg. After returning to Victoria in 1989, the dojo had just passed its 6th anniversary. Riding high off my success in Brockville and Kingston, Ontario, I was itching to get started with a new project. It took almost 8 months to research and create the new dojo at 1551 Cedar Hills Cross Rd in Saanich, BC. But the wait was worth it.

The West Coast was home and I had returned experienced, confident, and ready to show my skills to my peers. With recharged batteries, and again starting from scratch, the dojo got off to a fast start. It grew leap and bounds. I had brought a Brockville assistant named Gordon Holtrop with me to help with the teaching duties. When he got homesick after about a year, his departure made room for a young and talented protégé named Mike Croteau.

It was a dream come true as, within a few short years, I had again duplicated my eastern success. Mike's ability to teach and inspire mirrored my own and our relationship was more like father and son than business partners. He had been with me since he was 8 years old, so he knew exactly how to do things the right way. His motivation to learn and then deliver the programs was the best I had seen and what we did worked. Our combined passion to succeed and mutual respect should have carried us for decades, but it was not to have a fairy tale ending. That's where the ostrich came in.

Steve Sabol says, *"You can't soar like an eagle and crap like a canary!"* No truer spoken words were ever spoken as by 1985, with two dojos and about 500 local students, a shotgun-like blast ripped me in two. Mike Croteau, holding a smoking gun, had pulled the trigger.

My mentor, Harold Warden, was looking for a way to bring me back to life when he said, *"Let the kid do it!"*

Warden had been a paid advisor for over a decade and more than that, he was a friend. His help had always carried a price; there would come a day when his self-sabotaging nature would make the price of his friendship far too expensive. But that's a story for another day. This day, he was there when it counted – particularly in a time of need.

Following the grand success and emotion at the Royal Theater in December of 1994, the following year promised to be even better and grander. Why wouldn't it? From the outside looking in, as with the Castle on George St. a decade before, I had hundreds of students and all signals were positive.

We now had two full-time karate schools, with Kieran Baldwin running the newest one. My confidence was bolstered by a great staff of dedicated teachers, committed volunteers, and headed by my golden disciple. Mike Croteau was now a man, and he was everything I dreamed he'd be. He had a huge appetite for joy and his talent, now in full bloom, was accepted as the standard by which all others were judged.

Mike did not disappoint. Not only was he doing well at the dojo, but he also appeared to be doing well in life. As part of my promise, I had provided him with a home and all the tools for his future success. As a young man, he had a new girlfriend, a well-funded RRSP, money in the bank, and a new Toyota truck. With me, although conditional on the coming year's success, he also had a partial stake in a piece of real estate I owned and a well-earned opportunity to own shares in my company.

He was now the Sensei and, much like I had experienced a decade before, he felt the power to be all that he could be. I surrounded him with good people whom I trusted. They would assist him in leading and teaching, as well as the growing membership. With Sensei Kieran now in his own school, the established leadership of Peter Lindsay, assisted by Dan Holland and other dedicated Black Belt students, maintained the support I felt he needed. Many new parents/students, like Wendy Foster and Anita McFadyen, brought their energy and ideas to the dojo.

Wendy, as a former Early Childhood Educator, was creating great ideas for our new Tots program and helping build our reputation in the community.

With Mike firmly set as the acknowledged leader of the dojo, I also placed Leigh, now thirteen years old and ready for his Black Belt grading, as his primary assistant. Leigh, like Mike before him, would assist every day at the dojo. Mike mentored Leigh and was essentially his big brother. Leigh was developing his physical skills, learning to teach, and most importantly, learning to be like Mike. I believed that someday, as a result of the strong bonds they were building, they would share the ownership of the business.

It was the fourth year of a five-year plan, and we were about to execute the boldest part of it. This year I would invite others to share in our success and together we would begin two new franchises in B.C. - one in Colwood and the other in Langley. Also, having acquired a new and expensive family home the year before, I wanted to build an addition, making a private training retreat that would serve as my BC Karate headquarters. Like everything I do, I tore into these new projects with gusto and without hesitation. Mike Croteau would anchor the success of the Douglas St. dojo, and I would create future opportunities that would benefit us all.

Ahhh ... the folly of unbridled ambition, the best-laid plans of mice and men.

What was not apparent, particularly to me, was how the energy and good fortune was not anything like the year before. In my ambition to see my new objectives developed, I became blind to the needs of what I had already built. Similarly, like years before, it was a real estate decline that created questions as to the stability of what I was doing. Unfortunately, unlike the problems of 1981, this time I ignored the danger signs I felt and hid from the reality that whispered to me. All was not as it seemed.

The previous year I had bought a dream home just as real estate peaked, and as the market began to tumble, I would soon see my mistake. Equally devastating, the second karate school, located on Shelbourne St, had failed to duplicate the success of the Douglas Dojo. Profits were regularly filtered over to the newer school to make up for any shortfalls. The profitable business of the year before was now, at best, just a breakeven proposition. I had also kept my former home, turning it into an income property, and again with grandiose ideas, I leveraged it to buy the new property. Leverage works well to augment success when a hot market is going up and it works even better to accelerate failure when the market goes cold.

Worst of all, as I scrambled to deal with everything, I ceased to be what I needed to be - the Sensei. I was too busy being a leader to notice that my golden boy was not getting the only thing that he truly wanted and needed from me. Mike, still a boy, had come to Victoria so that I might continue as his karate teacher. He trusted me in every way possible and I delivered in every way, except one. Although he had the body of a man, what made Mike so special was he had the heart of a child. The innocent little boy in him yearned for the day-to-day praise and practice that only a teacher can give. I had ceased to teach and train him physically, like the deserving young man and keen student he was. I had changed.

Given his talent, I saw him as a peer and an equal, but he still saw me as the Sensei and the one person he needed to push and train him. In that way, I had abandoned him.

In the resulting vacuum, Mike filled his life by accumulating possessions, as he feathered his nest and began to truly create his personal life. I thought it was great and I applauded this new turn as being a positive and natural part of growing up. However, the innocent and trusting are also susceptible to outside influences. A dark force is often attracted to the bright and shining light. A woman named Claire entered the open space that I had left vacant. She cast a shadow that would become a dark storm of pain, and it would ruin his young life for many years to come. He lost his moral compass and all the goodness that had guided his life.

Even our collective martial arts training and great experiences together could not save us from being crushed. The coming fall would all but ruin me and mark him in a way that would haunt him forever.

By the end of the year, not aware of the impending doom, we were all reveling in the success of another great Christmas Concert. The concert was truly a bright spot at the end of a very tough and difficult year. The show had featured my very first tribute film and celebrated Sensei Mike's talent. He worked with Leigh and his Black Belt grading group to lead the show with our new Lion King demonstration. The concert that year was the only thing that seemed to go as planned – as everything else regarding the business seemed to be out of sync.

On this particular day, Mike and I were working at the dojo, cleaning up, and finalizing a few details before the holiday break. The Shelbourne dojo was up for its lease renewal and, as it had never created a profit, I had reluctantly decided to close its doors. Now, to regroup and return to profitability, we needed to combine the memberships of the two schools at the Douglas dojo. If this had been the year before, the idea of combining the schools would have been impossible.

At that time the Douglas school was running at peak capacity which, because of its success, had created expansion opportunities.

This year however, everything was off. Mike's registrations had been very weak since the spring before, and I had been feeding both schools from the company savings account. By the time we made it to the Christmas concert, we had nothing left in our bank's reserves. With only our line of credit at the bank to sustain us, I thanked God this year was over! Combining the schools would effectively cut our operating expenses by 30% and give us some breathing room, thus allowing our new plans to take effect. Although no one was happy about what we were about to do, we all agreed that we would stay the course and we would make it work.

I was busy opening a stack of mail, while Mike was sorting through our stock of uniforms and equipment. When I opened the current telephone bill, I was immediately drawn to the red stamp saying "overdue." This was the first direct telephone bill that I had seen in almost two years.

As part of my training system for Mike, I had set him up as his own business entity, teaching him how to be responsible for operating the affairs of the dojo. Mike was accountable to pay certain bills and I empowered him, daily, to make all but the most important business decisions. The income would be deposited into my corporate account, but Mike's sub-company would pay the bills. At the end of each month, Mike would submit a bill for all the expenses, plus his salary and potential bonuses. Then we would sit down and review what had happened and after going over his sales and the expenses, I would write him a check. He would then pay himself and all the bills from the previous month. I had done this several years ago with the schools in Brockville and Kingston, and it had worked like a charm. Sweeney and Coles had learned everything about their operations and because they were in control, they had been very motivated to make profits for themselves, as well as for me.

"What the hell? These guys must be crazy! Eight thousand dollars for a phone bill!" I said to myself almost chuckling out loud. *"Hey, Mike, check this out!"*... I began to say as I looked up from the bill and saw Mike's drained face quickly lose color.

"Mike???" my tone elevated. As our eyes met, I first saw fear in him and then felt it in myself, *"Mike, what is this? Is this real!? Holy shit! What the hell, Mike!"* I yelled. At that moment there were few words, only panic. I scrambled to open the hydro bill and then a few others, only to see the same type of red notices stamped on them. During the next few hours, I learned that we had over $12,000 in unpaid utility and advertising bills. Mike had been invoicing me for the full amounts and then, for some reason, not paying the bills as he was supposed to. Rather than grilling him to explain in detail, I gave him an excuse. I got it - he had gotten behind, and the money just got away from him. I understood because, although not to this degree, this had happened to me years before.

I heard myself say, *"Look Mike ... I know this is just a mistake, but do you know if it was anyone else, I would say this looks like embezzling – it's stealing! You are going to have to pay these bills – and I don't care if you have to cash in your RRSP to do it!"*

In the meantime, I went further into the company line of credit and paid the bills so that we were up to date. As it was Christmas, we would all be taking a little time off to reorganize and renew ourselves. With rest, we would reorganize and fix everything in the New Year. Over the next few weeks, I learned of more outright lies while dealing with an increasingly sullen and non-communicative Michael Croteau.

The New Year did not solve anything. During a fit of frustration and to make a point, I punched the doorframe into the business office, leaving knuckle marks, as I demanded, *"Mike! Get your head out of your ass!"* But he simply could not or would not. For myself, I simply couldn't understand why or what had happened; it was beyond belief.

A few days later, I arrived at the dojo to find Wendy and her Tot's class locked out. I was beside myself with anger! After opening the dojo for them, I phoned Mike, getting no answer, then went to his home only to find that he had moved out and was gone. I never saw him again, at least as the person I had known. I did, however, hear from him via his girlfriend, Claire.

Within days Claire was calling our students and distributing information about a new karate school that he would be opening. Mike had my students' contact information, and he knew all my operating procedures. To the students, he was still the golden boy that I had created, and he had the hearts and minds of the entire dojo.

What ensued was panic inside the dojo. This questioned my credibility as my students heard false stories about me. I was portrayed as an abusive business owner with corrupt business practices. What I heard created the worst kind of scenario – the kind where a person is trapped and afraid, being bullied and beaten "like the abused wife syndrome." And I was the bully.

Now it was clear, and I understood perfectly. Claire had been talking in Mike's ear and manipulating his mind for the past year. She had told him the classic story of how he was doing all the work, while I was making all the money. I suspect that he first took a little cash or hid a membership or two from me. Then, as she worked on him, he bought into her influence and became bolder. He stopped paying the bills, believing that he wasn't stealing, as it was money to which he was entitled. (Besides, I had plenty and probably wouldn't even miss it.)

I am equally sure that he came to see me in the mean light that she portrayed. After all, had I not punched the door? Had I not left Mike alone at the dojo doing everything, while I did nothing? She twisted him, and he bent with her every move. She wanted him to take my business so that she might have its prestige and status. She also wanted to destroy me, and Leigh, along with the rest of my family. She was jealous, vindictive, and, in my mind, outright evil.

My students were given an unpleasant choice. They could quit my dojo, and lose their investment by joining him, or they could stay, suspiciously, with me. Many left. Many stayed. But their trust and belief in my integrity were broken. No one had ever questioned my integrity before. Yes, I had made mistakes in the past - honest ones - and once realized, I made every effort to correct them. But this was different and inexcusable. How could I defend myself when called "abusive and corrupt?"

I was determined not to throw gasoline on the fire. I refused to add to the false accusations by trying to defend them. I said nothing, put my head down, and just went about my work. When questioned by parents and students, I simply stated that I had not done those things. If they would stick with the dojo, they could see for themselves in the coming months. I also said I understood if they wanted to leave, but there were no refunds to be had for mutiny.

I was crushed. I did not want to get out of bed most mornings, giving way to cramps of depression. Many, including Kieran Baldwin, Harold Warden, Leigh, and the rest of my family came to my aid, but this was as close as I had ever come to giving up on anything.

Slowly, as I distanced myself from the actions I could not control, I began to find some solid ground. I re-established myself, but I didn't have what it took to succeed. I was lost. As much as I tried to be the Sensei of old, I had lost my swagger and a lot of my confidence. Whether anyone else could see it or not is hard to say, but I knew that I was operating at a low-ebb and with no real desire. I was just trying to survive.

Harold did see it, and it was his statement that changed everything. *"Let him do it! He can. Trust me. He can! Let the kid do it!"* implored Warden, as he stopped me from going into the dojo. He had been watching Leigh teach the kids class and he saw the future, a future I was blind to see for myself. Yes, this kid could do this. Even at just fourteen years old, he had the right stuff. Let the kid do it. Perhaps he had been born to do this?

Croteau began a club on the back of the students who followed him, but he failed to attract new students. Although he failed, there was still plenty of pain for everyone as it took almost an entire year for me to recover. I legally sued Croteau to stop him and to recoup what he had stolen. Once my legal victory was assured, I didn't have the stomach to destroy him.

I fell short, abandoned my legal claim, and let him go. He would marry Claire, and within a year, they would divorce and she would destroy him - thus stealing the remaining shreds of his dignity.

Like the story of *"Jezabel"* from the bible, she had fabricated false evidence of blasphemy and she eventually brought everyone down around her, including herself. She left Mike with nothing but the pain of what he had done through her manipulation. He would have many sleepless nights in the coming years, as he ran from everything and everyone, looking for a place to be forgiven.

I soon forgave him and if he had asked, he could have heard it directly from me. Although I had not done the things for which I was accused, I had let him down. I had not been the Sensei he needed, and I knew it. The courage it would take for Mike to ask for and hear me forgive him would take almost twenty years. He was crushed, but unlike me, there was no earthly truth to save him.

I too had been crushed and ground into the earth.

Before the Christmas events of 1995, I had a net worth that exceeded $500,000. I owned property, had prestige, and I had the love of my community from my twenty-some years of good work. Within six months my reputation was tarnished, and my business practices were suspect. I was living in a rented house with over $75,000 in short-term debt, leaving me with an estimated net worth of about $25,000.

Yes, I had been crushed. But the truth, crushed to the earth, will rise again and again and again. I had invited Mike Croteau to be my "adopted" son and to be part of my family. Although I had, with the best of intentions, included Leigh, I made my son subservient in his position.

In some way, the universe took action to correct a wrong before it happened.

My son had also been burned and crushed into the ashes of the earth, and like a rising Phoenix, he emerged. The myth of the phoenix is modeled after the "sun" in the form of the regenerated bird that is reborn from the ashes. My "son", the phoenix, rose from those ashes.

When I, blind as an ostrich with its head buried in the sand, opened my eyes and looked around - I saw my son. The fire and the pain cemented a bond between us that was biblical in its proportions. As a teenager, a son rose to help a father, to save a dojo, and to claim the legacy that was rightly his.

THE NEXT GENERATION

LEADERSHIP IS CIRCULAR

I have granddaughters who have achieved Black Belts.

It's not the time that has passed so quickly that surprises me, it's the age of my children that bothers me. Yesterday, I had four sets of infant eyes looking to me for direction and now my four adult children are creating inroads to success that I never imagined. I already seek their guidance and revel in their abilities! Perhaps it is that way for all parents as you see your creation grow beyond your hopes for them. For me, I don't recall consciously doing much to influence my family, or for that matter anyone else's. My journey was just that: my journey.

To help myself, I instinctively knew I must help others. My thought was always if I gave of myself first, I'd be entitled to receive what I desired. In truth, it doesn't work that way, at least not directly or in a straight line.

Sensei Kim taught: the power of nature is circular, as in what goes around comes around. Man created the straight line. A man-made straight line is designed, like time, to only go in one direction. But the natural laws of cause and effect are circular in nature; what you do ultimately reflects back to you as its source. Social psychologists call it *"The Law of Reciprocity"* and it basically says that when someone does something nice for you, you will have a deep-rooted psychological urge to do something nice in return. As a matter of fact, you may even reciprocate with a gesture far more generous than their original good deed

In my experience, the reciprocal nature of the Dojo is true and profound.

The Dojo is the ultimate ecosystem to witness this cause-and-effect principle. For me it started by simply living my life. My cause was to feed my family by teaching an art that, as a young man, I barely knew. The ensuing effect was to feel the pressure to be "The Sensei". I believed that to be a worthy professional teacher I needed to be open to learning myself. As a result, I'd take on just about any subject that could assist me to be worth what I call *"the price of admission."*

The price of admission is: if you pay $10 for a movie, it has to be worthy of your expectations. Do you expect the show will be a "B grade" production or are you expecting an Oscar worthy story? The simple answer is that if you are going to invest your time and money to something, you require to get the very best for yourself. If you are a teacher, your students expect you're the very best you can be every time. And that requires personal growth. As such, I rarely missed an opportunity to upgrade my mental and physical abilities. Whether it was learning advanced Karate or training in a self-development seminar, I knew the more I had to teach, the more I could inspire.

My basic desire and teaching method stated, *"if I could inspire my students to be the best they could be, they in turn would demand more of themselves than they expected of me."* If they sought out the wisdom of what I taught, they would be more inclined to practice and develop their skills rather than simply rely on me to "make them better".

As an aside: Champions of anything create themselves, by themselves. It's a classic push or pull relationship. A trainer can only push so hard, or for so long. If the future champion is not driven, or pulled, by their ambition to succeed they will find a way to fail. They only use their trainers and teachers as guides. The sooner you can cut the apron strings of dependence, the farther you will go.

Bringing this back to my point: if a teacher only demands straight line thinking and action, they will need to continually spoon feed their students. On the other hand, if you demand a standard of excellence, but allow your students the liberty to discover their way, they will usually outperform your expectations.

It is the classic saying, *"If you give a man a fish, you feed him for a day; if you teach a man to fish, you feed him for a lifetime."*

I call it Dojo Calculus.

Dojo learning is a simple mathematical equation: one plus one equals "you". At first blush the equation looks like 1 + 1 = 2. It is finite and exact, with no room for judgment or error. If you add a technique or ability one by one you will learn, but only in a superficial and limited way. But Dojo Calculus is based on cause and effect, thus it is not measured by simple addition, it's multiplication. You teach two people who teach two people and what you do grows exponentially.

The exponential value of the dojo's cause and effect teaching and learning allows the teacher to offer instruction with the expectation that their efforts will continue to grow long after the lesson is done.

I believe this expectation is the single best reason that decades after I did my most effective teaching, my students have not only carried on, but far and away have surpassed me. The benefit of my Dojo calculus is that it has become generational.

And when it becomes generational, your effect on others raises itself to the 2nd power. Even if the typical straight-line give and take teaching becomes reciprocal it usually ceases to exist when the teacher stops teaching.

Sounds good, but can I prove it? Yes I can, and with one simple measurement. Starting with nothing in 1984 in Brockville, Ontario, I created two full time dojos with an annual membership of about 450 - 500 students. In 1989, having empowered two incredible young men to take over these schools, I made the tough decision to return with my family to my home province of British Columbia. Effectively, I led and taught full time for only four and a half years. Starting with Mike Sweeney and Dan Coles, I can count 19 direct students who were influenced enough by my efforts that they made Martial Arts their profession. Some people taught for only 5 or 6 years, and others are still teaching today. Along with *Sweeney* and *Coles*, the instructors include *Scott Bullard, Shelley Winters, Bob Noonan, Ed Comeau, Dan Wilson, Mike Croteau, Peter Townshend, Scott Hall, Gord Holtrop, Grant Joron, Bob MacNeil, John Wilson, Chris Greenwood, Elaine Luis, Drew Wilson, Chris Roberts* and *Leigh Mueller*.

I do not know anyone in the martial arts who can make a similar claim. I remind you that this is only for the short amount of time I was in Brockville, and from the people I taught directly, if only in a small way. They were all influenced by the multiplication effect of the Dojo Calculus. After my time there, many of these people influenced others to also make martial arts their life. Of the many accomplishments in my martial arts career, this referendum about my teaching, by far, is what I am most proud of.

Ok, enough theory. Organically, when my eldest son became the practical day-to-day sensei of Canada's Best Karate, he also took over my long list of responsibilities. Additionally, he molded his style of teaching to replicate the same Dojo Calculus I had employed. Using the power of cause and effect, his efforts have created five Vancouver Island Dojos from the original two.

In 2004, I fully retired from the Dojo. Leigh Mueller had already been running the schools for a few years, but with my stepping back he officially became the Sensei and owner of CBK in British Columbia. I remained only as his coach when he asked for my opinion or in the rare moment when he needed my help. He was free to make his own life and create his own mistakes and like all of us, he made plenty.

He also took what was left to him, then reinvented himself, and the CBK schools. Using the exact same formula to motivate students to work and rely on themselves, the Vancouver Island program has more than doubled under his watch. He has inspired many to become the best they can be and has developed leaders in Raj Bassi, Jordan Gieble, and brother, Kieran Mueller, to be independent franchisees of the CBK way. Together, they have approximately 800 families who attend and continue to grow The True North Dojo - Canada's Best Karate.

When I began writing this book, I intended to list the names of everyone who had achieved a Black Belt with me. When I looked at the list of first-generation people, I realized that I would need to include all the Black Belts from all the associated 2nd and 3rd generation schools. When the thought about the chance of missing someone occurred to me, I felt the risk was not worth the reward. Save to say there are somewhere between 500 - 700 people who have achieved that kind of success and I am proud of their accomplishment. I honor their efforts by telling the stories of the next generations.

The following stories are written by and about the 2nd and 3rd generations of our leadership. There are dozens and dozens of young people who represent the future of Canada's Best Karate. Today they are the cause and tomorrow we will see who they effect.

Did I mention I have granddaughters who are Black Belts?

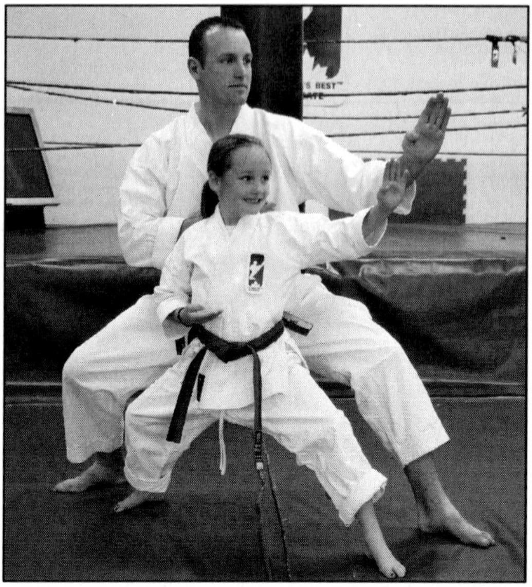

Leigh with granddaughter Maeli
Leigh with with Shannyn, Brooklyn, Dillon & Maeli

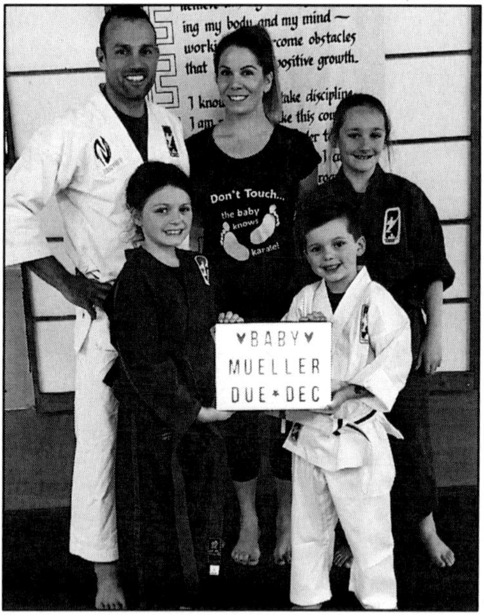

FIRST ENCOUNTERS OF THE DOJO

Leaders of the Third Kind

Leigh Mueller. The stage went black, and everything was dark from the back curtain to the audience. The show had ended with a roar of applause, and as the spotlight beamed down from the balcony all I could see was a solitary figure standing at center stage. Assembled on stage behind him were 300 seated students, their hearts still pounding, as the 917 souls in the audience at the UVIC Theater readied themselves for more. Collectively their heartbeats seemed to synchronize as they held their breath, wondering what would be next.

The light illuminated the white uniform, and his sweat soaked face shone like the North Star in the night's sky. Even from the back row you see his joy and as he began to speak, you could feel his intensity.

"My name is Leigh Mueller, and I want to change the world!" were his first words into the amplified space. After two hours of song, excitement and laughter, the 2004 Karate Christmas Concert had ended with his new demonstration of the Black Belt Finale and Tribute to Training. It had been a triumph.

The bold statement was followed by a powerful oration that, given the past hours of excellence, his proclamation seemed obvious and almost understated. He finished with his hand on his heart, and recited the mantra from the Black Belt Finale, *"I love my life, I am Unstoppable, I am a real CBK Black Belt!* Then he asked for all 300 students to join together in booming unison, *"I love my life, I am Unstoppable, I am a real CBK Black Belt!*

He followed the chant with more, *"Every person, no matter your age, your ability or who you are – if you stand with me, I will carry you – I will take you with me and we will go to the top together. That is where I am going. You can hold my hand, jump on my back, whatever you need to do – I don't care how you do it, if you want to succeed you can come with me, right here and right now. I am dedicated to take us, and CBK, to top and we will make a difference in the world, each one of us! We can change the world together!"*

The people in the back, the front and the sides stood. The standing applause was the loudest I had heard since the first concert held at the Royal Theater 10 years earlier. I stood, I felt the goose bumps and I believed.

All fathers believe in the goodness and the potential of their children, but when I saw this man on the stage, I had forgotten that he was my son. I just believed. I wanted him to take my hand and for a moment I said yes to myself, *"Yes! We can change the world!"*

I love big thoughts and global ideas, but I also know that you can only change the world one person at a time. The evidence had just spoke to me. I'd seen it before - over and over for 20 years – first in myself, and then in those who wanted what I wanted.

But I must say I was blown away by what I witnessed.

If you do the work, you can say, *"I am Unstoppable, I Love my Life, and I am a Real CBK Black Belt."* From that moment on I did not question whether Sensei Leigh Mueller could be a great leader, I just believed.

Rajan Bassi. Once again, he got to the same place in his Kata and his mind went vacant. Rajan Bassi had practiced this Kata successfully hundreds of times but when it came time to test, he blanked out again and again and always in the same spot. He knew the sticking-point meant failure and, given the gravity of earning his 3rd brown belt, he was obligated to fail once again. This was the third time in a row. The failure cost him his chance to challenge for his Black Belt. At thirteen years old it had been acceptable to wait, but now this failure seemed destined to make him quit.

At times like this a Sensei needs to try a little harder and do a little more. This meant having an extra meeting with Raj and his parents Cindy and Shirinder Bassi. Raj was just one student, but he was very important to me. I remembered him as a little six-year-old kid for two reasons: first were his big brown eyes and infectious smile and second, he was my first East Indian student.

When they initially came to the Dojo it was his Dad "Shin" that caught my attention as he, an Englishman from Britain, loved sports – especially soccer. He dearly wanted his son to love his favorite game too, but even at six years old kids know what they like and what they want. Raj wanted to please his Dad, but Shin could see that "football" wasn't for his son. It was the Ninja

Turtles that Raj liked, and Superkids Karate was what he wanted to do.

Up until this point in my life I had had thousands of students in Parksville and Brockville but never any Indian families. Victoria was a little different as there was a large Indian community and, with the popularity of kids Karate, it was just a matter of time before it became more cosmopolitan.

The Bassis were typical parents as far as I was concerned but, as they were of Indian descent, they had something "extra". This extra quality wasn't immediately evident, but after the Bassis joined the dojo, I began to attract a lot of ethnic students and that's when I began to notice something special. These people were the most dedicated family people I had ever experienced.

All parents, be them white, black, brown or yellow, love their children but the Indian family culture was the most involved I had ever seen. Each family serviced themselves and then extended that help to additional family and friends and ultimately their community at large. Hard working and impeccably honest is what I experienced over and over. I became a fast fan of this community and the Bassis were tops on my list.

They would meet with me yearly at renewal time. I enjoyed hearing Shin's football stories and sharing Cindy's determination to see Raj succeed. The wannabe six-year-old Ninja Turtle was a quiet, gentle boy who didn't stand out in class. He just fit in, did what was asked of him, and always came back for more. Other than the big smile, I don't remember much about Rajan's karate until be started failing tests.

"Well son, what are you going to do? Have you had enough Karate or are you going to pass this next test and go for Black Belt?" Shin asked. With three failures I wasn't sure what Raj would do, as he certainly was discouraged. The hard part was he was pretty good and near the top of his class, but he just couldn't remember this one particular Kata when the pressure was on.

Rajan looked serious. He clearly had been thinking about his dilemma, and as he prepared to answer I noticed his posture rise, "I don't want to quit. I want to get my Black Belt." Clarity is a powerful tool and that day I saw his future when I heard his determination.

The 2000 Black Belt Grading was the largest test to date. There were two distinct groups - an older contingent lead by a powerful woman named Cathy Quinn and younger teenage bunch of boys lead by Rajan Bassi. It stands out for me because my own son Drew had come of age by testing for his Black Belt that year, and this group had some very talented young men among them.

What I remember most was that, while each one of these teenagers stood out at various times during the 20-hour test, when Rajan Bassi took the floor to perform his Kata – he owned it. He was the leader that the others followed.

Twenty years later nothing has changed other than the quiet little boy with the big smile is now much louder and, as the Sensei of his own Dojo, he represents CBK in every way: mind, body, and soul.

Kieran Mueller. She slowed the car down as they approached Vancouver's roughest three blocks on lower Hastings St. Suddenly, it seemed like the street was without borders as the sidewalks overflowed with the homeless. Weathered faces full of rotten teeth and darkened eyes looked at them from under layers of dirty clothes. Drugs, prostitution, and hard luck told a story that no one wanted to hear, let alone live.

As she drove even slower, the street people, the lurching lost – people who barely had their most basic needs met, crawled closer to see if there was an opportunity or a handout to be had. Brittany Mueller was at her wits end, and Hastings Street was the last tool she had to make an impression on her little brother, Kieran. To help get him to talk, Brit had tried the Zoo, gone for walks and spent the entire weekend with her 12-year-old brother in hopes of turning him around. Her mission was the reason she had invited him to spend the weekend in Vancouver. Perhaps a weekend away from a mother who couldn't handle him and a father who wasn't there, would help him put him back on better path.

Kieran, at twelve going on eighteen, seemed destined for trouble. He was already dropping out of school and hanging with some rough kids. The Saanich Police knew his name. Divorce is a difficult thing for everyone involved but for the youngest, the baby of the family, it can be devastating.

Brittany, at 20 years old, was wise beyond her years and an old soul so to speak. While her mission failed that weekend, she planted a seed that made an impression on her little brother. Without acknowledging it directly, he understood that his sister was just a phone call or a ferryboat ride away. If he couldn't count on anything else, he could count on her.

Kieran Mueller didn't hit absolute bottom, but he came perilously close. The next five years saw him quit school, experiment with alcohol and time after time, antagonize the police. He was the classic "good kid" going bad. Everyone could see it and no one or nothing, including the Karate Dojo, could seem to get him to fight against it.

It took a last-ditch plan from his older brother to finally break through Kieran's self-destructive behavior.

Leigh, as Kieran's Sensei, stopped telling his brother what to do or what to think – instead he took a different approach and asked Kieran for his help. Leigh created a need at the dojo, saying that things were going poorly at the second school and he needed someone he could trust. Being trusted and valued without having to endure being lectured was something Kieran hadn't felt for some time. Within months the wrong path turned into the right road as the black cloud of confusion lifted.

Kieran found his self-worth and, back again in the dojo, he found that his martial arts ability made him valuable. Not only was he a talented fighter, but now his struggles became an asset, and his self-imposed ordeal prepared him to become an excellent young teacher.

The dojo does not always create a clear path to success and sometimes it seems that the training has missed the mark. But it's the beauty of the lessons learned early in life that come back when they are needed the most.

The little brother who needed to be needed quickly became a force on the floor, and within a few years he was leading the flagship CBK dojo and making it his own. In a family of high-ranking Black Belts, he is arguably the best athlete with the kind of speed and power that is rare. When you have natural talent combined with a strong work ethic you get a leader in the making. A decade later, in 2013, Kieran Mueller's hard work and dedication earned him his Sensei title. This was not an easy accomplishment for a Mueller as the bar is always set a few pegs higher for family.

He has become the kind of mentor that all kids look up to and all parents respect. He walks his talk and because his path was full of setbacks and stumbles, he is the epitome of the old Judo maxium: *"fall down seven times and get up eight"*. It's not that leaders never fail. They just never fail to lead!

Like his sister, he is wise beyond his years, perhaps decades.

Jordan Gieble. Seated beside Professor Jacob, I held my breath as Jordan took the ring for the JuiJitsu open grappling finals. It had been another hot day in Port of Spain, Trinidad. Our host, Don Jacob, was sponsoring his first World Championships in over five years and CBK had brought a good team to represent Canada. With over 50 schools and 25,000 Purple Dragon students globally, the Professor didn't need any foreign Dojos to round out this global tournament. But, as we were friends who had long ago twinned our organizations to a similar heartbeat, we were welcome guests.

Friends, that is, until you step into the competition ring.

They don't like to lose in Trinidad and most often they do not. It's not unfair to say that there is also a big hometown advantage as the judges are often swayed by their fierce loyalty to their own schools and ultimately the Donjitsu System. It happens regularly between their intermural dojos, and even more with any foreign competition.

That aside, Canada's Best Karate had a very good day by winning its share of medals. We had a proud team that year, as Sensei Leigh had prepared all our competitors to accept the hard scrabble rules and competitive spirit of the Trinidadians.

As you might expect, CBK did very well in the traditional Kata divisions and made a good showing in the always Trini-rough point sparring matches. Notably, Sensei Kieran was disqualified from the Black Belt Finals for excessive contact. His opponent rushed at him hard during the opening bell trying to rough him up. His blood up, Kieran Mueller made a statement. After the first clinch, his full contact ring experience took over and he knocked his opponent out cold. It's one of the few times a 2nd place trophy felt justified and therefore satisfying.

I, along with Billy Blanks of TaeBo fame, Don Warrener, and of course Professor Don Jacob, watched from the sidelines. That's what old men do - even some of the best to ever don a karate-gi must limit themselves to watching, as everyone eventually gets too old to compete.

With over 1000 competitors and all the fast-paced action, one person caught the attention of all four of us at the head table. CBK Sensei Jordan Gieble had fared well in the usual Kata and Kumite divisions but decided to take his Trinidad experience to the next level by entering the Juijitsu Open Grappling Ring. In these matches there were little kicking and punching allowed as the focus was grappling.

Grappling had also become an added focus in the Dojo over the past decade as Sensei Leigh had added both kickboxing and grappling to the CBK curriculum. The goal was to expand the dojo's overall fighting skills and abilities. Fifteen years prior, Leigh himself had earned a Donjistu Black Belt directly from Professor. That experience had him appreciate the importance of a multi-disciplined approach to training and now CBK was benefiting.

Perhaps discipline should be Jordan Gieble's middle name. He is about as clean-cut a person as you could want in your family or to head up a Karate School. Ethical, determined, and patient, he is the kind of guy you would like your daughter to bring home. As with most people who appear to be like a boy scout or straight arrow, he also tends to get underestimated much of the time. As a teenager he had developed knee problems that inhibited his flexibility and kicking dexterity, so to compensate he focused on developing his strength and power.

In jest, his fellow training mates, Kieran Mueller and Raj Basi, dubbed him *"Tin Man"* for both his stiffness and his ability to keep moving forward no matter what. The more success Jordan experienced the more the nickname stuck. And he succeeded a lot!

The nickname was more than just a comment about his fighting style, as it also represented the heart of the man. He never gives up, no matter what the odds, and he always keeps moving forward. This "never say die" attitude has served him well at his Duncan, BC Dojo and in his life. It's a matter of pride that if Jordan says he can, he will – no matter what!

As I watched him during the daytime eliminations, his basic skills were enough to keep him even with some highly skilled Trini grapplers. However, it appeared to me that during each of his fights he would find himself repeatedly over matched. Then on the brink of losing, his will to endure would kick in and he would find another gear. He not only out-muscled his competition, but he out-survived them long enough to bring each match to an end by tapping his opponent out - effectively knocking them out! What was interesting to me was how he first wore out his opponent then skillfully positioned them to lose.

Unlike boxing or a striking contest where you might be overwhelmed by your opponent or suddenly knocked out, grappling fights require one man to submit. Usually, it happens because you are in danger of a limb being broken or a fight-ending submission chokehold. Either way, the danger is so great that you must give up or be knowingly injured.

His efforts and will to win all day led him to a berth in the finals against a very tough opponent. I was already nervous for him when Don Jacob leaned over and whispered in my ear, *"Don't worry man, I won't let your guy get hurt - I'm watching my guy like a hawk. This man is dangerous – for real! Last year he got attacked on the street and he killed a guy in self - defense. Don't worry. If it gets rough, I'll stop it!"*

I'm not sure whether I felt reassured or more worried by Professor's promise.

Once in the ring, Jordan's lily-white skin and nice guy nature seemed to completely contrast with the black man I now knew to be a killer. To me, the opponent looked bigger, stronger, and certainly meaner. Frankly, I don't like to be pessimistic, but I gave Jordan zero chance to win against this man. My best hope was that he would lose quickly, without getting hurt.

As the match began, Jordan Gieble suddenly looked bigger in every way to the Trinidadian fighter. Instead of being dominated like he had at the start of his elimination matches, Jordan moved in, positioning himself well, and then took his opponent unceremoniously crashing into the mat. While he was unable to force a submission, he clearly dominated while on the ground. In these matches the fighters have about 30 seconds to affect a submission before the referee breaks them up and restarts the fight with both men back on their feet. Knowing that he was in trouble, the Purple Dragon fighter began bloodying Gieble with left jabs and various strikes. Without wavering, the "Tin Man" moved forward and took the blows as he forced the fight to ground.

Sensing the desperation, the all-Trinidad home advantage audience roared. Although they cheered for their man, the ensuing energy and applause emboldened both fighters to go all-out. At the end of the 5-minute round they had fought to a draw and as such, an overtime round was required.

The pattern of Trinidadian striking, and Canadian takedowns remained consistent, with Jordan being the aggressor and fearlessly dominating the fight. But there was no submission and no win. The Purple Dragon man was equally determined and highly skilled, as he kept himself out of Jordan's locks and positioning pins. By the end of overtime, the fight was still deadlocked and there was still no clear winner. With both fighters exhausted and out of gas, they were told to turn their backs towards the 5 judges. Then the center referee called for a vote where three arms pointed to Trinidad and two nods for Canada.

Professor looked at me smiling with his big broad smile, shrugged his shoulders, and we both loudly applauded the match. The crowd roared its approval as I sighed and exhaled with relief. I also felt a CBK father's pride as I truly saw Sensei Jordan in a new and unexpected light. This Tin Man had the heart of a lion. It is said that *"nice guys finish last"* but in the case of Jordan Gieble, it's more appropriate to say, *"nice guys are the last to finish."*

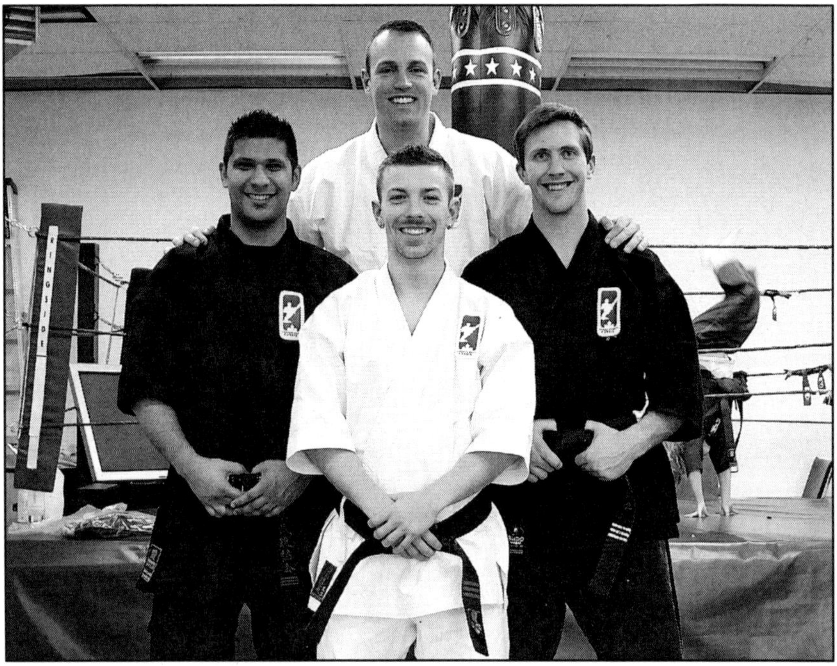

Leigh Mueller
Raj Bassi, Kieran Mueller, Jordan Gieble

THE STAND

BY LEIGH MUELLER

"Where's Sensei Mike? Is something wrong? Has there been an accident? Why is Sensei Kieran Baldwin teaching?"

These were the Dojo questions on everyone's lips. It was a cold, cloudy day Tuesday, January 7th, 1997 - a day that still burns in my memory. I was 15 years old the day my life was turned upside down. I think it still haunts and drives me.

It began like any other normal day as I entered the Douglas St Dojo. Since earning my Black Belt, and for as long as I could remember, I had been at my father's Karate School assisting my mentor and best friend, Mike Croteau. It seemed that I was always answering questions, helping students and parents - always preparing for the days' classes. But today was different. The usual buzz and excitement of starting a new year seemed dark and foreboding.

Sensei Baldwin, another man I respected greatly, took me aside, whispering, *"Mike's gone, nobody knows where he is."* His eyes narrowed as his face took on a very Sensei type expression, *"But your Dad says it's bad - looks like Mike stole a bunch of money and ran off!"*

My mind spun 360 degrees, but there was no time to say or do anything else. Classes were starting, and I was still in the dark. Communications were different then, no Facebook or social media, just the good old-fashioned rumor mill and it was grinding hard today.

Dad picked me up after classes finished saying, *"Leigh, I need you to teach all kids classes tomorrow."* It was one weird thing after another. When we got home my parents told me that Sensei Mike had been stealing money, embezzling was the word they used, out of the dojo and was trying to open his own club. Sensei Croteau wanted to take us down.

Before telling you what came next, it's important to realize who and what this person was to me, and to my family. Mike Croteau, in Dad's words, was the most gifted student he had ever taught. Mike had been with our Karate School for almost 20 years. He was the golden student, who at 19 years old had moved with us from Brockville, Ontario to Victoria, BC to be Sensei Mueller's protégé. He was everything to our family and especially to me. I looked up to him like my older brother and, as he lived with us for over 3 years, he became a brother. It seemed to me that he was also Dad's favorite son. Sounds like something you'd hear from a teenager doesn't it. Regardless, I loved and respected him, his dedication and ability. He was amazing in so many ways that I understood why Dad had trusted him so deeply.

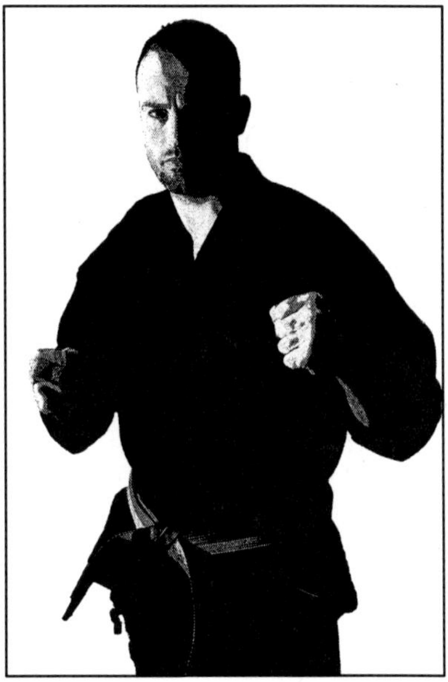

When you are told at 13 years old that *"your brother is trying to hurt the family and ruin your business"* it hurts. The next day at school, my ESL teacher, Mrs. Boyd, one of the only teachers who ever understood why I needed learning assistance, saw the pain on my face. After I explained the situation, she told me to not attend any other classes - just stay with her in homeroom class that day. Mrs. Boyd said, "*Write your feelings down, and it will help you deal with the situation.*"

All-day I wrote and re-wrote letters, affirmations to myself, I cried, and ultimately decided that this was my moment. I was going to defend my family, start making my mark, and truly get noticed by my Dad.

Powerful thoughts and actions come to you when things get real. I wrote about my confusion and my anguish. Why would a person who had hundreds of people admiring him be so cold-blooded? Mike told me often: Karate people are the most disciplined in the world, and I believed him. He said don't do drugs, don't smoke, and don't drink, and I believed him. But then he did the unbelievable. It turned out that the rumor mill had been right - he had, without cause or warning, lied, cheated, and stole from us. No integrity and no honor - that was how it felt to me. It was hard to write down my feelings, but that was the first day I truly shaped my own character. While it took decades to realize, it was the best thing that could have happened to me.

That said, the destruction he caused was truly terrible. Croteau set off a chain of events that affected all my family. During the next years, my parents lost their marriage, their property, and their savings. We had to start again - almost from scratch. Integrity and action are big things for CBK, as well as in my family, and while it took some time, we earned the trust of our community back. It taught me a lot about how to be and how to act.

While I never spoke to Mike again, I saw him a few weeks later when he held a meeting "to explain" himself and ask our students to quit CBK. My father was both disgusted and heartbroken saying to leave it alone. Yes, he was worried, but he said, *"I won't engage with these lies - we will just do our job and show people who we are. But I understand that you need to see for yourself. Sensei Kieran will take you to the meeting if you want to hear what Croteau has to say"*

Mike held a press conference (actually, it was more of a membership drive) at the Velox Rugby Club and invited everyone from the dojo to come. I had to go. I needed to confront him and ask him why? From the audience, I asked him directly why he had left. When he saw who had asked the question, he couldn't face me. He looked away and cried saying he was sorry for how he left, and that he didn't mean for things to happen this way. My pain turned to rage - my rage.

I had made a decision, weeks before in Mrs. Boyd's class, to take a stand. I, Leigh Mueller, was going to be a Sensei. Not just an ordinary teacher, but the very best I possibly could be. I decided I needed to take on a leadership role for my family. Mom and Dad needed me to step up and work the farm. So, I dug in.

Croteau's meeting was a sham and thankfully it turned out to be a bust. He lasted a few months before the disgrace caught up to him – then he left town.

This sad story is true, and it haunted me for a long time. Another truth is: when you learn martial arts as a child you develop maturities in unexpected ways. For me, it meant that I knew how to confront problems and look for solutions. More importantly, I knew to look for the meaning behind the problems. You can't solve what you can't see.

I can state without a doubt that our dojo and I would not be what we are today had that terrible event not happened. I learned from my father's pain and my disappointment. The virtual gut punch that Croteau delivered started a fire in my belly that has sustained me through thick and thin.

The English translation for the word Samurai is: "to serve." I dedicated myself to first serve my family, and then to serve my dojo community. My passion to train also served my desire to compete. That subsequent drive to learn has taken me to exotic places like Trinidad & Tobago, Thailand, India, and many American dojos. Whatever discipline, be it Karate, Jiujitsu, or Muay Thai Kickboxing, I've always wanted to test it and myself to find a way to compete. Measuring myself personally is always top of mind as competing against great opponents shows you where you stand. I believe it's a kind of reality check. As the old masters always say, "Know yourself and know your opponent and you will be victorious 100% of the time."

As a kid, some old masters were pretty close to home! Having your father as your Sensei, the most important person in the dojo, is not easy. While he always supported and encouraged me, he's never been easy to please. As the firstborn, much was expected, and as such, much was given. I think the best thing my Sensei Dad gave me was an opportunity. From the age of about 10 years old, he took me to numerous places with him, so I could experience many martial arts masters. As a kid, I was in the room with Hanshi Richard Kim, Professor Don Jacob, Sensei Jim Macdonald, and many others. I might not have always understood what they were talking about, but I experienced it and I learned from it.

When he needed my help to overcome the damage Croteau had caused, I stepped up and I played a major role in every aspect of our recovery and the subsequent success. Sensei Dad is a tough taskmaster and serious martial artist, He holds himself to a high standard in whatever he does, and he expects that of me. When I realized that his high expectations were his way of acknowledging me, I saw the Sensei in myself. That's when it occurred to me just how much he had noticed my contributions over the years.

I feel that my biggest contribution to Canada's Best Karate has been my desire to compete. And I don't mean just being competitive. I want to win - to be the best at whatever arena I enter. To do that I will outwork, out-think, and commit myself totally to what I'm doing. I believe that is the CBK way and in that, I have come to lead the way.

To be a great leader you must start as a great follower. I entered my first Karate tournament when I was 5 years old. I love to compete, and I love to fight. It's funny – for all the expectations

Dad had of me, he never pushed me to compete or cared much about competition. I was always pushing him because I wanted to win. It's not like he had never tested himself in competition, as I know he competed in over 100 tournaments - winning more than his share. But he did it out of obligation to his dojo and teacher, Jim MacDonald. Winning tournaments was okay, but not high on his list of priorities.

He likes to tell the story about my first karate tournament. I placed 8th out of 8, dead last. As a judge, he knew that I had been the youngest in the group and my last-place finish was correct. He believes in fair play and that being gracious in defeat is an important life skill. On the other hand, he had a tearful boy coming to his Dad for support. After a hug and a couple of atta-boys telling me how well I did, he tried to make it a teaching moment. He looked at me carefully saying, *"Hey, did you see how good the older boys' stances were? Those boys were really good - weren't they?"* In his uplifting way, he tried to soften the loss and dry the tears by changing the subject.

Wide-eyed I nodded, looking right at him, and said, *"Yeah Dad, theirs' were good, but mine was better."* I wasn't having any of it.

Whatever I have competed in, I wanted to be a champion. Perhaps I got it from my godfather, Jimmy Mac (Dad's original Karate teacher). He and I share a November 2nd birthday, so it figures I must have got my love of competition from him. Maybe it skips a generation! During Sensei Mac's last tournament, a year before his death at 57 years old, I saw him, as an older man, spar a bunch of younger guys and win some matches. Even though he left with broken ribs, I heard him say, *"I think I am too old for this, but I sure had fun."*

My favorite day as a Karate competitor was April 21st, 2001. I had been competing for many years as a teenager, but when I turned 17 it was time to step up to the Men's Black Belt Division. That was fine with me, as I wanted to prove myself at the top level. I won a lot in both the fighting and kata competitions, but there was one person I couldn't beat - Jon Fung. Fung was rated internationally as a kata top contender. When he walked into a tournament everyone knew they were competing for 3rd place, as I was taking 2nd! On that day in April, at the BCIT Gym in Burnaby, I ended his winning reign – first place was mine! The first winning phone call was to Sensei Mac - he was proud and happy for me. It's a moment that still rates high for me.

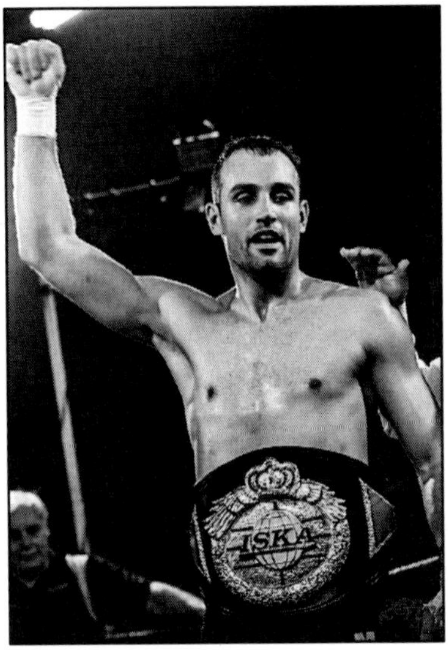

2005 brought new challenges, as I added both formal Brazilian Jiujitsu and Muay Thai Kickboxing to my list of desires. Although I held Black Belts in Japanese Shotokan and Purple Dragon Juijitsu, the joy of learning a new style was irresistible. In typical fashion, I decided to add learning two very different major styles at the same time. To accomplish this I traveled to California multiple times for Gracie Jujitsu lessons, and to Thailand over two summers for training and ring fighting in Muay Thai.

Devoting 4 years to these arts, I fought any and all fighters across Canada. I would take any match offered, and many times I was in over my head – but I learned and took myself to the top. I never pulled out or cared if the opponent missed weight (once by 12 lbs) - I just wanted to earn respect for my CBK Dojo. Notable fighters like Josh Jouncy, ranked top 5 with Glory Kickboxing, (the highest-level league) and Hakeem Dwadu, a top-10 UFC fighter, took the ring with me. I earned their respect, if not the win. I needed to fight for myself, and for respect.

For years I had heard many "fight gyms" say "Karate sucks and doesn't work". To prove a point, I entered every fight ring wearing my traditional Karategi. Win or lose, I won their respect. Answering the bell in 27 fights, my ring record was 17 Wins – 8 Losses (lessons) – 2 Draws.

My career concluded with the B.C. Amateur Kickboxing Championship Belt and a World title shot as a welterweight, fighting Kalon Melin, a tough, tall Australian. I won my fight against Melin, and the ISKA World Championship Belt, with a unanimous 5-round decision.

I wanted to prove the "haters" wrong. And I did.

While I was born with a willingness to compete and challenge myself, I know that a great deal of what the Dojo and I have become happened because of the vacuum created by Croteau. Would I have driven myself so hard without him? I can say yes, it's likely - but not guaranteed. The Kune of Life is that there are no guarantees. Everyone has opportunities, but if you don't act on them, they are worthless. The way of the Dojo states: Nothing is Free, all start at the beginning, and everyone works.

Everyone works - my goal in life has always been to outwork everyone. It's what makes me a Real CBK Black Belt.

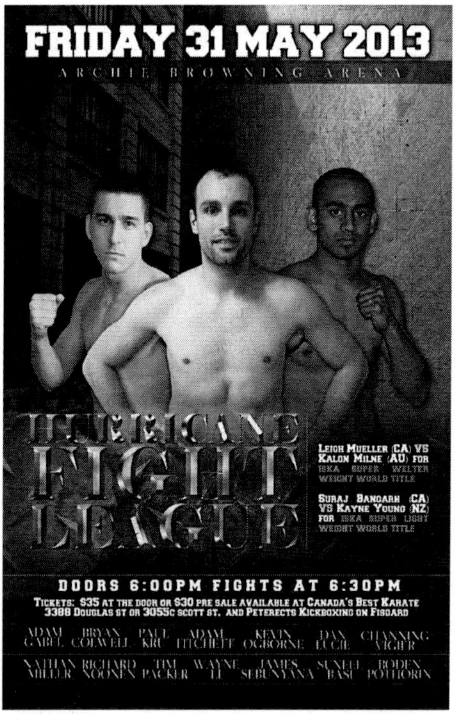

THE EXPERT FAILURE

BY RAJAN BASSI

The dictionary says that: *"Failure is the lack of success, an unsuccessful person, enterprise, or thing."* Failing can also be the omission of what is expected or a required action. Wow, why would a person claim to be an expert failure? Sounds crazy but it sums me up quite nicely. Do I take the word failure in a negative sense? No, not at all, as my experience has always been to turn that word failure into success.

As I look over my long martial arts hobby, career, and passion I realize that many of the best lessons and many of my greatest triumphs came directly after a failure. Those failings taught me more about myself, and the situation than winning right way ever could have. I started my martial arts journey on the back of other sports failures.

As a kid, I was the slowest, smallest, least athletic little 6-year-old with asthma you could imagine. Asthma did not set me up to succeed in the world of soccer, my father's favorite sport. My dad had played semi-pro ball in England, so I felt the pressure to follow in his footsteps. It proved to be a pressure I couldn't take. However, what I didn't know was that my dad wasn't concerned with me being great at soccer. He just wanted me to do "something" besides sit around at home, and I remember one day after running nonstop after a soccer ball I could never catch, he asked me *"do you like this?"* It was easy for me to say, *"Yes dad I do!"*

But I have a very good and smart father. He looked me up and down, and then said, *"No you don't. Why don't you pick something you want to do?"* When I tried to reassure him that I liked playing the game he loved, he said again, *"No, I want you to find something you enjoy as much as I enjoy soccer." If you can do that, then I'll be happy! And I'll know when it gets hard you'll push through the tough spots and you'll enjoy the sport so much more."*

At that time in my life, all I knew for sure was I wanted to be a Ninja Turtle like I had seen on TV. My family agreed, so I set my sights on karate and when my parents found Superkids Karate I found something I loved.

After a couple of years of training, I became more confident and was becoming more outgoing as I made dojo and school friends. Riding high with my small group of school friends, it was only a matter of time for a bully to begin targeting us. When it happened, I thought, no problem guys I got this; unfortunately, my first life lesson proved that I didn't have this! Not only was I beat up pretty bad and thrown down some stairs, I didn't even really stand up to him. I froze - I didn't say anything and I didn't do anything! Karate training doesn't help much if you don't use it!

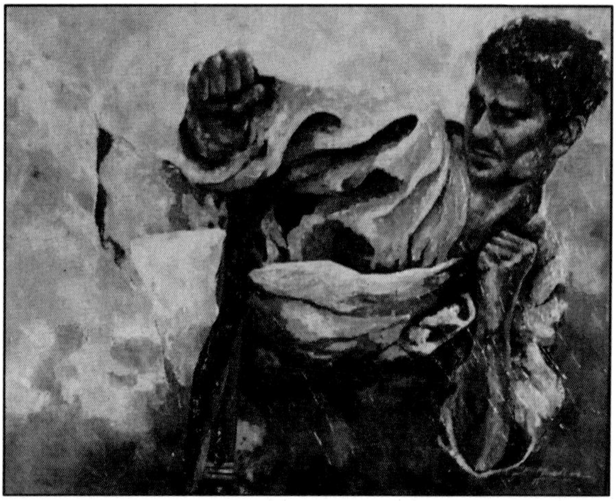

I felt like a failure - failure to act, failure to protect, and failure to do anything at all. I was discouraged and when I talked to my parents, I told them I wanted to quit. Their answer came back *"You're not allowed to quit. You made a commitment to training,but if that's how you truly feel, you'll need to talk to your Sensei."*

Talking to Sensei was a scary thought as I imagined how mad he might be! But surprisingly, he wasn't mad at all, rather he supported me by saying that I had been brave to stand up to the bully. I learned a big lesson - martial arts isn't about fighting and being the best fighter, rather it's about being the best person. I learned that all my training to that point had helped me a lot as I'd gained confidence, self-respect, and some self-esteem to not only make friends but to also stand up for them. Did I win the fight? No, but I did take a step in the right direction of being confident and secure in who I was, and the kind of person I wanted to be.

Later, as a teenager, the 14-year-old me was riding high with more confidence than ever. I had lots of friends, and became the funny, outgoing guy that everyone wanted to hang out with. I found my place in other sports as well and felt like I could do no wrong. I played volleyball, basketball, did track and field and it seemed like I was winning at everything. The next big goal was to get my Black Belt in the summer, and nothing was going to stop me - until it did.

Overconfidence can cause many problems, just like lack of confidence. I put myself in a spot where I didn't focus on my training as much as I should, mostly because "I was already awesome" and I'd just wing it. Knowingly, Sempai Leigh and Shihan Bob Mueller put the brakes on my plans as they told me that I wouldn't be receiving my 3rd brown belt. That meant I'd have to wait another full year to try for Black Belt.

What was their reason? They said, *"You can do better, you're not applying yourself enough, and most importantly you could be one of the best on test - but right now, because of being lazy, you aren't ready!"* Were they right? I didn't think so at the time as I was mad, embarrassed, and again contemplating quitting. Three others who also didn't pass the brown belt test did quit when they were told they weren't to test. When I wanted to join them, good old mom and dad said, *"Nope. You're not allowed to quit. You have come this far and you need to fulfill your commitment. You need to earn the Black Belt and then afterward you can quit."* With no other option, I brushed myself off and as I had a point to prove, I said to myself, "Ok I'm going to be the best on the test. I'm not going to be lazy anymore. I'll outwork everyone. When I get my Black Belt, I'll show them that they were wrong to deny me, and then I'll quit." I began showing up at the dojo at 3:30 pm every day and did every class whether it was assisting or training until 8:30 - 9:00 pm and repeat. While they didn't say so, I could see how proud my parents were of my effort. I was doing what my Dad had asked of me many years before by applying myself when the going got tough!

One year later, I earned my Black Belt, and yes I felt I was the best on the test. However, I also felt humbled and grateful, rather than boastful. Instead of saying I got this, I learned to respect the process, and ultimately, I recognized my lesson. Failure, when accepted, leads to humility and from there you can find a way to succeed. Before then, I thought I was doing all I could, but it was the push from my Senseis that motivated me to become successful.

Now into my third decade of training as a Sensei, Dojo owner, and leader, I still employ the hard-learned lessons of my youth. I also recognize myself in many of the kids who are now my students, and I look for ways to give them the kind of support that I received from my family and the teachers.

The only true failure is quitting, particularly quitting on yourself! As an adult, I could have quit many times on many things, but my training has given me the strength, the support, and the means to keep pushing forward and to keep striving past the struggles. Every failure made me hunger to win, while every success has made me humbler. When you find your true passion, you'll build a better you, and you'll find yourself reaching for your true potential.

As my dad said so many years ago *"Pick something you want to do and enjoy, then you'll be able to do the hard work!"* I believe when you pick martial arts you are picking a winner to become a winner in life!

STRUGGLES OF A DOJO FAMILY

BY KIERAN MUELLER

I'm not sure how old I was when my father brought me a special book to read. My best guess is that I was about six years old.

Calling it a book wouldn't be quite right as, with 40 pages and lots of pictures, it was more of a comic book. But it was perfect for me. I'd say it was a kind of superhero comic, but it was about a real person. If you know anything about my family, then you know superheroes are big with us.

The book told the tale of Professor Don Jacob, about his life, and his Martial Arts. My young mind was captivated by everything about him. He grew up in on the small island of Trinidad & Tobago, where he battled poverty and many challenges. Professor was born in the ghettos of Port of Spain, and because he was from a broken home, he was raised by his grandmother. I liked that he, like me, also lived on an island. Even at six years old, I felt lucky to live in a safe and friendly place like Victoria, British Columbia.

Don Jacob's story explained how he went from the toughest of circumstances in a third world country to becoming an internationally renowned JuiJitsu master. His comic book told how, as a young boy, he was saved when he was introduced to Martial Arts training, how his Senseis molded and influenced him to find his greatness and teach him to not have a "*ghetto mentality.*" He said, *"I was from the ghetto, but I was not part of it."*

This small comic book was the greatest inspiration to me. I must have read that book a thousand times, turning every page and never once losing my excitement.

It turned out that this superhero was a friend of my dad!

I remember the day my father invited the Professor to stay in our home. I introduced myself, and he smiled with his big white teeth. He picked me up in his long arms, hugged me, and then spun me upside down making me do a backflip! It was awesome! To me, he was a 7ft tall giant, with the biggest hands you have ever seen! He was an imposing character in every way, with massive superhero muscles and a huge personality.

In reality, while he is a big man, he is not very tall, and not as imposing as how I pictured him as a child.

But my childhood memories reemerged when, years later, he stepped onto the mat of our dojo. He was there to teach and demonstrate and it was incredible! There was silence as everyone, including my dad ,waited for him to speak and teach his art. Professor's story and ability made me want to train and be like him. This man is my hero.

Some of my heroes live a little closer. I am the youngest of four, with one sister, Brittany, and two brothers Drew and Leigh. I believe that I received this book just before my mother and father divorced. Until now it never occurred to me why Dad gave me the book. When my father moved out, my eldest brother Leigh became a surrogate Dad for me. This made our relationship kind of odd. Leigh and I are separated by 10 years, but even when he was a teenager, he was never too cool to sit and play toys with me.

I began my Karate, like my siblings, when I was 4 years old. My father told us that we needed to start young, but we could quit whenever we liked - that is, *"after we got our Black Belt."* It was the family rule and we all abided by it. Dad never taught us directly, as he didn't want the appearance of any family favoritism in the dojo. As such, Leigh has always been my teacher.

Outside of the dojo, he was always a fun and playful guy, but, as the Sensei, when he stepped on the mat, he became a different person. Does that ring any bells? I know he had something to prove as a young man running a Karate school, and it was his goal to make his students the best. I have always admired his drive and intensity. Leigh was a very tough and strict teacher and I believe he added a little extra dash of toughness just for me (thanks....). I also know he did that because he wanted me to be a top student like him. But sometimes, when he was around, it put me on edge, as I constantly thought I was doing or saying something wrong. A step out of place in the dojo and he'd send me to the wall to sit in a chair position until my legs screamed or do pushups until my arms fell off. I knew he always had my back and cared for me, but I'll admit that sometimes he scared me.

In the dojo, there were always great events with cool demonstrations. I loved these demos! Leigh, as the Sensei, was always the main event. He would throw his ukes (attackers) around like it was nothing. He had learned JuiJutsu directly from Professor Jacob in Trinidad, and now he appeared like a superhero. I am sure everyone who saw those demonstrations thought so too! It was during a demo one day that I remembered "The Book". That's when I saw the spirit of my hero in my big brother. I was in awe, as I had found another hero.

Sandwiched between Leigh and me, our family has two other Black Belts you may not know of. Closest in age to me, by five years, is my brother Drew, and we have that classic brother bond. We were good buds as young children, sworn enemies as teens, and best friends in adulthood. I idolized him, as most little brothers do with their older siblings, and I thought everything he did was the coolest - right down to his name. I was always following him and copying everything he did. Drew was a tremendous martial artist but modest and quiet, making him in some ways, the black sheep of our clan. To that, I believe he is also the most talented member of our family.

Between Drew and Leigh lies Brittany. My sister is the toughest of all of us kids. I don't remember much about my relationship with her, save for the regular sisterly things a girl might do with the baby of the family. I believe I found myself in many dresses and with painted nails! Brit, like an unbridled mare, left home as soon as she could. Not because of unhappiness, but at 18 years old, confident and ready for the world, she needed to test herself to see what she could do. To this day she has never stopped - or in dojo terms: she is unstoppable. She found an amazing and somewhat famous life in Vancouver. I'd say that she has maximized her Black Belt training with a life philosophy and outlook that we all lean on. Although she was a ferry ride away, she was always there if I needed help, like learning how to drive or with some of the teenage issues that almost ruined my life.

I say, honestly, that I am a mommas' boy, and my mother is the best. She is the only one in our family who does not have a Black Belt. But when angered, her 5' 3" stature and 95 lbs is a force of nature. I'd say she is as fierce a warrior as you might care to meet. Mom was the disciplinarian. No matter what, she did everything for me and has always been there. My stepdad earned my love and my respect. But, as a teenager, I put him through hell. He knew I didn't want him, but he taught me a lot about love and perseverance. Through all the crap I put him through he could have left me for dead. But he didn't, he stayed true and hung in there eventually winning us all over. As a man, and when I was becoming a Sensei, I told him exactly what I thought of him - a great guy I'm proud to have as my stepdad.

As mentioned, my father moved away when I was young. He was always in the background and in my life, but I didn't get to see him very much. When I did, he often told/taught me things that I didn't particularly understand at the time. Surprisingly tender at times, he was always the Sensei. You might say he was born to lead. He told me many times, in many ways, "You have to look out for # 1." His exact words were *"People do not do anything for anyone else. They do everything for themselves!"*

I have seen many shocked looks when he has said that to others, and admittedly it took me many personal lessons to understand what he meant. At first blush, it sounds like he is saying people are all so self-absorbed that they don't care about helping others. That is a misunderstanding.

That saying can mean many different things, whether you look at it as being selfish or see it as being your best self. I have been through the life-wringer enough to squeeze out its meaning, and again it was the dojo that revealed to me the truth of what he meant.

That, however, took a very dark path of understanding.

You could say, as a kid, I was attracted to trouble. I was drawn to people who have had tough lives. I was always interested in knowing about people in dark places, seeing what they had gone through, then comparing them to myself - but not in a good way. It's fair to say that as a confused teenager, I would describe myself as a hoodlum.

I was a pretty good kid up until grade 8, then for some reason, I wanted to make everything harder. I decided I disliked school, started smoking, stealing alcohol from my parent's liquor cabinet, and ultimately having the police visit my home many times. I was a messed-up nightmare of a child from the age of 12 to 17. The world was seemingly against me. I thought my family hated me, and that they didn't care or wouldn't help.

At the lowest point that I can recall in my life, my brother Leigh asked me to help him. Me, help him? How in world could I do that? You see, I was on probation for assault and robbery. I had been hanging out with the wrong crowd, and everything was pointing to a life of dead-end jobs, bad behavior, and perhaps even jail. Leigh, for some strange reason, needed my help. He said he was in a jam at the Karate School and he needed a person he could trust and depend on.

I said yes, but without thinking much about why. I figured I could go and teach for a year, maybe two, make some money and then figure out what to do with my life. The change truly happened for me when I walked into our old Douglas Street dojo to meet a former teacher of mine, Sensei Raj. Leigh had set it up. I was going to assist Raj and in turn, he would prepare me to teach full time at the Cedar Hill dojo. He welcomed me with open arms! We became friends instantly, and then training partners for life. Looking back, I see how Sensei's philosophy of "everyone only works for themselves" happens. Sensei Leigh had a good teacher. He knew that if he had said, "Kieran, you need the help and you need to clean up your act" that I would have most likely refused his offer to help. Instead, he knew the only way to help me was to help himself. I couldn't refuse him. He said the dojo needed me.

Sensei Dad said *"When you give someone a present, do a favor or a good deed, who are you really doing it for?? Kieran,*

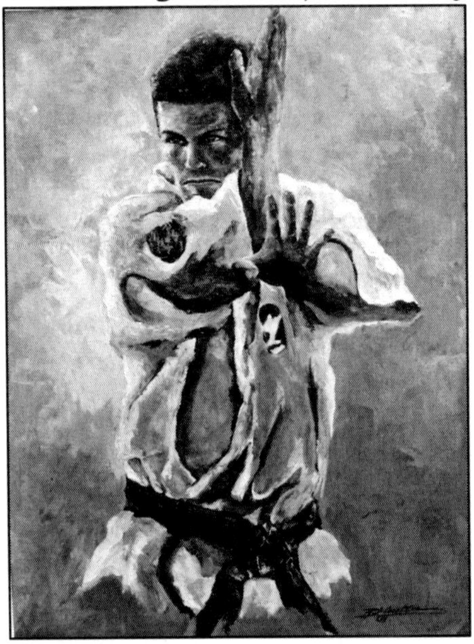

there aren't many saints like Mother Teresa in the world - everyone only does things for themself. Helping someone in need, makes you feel needed. Let me ask you, how do you feel when you give someone a gift that you know they truly want? Is it more fun to be the giver or the receiver? When you give to others, you are giving to yourself first. The more you give, the more you get. In my mind, you do selfless acts for yourself. Your reward for helping others is how it makes you feel about yourself. You are putting yourself first by being able to give to another ... right?"

That is the essence of the dojo. Interestingly, the word Samurai (Japanese warrior) actually translates to English as "to serve". To that end the meaning of the Sensei and the role of the dojo, has become clear to me. Perhaps I have evolved and finally figured out that perplexing statement my father taught me; *"You must take care of yourself before you can take care of others."* I know that is a common saying, but how many people have truly figured that out? I have yet to see this in myself, but I have seen it in my father. As a confused teenager, I thought that he was selfish. He had left me, and he left our family, but at the same time he cared for us through the dojo. I guess it's easy to see how that was confusing for a confused kid.

In reality, he took care of himself to be a better person. He put himself in a position to ultimately help out his family and the others who would become part of it. And there are many.

Through the dedication of my brother and the help of my friend Sensei Raj, I slowly changed into to the person I was meant to be. My personality, my character, and my strength came from the same source that my entire family had used for decades: the dojo. The harder I worked, the more I put into it, the more I did for my life – the more I could give to my students and the people important to me. The more I gave, the more I received.

That's when I became a real Black Belt. I found out what martial arts are and what this training means to me. This isn't my brother's version, or even my father's, as everyone has different views. I own this one.

My martial arts journey begins and ends with family.

It took a while to figure out that my family has always been there, even when I thought they weren't. Leigh being a brother and a father to me, my mother being the disciplinarian, Drew being my friend by encouraging me, and Brittany being a rock, with no judgment.

My stepdad showing me what hard work and perseverance means, and my mentoring father, ever the Sensei, with his strange way of teaching about the meaning of "being" number one. Lastly, my brother-from-another-mother, Sensei Raj, for showing me equality and how to trust true friendship.

For me, it began with a comic book about a great man. Today, I am beginning to see that hero, as seen through the eyes of my dojo students, in me. I walk my talk with my martial arts, and I believe in family. The dojo is family, and yes, families struggle, but when they use this place to better themselves, they enhance the lives of everyone around them.

A good dojo raises all involved, like a high tide raises all boats.

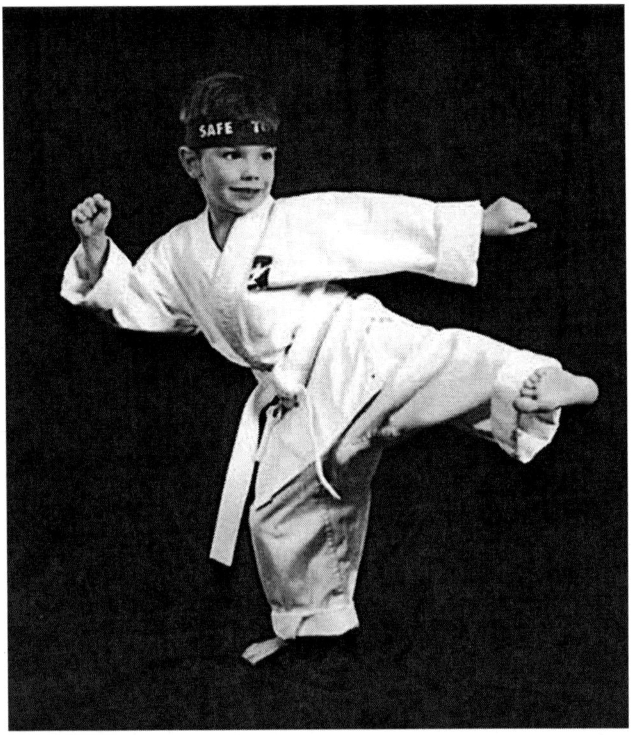

Kieran Age 5

DUNCAN DOJO: THE FAITH TO SUCCEED

BY JORDAN GIEBLE

Everyone has those moments in life where they think, *"What am I doing?"* or, *"Will this even make a difference?"* As I sat in my brand-new Duncan dojo, empty of students, I could not help but think the worst.

It was January of 2012, when I remember the first meeting with Shihan Leigh Mueller. He was my main instructor and mentor since starting Karate in 2001. His teaching was the catalyst that became my love for martial arts and helped me work towards my first huge Karate achievement of my Black Belt in 2005. He continued to help me to become an instructor myself. Side note: Leigh helped me achieve MANY other martial goals over the years, but that is not what this story is about.

Growing up we always heard Leigh say he wanted Canada's Best Karate anywhere and everywhere. If an instructor was someone of quality, and stuck true to the beliefs of our dojo - he wanted to help them. Our meeting was about having me open a Canada's Best Karate School, independent from a Mueller family member.

"You could go to Vancouver and do it all on your own. Or you can go up island and I can help you when needed." He has always been very straightforward. However, at 20 years old, I had little idea what was expected in opening and running a business. What I did know was - I wanted to do it! Vancouver held little appeal for me, as I knew nothing about the mainland martial arts community, so I quickly said, *"Let's go up island."*

Together we decided Duncan was the right spot. It was a short drive from Victoria and had no other schools offering a quality program like ours. We thought it could be a great opportunity for a CBK dojo to make an impact on the community. Collectively we started to look for a location. We found it at 81

Trunk Road! While small, it was a great prospective location: high visibility for street traffic, across from the main mall, and easily accessible by foot. We were both excited!

All of September 2012 I spent my time building, painting, and preparing the new dojo. The few small setbacks I met along the way simply fueled my impatient dojo desires. As I started to make some headway, with the dojo almost finished, I showed up to find the ceiling being torn down and all the lights being taken out. *"The inspector says it's not up to code."* the owner told me, adding *"But, we'll will have it fixed in no time!"* I worked around them the best I could, trying to protect what I had already finished, while the building owner corrected their mistakes.

When I wasn't at the dojo, I did the next best thing to help get a good start - I'd promote the new business by introducing myself door to door! I took to the streets with hundreds of flyers. I walked everywhere in my area sliding fliers in mailboxes, under mats, on door handles, anywhere the owner would not miss it. I remember Leigh saying, *"Just go pound the pavement! Someone will call in no time. Be ready!"*

Now the dojo was finished, and I was ready to teach. Starting that Monday, I walked four hours a day handing out flyers. By 2:00pm I'd shut it down, go back to the dojo and change into my Karategi and wait. I had no one to teach so I had to wait for a call or a person to walk in to ask questions. Once the phone started to ring, I'd be on my way with my first student learning on the new dojo floor!

Day 1: All I did was wait. After all my waiting I drove back home to Victoria, ate some dinner, and went to bed. When I woke up, I had breakfast and got right back to what I did the day before!

Day 2: All I did was wait.

Day 3: All I did was wait.

Day 4: All I did was wait. It was at this point I remembered something I had heard before we had started: Duncan had never had a professional martial arts school succeed long term. I had dismissed it then, but now I wondered - was I just going to be another failed attempt? A few weeks ago, I was full of energy and excitement. Now came the doubt, and a deep sense of loneliness. Charles Dickens may have put it best - *"It was the best of times; it was the worst of times."* I was feeling it was the worst of times.

Day 5: Finally, on day 5, after handing out hundreds of flyers, I was sitting at the dojo having my lunch, with the commentary of the previous 4 days running through my head: *"What am I doing? Is this even going to work?"*

Then it happened: the moment I was waiting for - the phone rang.

Never have I been more excited and nervous to answer a phone. *"Canada's Best Karate!"* I said with anticipation. The excitement quickly evaporated as I heard my mentor's voice checking in to see how things were going. Like the nosedive of an Olympic diver into an empty pool, my enthusiasm hit bottom. *"Not the best."* I remember feeling jinxed as I stated, *"You were the last person I spoke to..."*

Since his Monday call, I had spoken to no one, and now it was Friday. All I did was hand out papers, eat, and wait, hoping that something would happen. Almost 5 full days of not speaking to anyone, was discouraging, so I finished my day a bit early and made the lonely drive home.

The following Monday is when everything changed. Leigh came to Duncan to help complete some finishing touches. When I arrived, he was already there cleaning the dojo, and with a smile he said, *" We got one!"*

Of course, with all my work and doubts the week before, this fate felt a little cruel! It was like a paper cut - I should have been the one to receive the initial call that would get us started. Shihan had returned a phone call from the weekend, the jinx was broken, and our first student was coming to try a class!

Her name was Ciara.

When Ciara arrived with her grandmother, she hid behind gramma, not saying a word. Hiding as if I was a dragon, coming to eat her. She was shy - but I was determined. Slowly but surely, I got her to the dojo floor and had her participating in our class of one. I had someone to teach, and it was thrilling but also terrifying at the same time. What if she was too scared to join? By the end of her first class, she was standing a little taller and had a smile on her face. She still did not speak, but I knew we made some good progress. I had my first student!

After that she never missed a class. Ciara started smiling more and more and actually began talking to me. Soon she, as my senior student, was welcoming other new kids as they slowly started to trickle in. By the end of December 2012, the dojo had 9 students. Not exactly what you would call a fantastic start, but it did not matter to me. I taught every class as if my life depended on it!

Even as the dojo started to gain some students, I still had this lingering shadow behind me. *"Will this even matter?" "Can I make this school succeed?"* I had rent, bills, and myself to pay!

With the support of Shihan Leigh, and the new students who depended on me, those thoughts started to fade away.

Everything is a process when you start from scratch. As the dojo began to grow Shihan had a great idea. He suggested I go to the Duncan elementary schools and meet with the principals. He said, "Offer them a program for the entire school, all-volunteer on my part. Then donate of 100% of the small teaching fee charged, thereby giving it all to the school." Leigh and I visited the first school together so I could, "get the idea". We sat in the lobby for an hour before the front desk administration said, *"We are just too busy today, we will call you."*

I was excited to hear that they would at least give us a chance! Leigh quickly turned that around saying, *"They won't call, but at least you know how to do it now! Go visit some more schools." Still* very unsure of what I was doing, I just treated it like any other meeting with students. I gave it my best effort.

One of the schools, Tansor Elementary, had a progressive principal at the time named Joseph Boudreau. He not only was the first and only principal to take my meeting, but he truly engaged with me. He asked questions and got excited about my concept. Unfortunately, as there were other known commitments, he couldn't have me set up an after-school program. What I did not know, was how this meeting would change the dojo forever.

In January 2013 Mr. Boudreau brought in his son to the dojo. Isaiah, a small boy, was filled with lots of energy, but like most of my students, he was shy. They had tried many other sports with no luck getting him involved. Joseph had kept my package of information about the CBK program and decided to give us a try. After seeing the work I did with his son, Principal Boudreau invited me to his school as a "guest teacher" for P.E. classes and begin an afterschool program. Year after year, I did P.E. classes, after-school programs, and funfair events. My volunteer efforts brought many new students from his school. When Joseph moved to Bench Elementary, I moved with him! As I write this now in 2021, I can reflect on Isaiah's journey with the dojo. He is still here and now, as a leader, he is going strong! Today he's Full Shodan, (first-degree Black Belt) and he's a grown to be a confident martial artist and a great young man.

My first homegrown Black Belt was a boy named Ryan. He, along with my wife Jenni, tested in 2017. Jenni had been doing dual training at the Langford dojo, and she was full time in Duncan as well. I finally had my first Black Belts - one grown in the community, and one as a family member who had earned their spots as leading representatives for our dojo. This was huge for me, as it felt like I was making great progress with meshing my family life, dojo, and new community all into one.

My success thus far in life would not have happened if it were not for all these things coming together as seamlessly as they did. Lucky for me, my family is always supportive of what we are doing with the school as well as adventuring in our new community. Jenni is a Nidan (second degree) Black Belt. Our oldest son, Hayden, is also a Nidan and helps me with the teaching. Karis, the middle child, is a full Shodan and part of the CBK instructor program, and lastly our toddler, Jaxon, is waiting impatiently to get onto the dojo floor.

As for Ciara, she ended up moving to Alberta with her family shortly after earning her green belt. I still smile thinking of that shy little girl slowly letting her guard down and growing in the dojo.

After the success with the school programs at Tansor and Bench Elementary schools, more opportunities opened up as the dojo made an impact on the community. Many of my students are members of the various local Tribes. The Cowichan Tribes support their students with their Youth Recreation Programs and asked me to be a guest instructor with their summer camps and special events.

Through the years, working with Cowichan Tribes has grown into an incredibly important relationship for the dojo, and to me personally. Many parents have invited me to take part in school events and cultural ceremonies and many have come to classes themselves! There are numerous examples of wonderful families that have children in our school, but one recent story stands out.

Hunter has been a student at the dojo for 4 years, and recently earned his purple belt. His older sister, Rosie, has taken kickboxing classes in the past, while his best friends, John and Nate, have progressed side by side with him through the CBK program. His mom, Angela, has been in the kickboxing class for over a year. Angela is also the principal at Quw'utsun Smun'eem Elementary School and has helped facilitate online Zoom classes for her school. Instead of regular P.E. classes, she opted to use CBK to teach when the Covid 19 pandemic closed her school. This is just one example of how supportive our families are, and how a Cowichan Tribes family has consistently gone above and beyond to support our community dojo.

The trust and appreciation the community has for the dojo is a huge factor in our success, and together we have worked through the recent tough times. I am incredibly happy to say that I continue to work with many members of this community.

Favorite community events for myself and my students have been the "39 Days of July" and the "Duncan Dayz Parade". Our Duncan Dojo won favorite group as voted by the community during the last parade. We had over 40 members of the dojo participate and represent CBK in the parade. Community pride and consistent effort has made CBK stand out. Our school has become what Shihan Leigh and I had hoped it would be - the one that became a long-term success.

Now in our 3rd location in Duncan, I can proudly say I never again asked *"What am I doing?" or "Will this even matter?"* I never have the doubts I experienced in my first few weeks of opening the dojo, even working through the pandemic of 2020 or changing our platform to an online base. We have stuck together! The dojo community trusted and followed our decisions. They supported the school and adapted to the "new world" we are a part of. Instead of questions around doubt, I now think, *"What can we do next?!", "How can I make our program better and grow even more?!"*

The progress that has been made so far is more than I could have dreamt.

The strength of our community makes me feel truly lucky. The fact that I get to be involved every day with my school, family, and friends means the world to me. The continued growth of the dojo proves to me that given enough hard work, some patience, and a lot of persistence ... those first 5 days of waiting were worth it!

Anything can be done with the right opportunity, and a little luck!

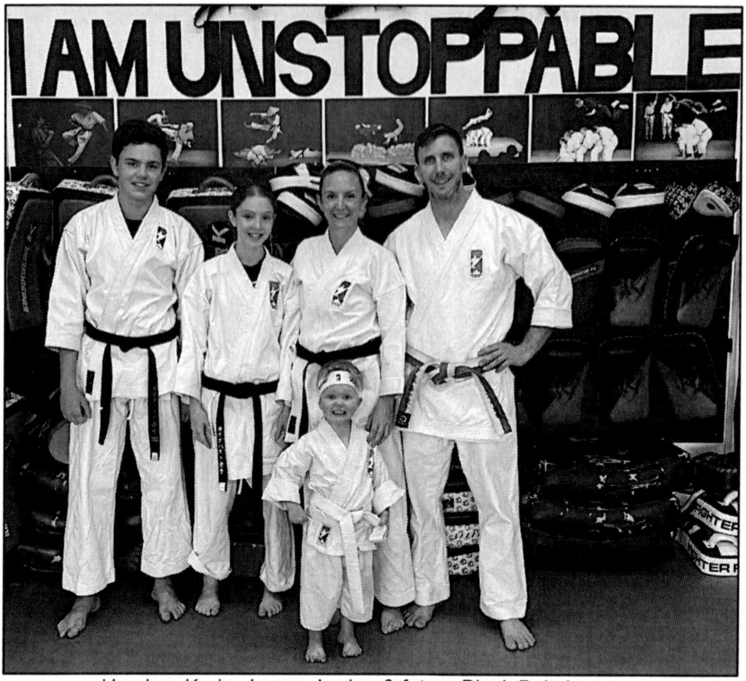

Hayden, Karis, Jenny, Jordan & future Black Belt Jaxon

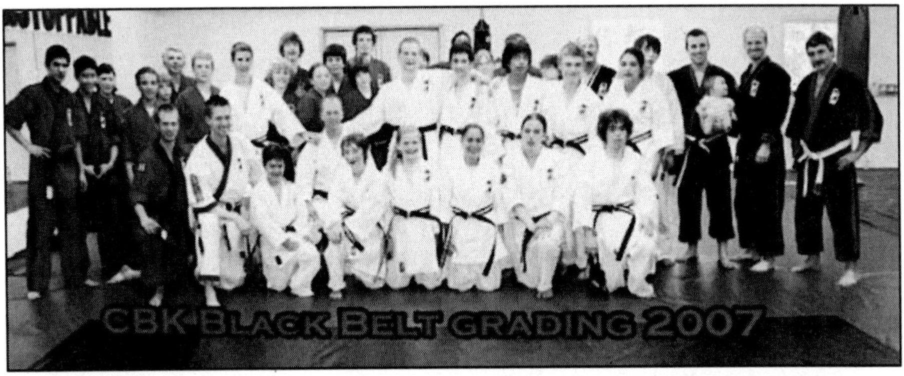

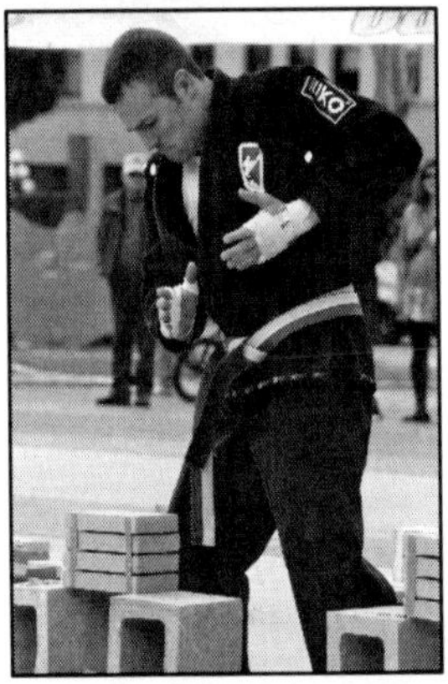

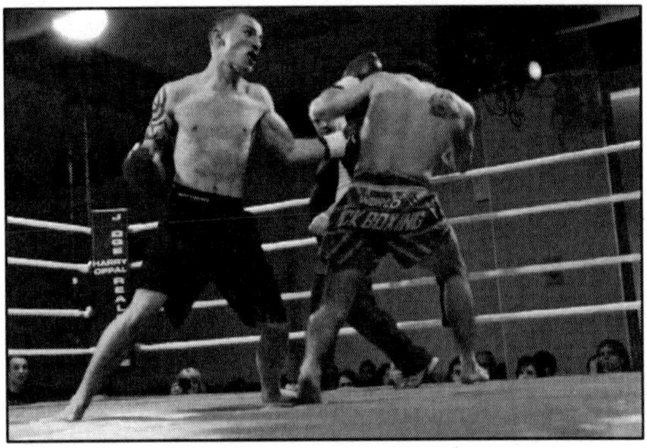

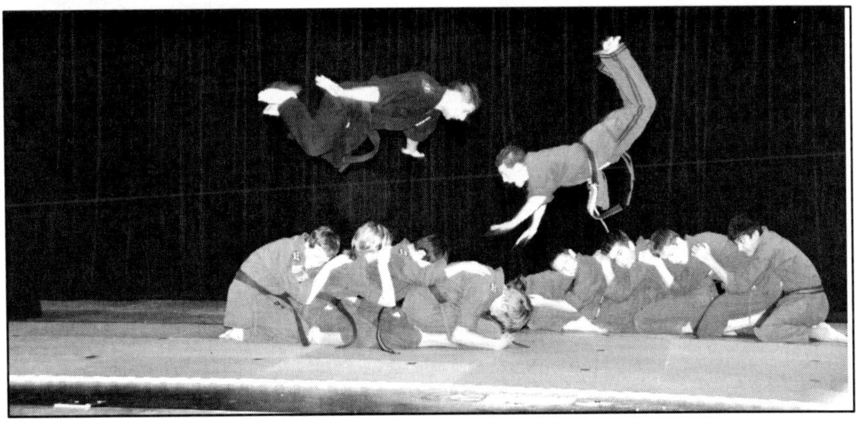

Black Belt Group 2007,
Leigh breaking 500 bricks 2015, Kieran KO
Raj & Kieran Dive Roll Demo 2010

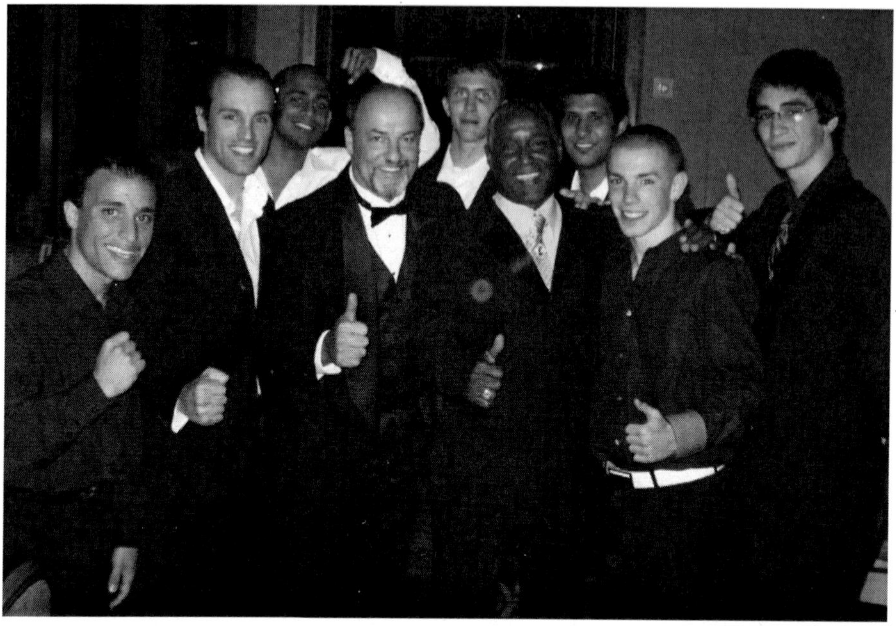

T

Team Trinidad 2010

Mueller Family 1990, Raj Bassi 2016

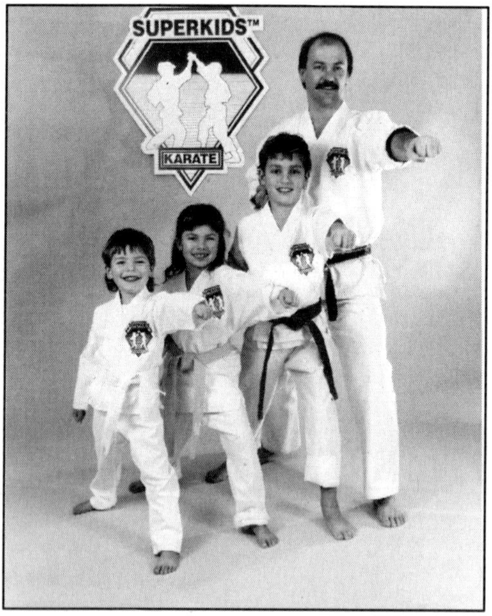

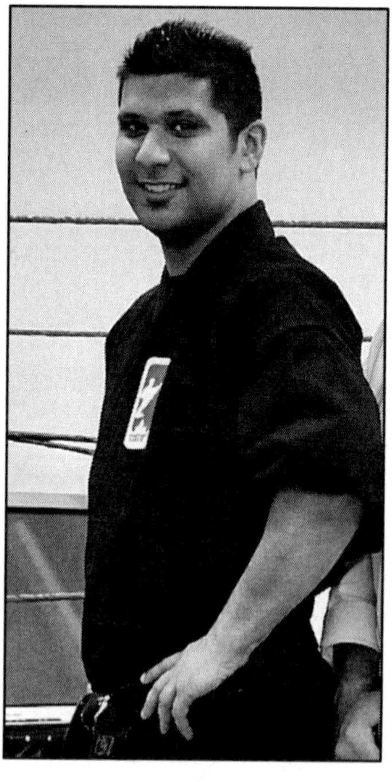

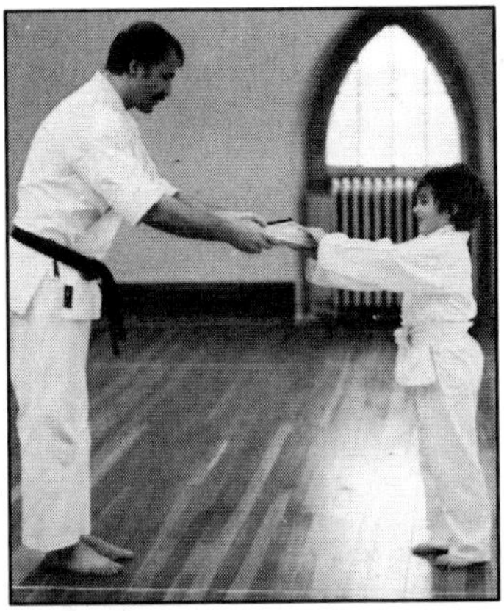

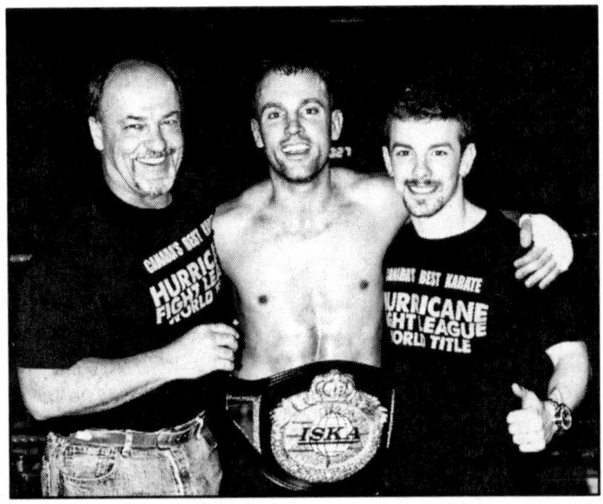

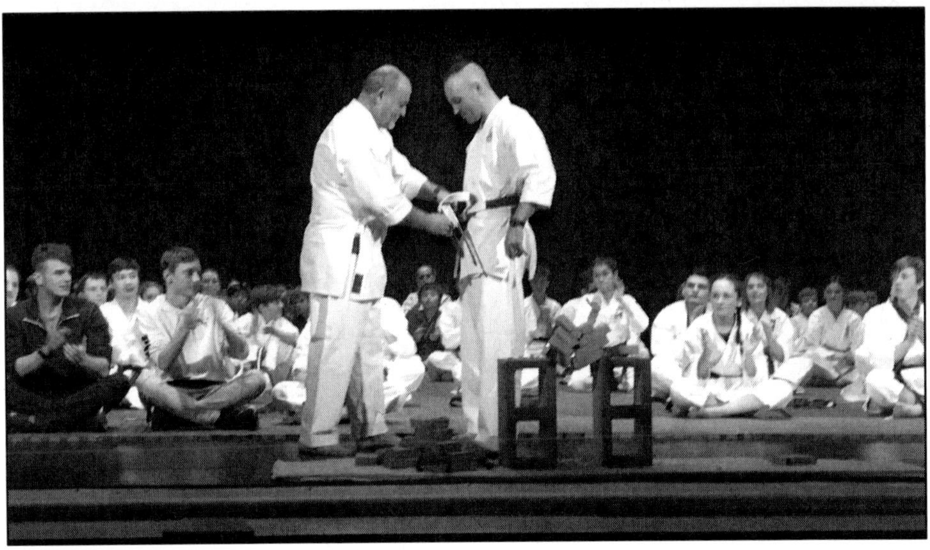

Leigh Mueller 34-year Odyssey
Receiving Yellow Belt 1985, Winning World Championship 2013
Awarded Shihan Rank 2019

THE DOJO COMMUNITY

Notable Contributors

Shaun Emery. The cheque was returned NSF (Non-Sufficient Funds) again. It's one of those annoying troublesome problems you must deal with when you run a business. The student was 14 years old, and if I had to describe his circumstances, I'd say he was raised on the *"other side of the tracks."* Shaun Emery's mother was a very nice lady who presented herself well, but she and her husband supported 3 kids in a two-bedroom apartment residing in Blanchard Courts. Even with the government assisted living help there was always more month than there was money.

Usually the bounced cheque issues, while annoying, were more of a mistake on the part the issuer rather than a habitual event. With the bank adding a $25.00 service charge as a penalty for the dishonored cheque, each transaction became very expensive for a good kid with no money. I also had a 3-strike policy where after the third NSF cheque I wrote off the loss and cancelled the membership. Continuing the baseball metaphor, Emery was long past the 3-strike zone but still in the batting order, so I needed to act.

The real problem for me was I really liked this wide-eyed kid. He was bright, polite, willing, and very able – just poor. Shaun, at orange belt, was the hardest worker in his class and the type of kid that you just knew was all-in every time he was on the floor. In the past I had found jobs for students or asked relatives to assist with tuition and even sponsored a few people myself in various ways. Thus, I looked for a solution to help the family.

After a morning of arguing with myself about what to do, I set up a meeting with the family. They arrived with a fresh cheque in hand and the desire to make Shaun's training a priority. Normally, I would have been pleased and accepted the family commitment, but I knew we would most likely wind up here again next month. So, I took it away from the parents and turned to teenage Shaun saying, *"How would you like to work for me at the dojo?"*

He looked at his parents, then back at me, and without questioning he said *"Okay"* With that, Shaun took over his family's commitment by sweeping and cleaning the dojo floor after classes each night he was there. It didn't take him too long and while he performed his tasks, I cleaned up the evening's business details.

Occasionally I would drive him home, or he would take the bus and if he didn't have any money he walked, but he never missed a day. Committing to working for his dream of being a Black Belt was easy for Shaun Emery. He was an excellent student and kept his word. He never complained or explained; he simply trained, working on the dojo floor during and after class.

After Dan Holland in 1993, Victoria's first Black Belt, Shaun, along with three other teenagers, Tim Bown, Derek Low and Brian Lim became the second graduating Black Belt class for the new Dojo. All four kids were talented and worked hard, but I had a soft spot for the one who said *"Okay."*

Twenty-five years later, you'll find Sensei Shaun Emery and his family of girls at the Langford dojo. To me, he is still wide eyed, and no matter what is asked of him, his answer is always "yes." I'd like to think that his martial arts training helped him develop into the successful man he has become, but in truth I think he had the right stuff from the beginning.

Sensei Emery has distinguished himself in many ways. He holds is a CBK 3rd Degree Black and has a Kung Fu Green Sash with many awards for the work he has done with outside organizations. It takes a lot of will power and dedication to be a lifetime learner and leader in the martial arts field. When an opportunity comes his way, he has always stepped up and affirmed his commitment to improve himself and those around him. Sometimes it's as simple as saying *"Okay, yes I'll do that!"*

Most of time with good people they don't need a handout, just a hand up and Shaun is the best example of a man rising above his circumstances that I have experienced.

He doesn't clean the floor anymore but if someone needs straightening up or out, and perhaps a little extra help - Sensei Emery is your man. His martial arts journey has taken him to different styles, trainings, heartbreaks, and consistent advancement. When he returned home to CBK, he became a leader and brought with him the wisdom of a man who had been there and done that.

When a few years ago he renewed his commitment to training with CBK, it was like he had never left. Like my other adopted sons, I am very proud of this one.

Wendy Foster. The question was posed: *"Who is the best Karate Tots teacher CBK ever had?"*

Sensei Leigh Mueller was quick to answer, *"That's an easy one, Wendy Foster was the best!"* And, as he was a teenage assistant to everything that CBK did in the 1990s, he would know better than anyone else.

The Tots class began as a simple program to allow preschool kids to experience some Karate. It was forced upon our school as many of our students had younger siblings who were eager to "do Karate". With the growing demand, we put together a simplified program that seemed age appropriate. At about the same time a young mother was looking for something challenging and different for her 4-year-old daughter, Kaleigh.

Enter Wendy Foster. Within months she and Kaleigh were doing classes and learning Karate. While the precocious Kaleigh was a natural, her mother was not. At first, Wendy, never having been an athlete, struggled with the physicality and the demands of the training. To improve and understand more about her own training she offered to "assist" Leigh and Mike Croteau with teaching the new Tots classes. The saying *"you can only help others, when you help yourself"* was exactly what happened, as after a few sessions she revealed that she was an early education expert. It was an expertise that CBK quickly added to the curriculum as she helped make what was a good program become great. The more Wendy applied herself to her own training the better she understood how and what was needed to take CBK's preschool classes to the next level.

When asked, she donated her time and expertise into creating one of the best tot's preschool karate programs in the country. I can confidently say that CBK had the best program available anywhere, as our organization was the first group in Canada to take on teaching four- and five-year olds within the "Supertots Karate Program".

What was most interesting to me was, as I saw our tots program grow and improve, I also saw the athlete she had never been come out of Wendy Foster. The more she taught the kids, the better her abilities became. Confidence is an interesting commodity and in Wendy's case, becoming a leader first helped her personal development. The more she led the kids, the better follower she became in her own training. So much so that by 1998 she had become the consummate Karate student as she qualified for and passed her Black Belt test. I remember the grading very well as it was the year that my only daughter, Brittany, also earned her Black Belt.

Many people have achieved a personal best by earning a CBK Black Belt. It's quite an accomplishment to do that, but to be remembered as the best ever? That's quite a different thing. Decades later when the question was asked, she is still remembered as "*the best tot's teacher ever*". Wendy's time on the Dojo floor was well spent and many of her teaching ideas are still used today.

Lucy Peel. Proud and confident, she shook just a little when she answered *"Yes"* to the visiting Shihan's question. Almost like she wanted to look behind herself to see if there was someone else who was supposed to answer.

How was it possible that she, a woman, and an immigrant from Zimbabwe, could be asked such a question?

It was true that she, along with her husband and two children, had been at the Vaughan, Ontario CBK Dojo for almost as long as they had been in Canada. Along with their faith, they had used their Karate training and experiences to become naturalized Canadians.

Like many immigrants, they were intensely proud of their adopted country, but they also knew the naturalization process meant they had to outwork and over perform. Unlike many Canadians, they didn't take our liberties for granted, as they knew that liberty can quickly be swept away. Even highly educated people can wind up on the wrong side of bad governments and corrupt policies. Regardless of why, when the opportunity to move Canada presented itself, they took it.

It was the same when they met Sensei Scott Bullard. After researching many different dojos, they decided that the Canada's Best Karate system was the one for them. Fifteen years later the entire family had earned Black Belts, and while husband Adrian and now adult children Daniel and Andrea had moved on from their training to pursue other interests, Lucy Peel soldiered on. She accomplished her Shodan in four years, then Nidan, and Sandan, Lucy took on every Black Belt test and each new challenge with a confident smile, and a determined look. Karate-do was for her.

When she couldn't get enough training, she volunteered to teach and assist at the Dojo. She rarely missed any kind of event, and never a Grading or the opportunity to train with guest instructors like Shihan Bob Mueller.

Generous people like Lucy Peel, while they serve without compensation, do not go unnoticed. Of course, they know they have value, but perhaps not to the degree of their actual worth. Often opportunity falls to those who are present and willing, as the Dojo is a place that values effort. Nothing is free, but when you do the work, the rewards far exceed the costs. For Lucy, being present is a natural state and her willingness to serve is felt by every person regardless of their rank, stature, or gender.

The Dojo, when done correctly, is a true meritocracy - everyone works to earn their place. Equally true, everyone starts at the beginning, as a white belt. Whether you are white, black, rich, or poor you start at the back of the line and earn your way to the top. For Lucy, this was simply common sense as she knew that anything of value was worth working for. The reward was always in the work.

But now, blank faced at Mueller's question *"Would you like to be Shihan Bullard's partner and an owner in CBK"*, all she could muster was a quiet *"Yes"*. Humility and honestly comes naturally to the good ones and Sensei Lucy Peel is one of the good ones. Today she stands beside and with her teacher with the same pride, and confidence that brought her from another world to succeed and made her a positive force in the Dojo.

Jason Sikora. Some of my most talented and promising students did not become full-time teachers, start their own dojo, or make martial arts their career. But just because it didn't become their living doesn't mean that it wasn't their life.

Near the beginning of Superkids in Victoria, a thin little 7-year-old boy, with thick coke bottle-type glasses joined the new kid's class at the Cedar Hill Dojo. Quiet and kind of bookish, he didn't seem very athletic but sometimes it's the silent ones who surprise and impress the most.

When Jason Sikora added braces and a gangly growth spurt to his package as a pre-teen I knew his name, but other than his constant attendance I didn't notice him much. I did however get along well with his parents, Greg and Laura, and enjoyed talking to them any chance I got. They were highly educated, enthusiastic, and completely dedicated to the Dojo, so it was very easy to like them. Jason, a well-behaved only child, gave a good solid effort but other than being likeable, there wasn't anything extra special about him.

Leigh however, as a young Dojo leader, befriended him and I noticed Jason was around more and more when I was at home. The closer they got, the more I noticed things about young Sikora. He wasn't a wallflower, rather like his dad, he was bubbling with energy and whenever the kids played a game he seemed to win. Then, seemingly the next day, the glasses disappeared, the braces had done their job and the skinny kid turned up tops in his karate class, getting the best grades on his belt tests.

As a Sensei with hundreds of students, you tend to only notice the extra good ones who start fast, or the troubled ones with discipline problems. Everyone else, as they say in school, gets graded on a curve. For me, this was compounded by the fact that I was the leader of four additional franchise schools in Ontario to which demanded a lot of attention. As such, it took a while for average, well-mannered students with good work ethics to be noticed.

Then it happened. During the Black Belt qualifying trials, Jason beat everyone, including Leigh, on the fitness run. Not only did he beat them, but he lapped more than half the field as he performed what I can only describe as a mile and half sprint! Most of the rest of the top candidates completed the six-lap run at about the 7:30 - 8:00 minute mark - Sikora was sub 6:00 minutes! Wow, was that kid fast!

The next thing I knew, seemingly out of nowhere, he was much better than the pack. First with his evolving Kata excellence, he then proceeded to best everyone at sparring as well. It was like this new Sikora kid, now Godzilla-like, had eaten a younger brother or something and become a monster in the dojo!

He was still slight of build, but his technique was impeccable, and he was so athletically talented that he now looked like a natural. It had just taken eight years for him to do it, or as likely for me to finally notice!

For the next ten years, Jason Sikora was a mainstay Dojo leader, becoming Leigh's constant training partner, best friend, and one of our top students. Whenever he took the stage during a concert or a demonstration he dominated the floor, as you couldn't take your eyes off him. When someone has the "IT" factor they seem to shine everywhere. Jason did it all and tried everything from competition to teaching, eventually earning the rank of Sandan - 3rd Degree Black Belt - and the title of Sensei. At one point he joined Sensei Raj, as they operated the Cedar Hill Dojo together, sharing all the teaching and administration duties.

But great talents also have great options. Along with his Karate talents he, like his parents, pursued higher education, earning an MBA at Royal Roads University. His twenty-year Dojo stint that began as a seemingly shy boy, culminated with him being wanted by everyone; by us at CBK and the banking/investing business world. The world won.

We, however, didn't lose either, as he took the Karate success training he had learned and applied it to his life and all his future ventures. Jason Sikora is still a CBK ambassador at large. He is constantly promoting our good works and talking up the Dojo. His children are now CBK students and to keep in touch, he formed an executive martial arts training group that trains weekly at one of our Dojos. Like all my boys, this adopted son holds a special place in my heart.

The Perkios. It is usually individuals who tend distinguish themselves through their martial arts efforts. Rarely does an entire family that make a mark so deep that they become important to an organization's history. The Perkios are such a family. First Eric, then daughter Christine and finally their father, Ron, came to CBK in their own time and for their own reasons. The collective result made them leaders in the Dojo for about twenty years.

Their story is also a vehicle to discuss the fact that things happen in life that cause people to move on or force them to quit. Professor Don Jacob teaches that along with your training you must pass three challenges to successfully make martial arts your life. Everyone will at some time be disabled by injury or sickness. They will need to overcome envy or ridicule and finally, they need to accept that training is a privilege and rank is not an entitlement. Once you experience these three tests and find your way to continue, you can make martial arts a lifetime study.

Eric Periko enrolled as a preteen at about 10 years old and as an ordinary looking kid, he had average ability. His friendly demeanor and good work effort saw him advance quickly and by the time his was ready for his Black Belt he had transformed into a top athlete. What made his Karate exceptional was his speed and incredible quick twitch muscle fibers. In fact, of the thousands of CBK students I have taught, I can count on one hand only a few that had his kind of quickness. When he discovered the bo-staff he found the medium to demonstrate ability.

His talents and athletic prowess allowed him to compete with the other young guns of the dojo, like Jason Sikora, Raj Bassi, and Leigh, then Sempai of the Dojo. However, at about the same time as he was coming into his own, he discovered he had a medical problem. An enlarged spleen, while not life threatening, had created issues in his body. As such he had to limit his martial arts to practicing forms and kata to avoid any unnecessary internal danger. Eric found a way to continue training ultimately achieving his 2nd Degree Black Belt with CBK. Unfortunately, Karate ended abruptly for Eric when an inattentive driver blindsided him while he was driving his motorcycle. The crash was severe and almost killed him. The combined effect of the injuries and previous health issues effectively ended his promising martial arts abilities and potential career.

Ron Periko, a retired RCMP Constable turned CSIS Intelligence Officer (the Canadian CIA), had always been interested in martial arts. He'd also been an eagle scout as a kid and he loved badges and the symbolism of ranks and titles. Ron was a good guy who turned out to be a good friend. After seeing his son's success, Ron inquired about starting a Karate Program on the mainland of BC. When he moved to Langley BC an opportunity appeared and within a year, he applied his expertise into operating the first CBK franchise. Once the new Dojo was launched, he began formally training in Karate. As part of the start-up, the Dojo needed a teacher to be the Dojo leader and handle the daily classes.

That opportunity fell to **Tim Bown** and he became the Sempai of the new school. Tim, an unusual talent, was part of the first Victoria Black Belt Grading in 1994. He was tall and lean with an exceptionally quiet and cerebral demeanor. Perhaps that's what attracted the intelligence officer to hire him and make him part of the Perkio Dojo family.

Tim was quiet, that is, until he took the floor to teach. As the Sempai, his leadership role transformed his reserved nature into one of an enthusiastic and confident teacher. He grew, as did the Dojo, and eventually earned his 3rd Degree Black Belt and the rank of Sensei. He was loved and very successful as his teaching style created many top-quality Black Belts for the Langley Dojo. Shockingly though, Tim Bown was struck down at the age of 32 by cancer. His death left a deep and sad hole for all who knew him.

Although Tim's passing was the final blow, Ron had decided months before to leave CBK due to a financial disagreement. It was the last straw in a long slide away from our CBK Traditional Karate teachings. A few years earlier Ron and Tim had gotten involved an American Self Defense System and they began teaching an alternative program. While it had some effective training ideas, it lacked the kind of values that make learning CBK karate a life skill. The egos and undermining influence of the American group leader wasn't a fit for CBK and as such Ron gave notice to move on. Ron acquired honorary titles and ranks as he continued as an independent entity called Safequard.

Christine Perkio was an amazing talent. As a former ballet and dance student she knew the kind of training involved when you study the arts. She fueled her flames of martial arts desire as she watched her brother and father from the sidelines. When the opportunity was right for her to start training, she applied herself like no other. At 5' 3" and about 100 lbs she was petite and graceful but as William Shakespeare said in his play "A Midsummer Night's Dream" - *"Though she be little, she is fierce!"*

Christine applied her dancer's poise and grace with intensity. By the time she achieved her Black Belt in 2002 she set the standard for women at CBK. When I graded her for Shodan I rated her as the best female karateka in our entire CBK history. Unfortunately, she had damaged knees when she came to the Dojo and the opposing forces of dance and karate training progressed the injuries to her knees further. On the advice of her Doctor, she was forced to stop shortly after accomplishing her Black Belt. I would have liked to see where she could have taken her skills.

Valerie Bates Perkio was also a force to be reckoned with. Outside of attending a few CBK seminars and events, she didn't train at the Dojo. Along with being a great Mom, her talents were applied as a respected business expert and speaker. She, in her capacity as a business expert, attracted the attention of a famous international businessman. Valerie married Mark Yarnell and brought him to Victoria where he became part of the legacy that made their family's contribution to CBK unique. Mark and Valerie were constant contributors to the CBK culture and created a lasting impression for their efforts.

As a family, the Perkio's were a blend of talent and determination. The fact that injury, sickness and entitlement ended their tenure with CBK does not diminish them at all. It's part of the process, as for twenty years they made a positive impact on CBK and set a good example as a family unit.

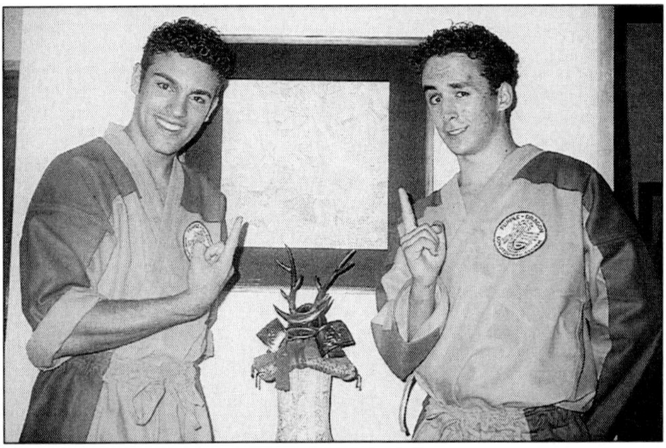

Leigh & Eric preparing to travel to Trinidad

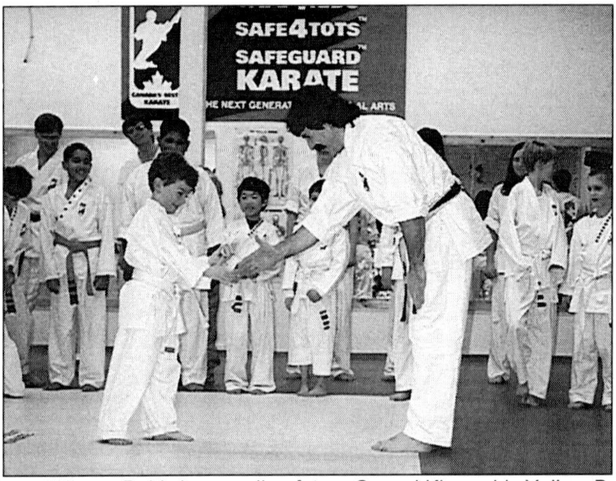

Sensei Kieran Baldwin awarding future Sensei Kieran his Yellow Belt

SHOSHIN: THE BEGINNER'S MIND

BY SHAUN EMERY

I was fourteen years old when my curiosity opened a door for me. We were in class working on a one-step sparring application when I asked Sempai Gord Holtrop a "what if" question. My instructor was a new assistant teacher, and he was also a student of my Sensei, Bob Mueller. As such, he didn't know how to properly deal with every situation. His answer was to have me do the attack on him and WHAM!!! Without warning my face hit the mat before I even completed the technique. I clearly got the message that he didn't like the question. I would find out later that the "No questions" mentality was rampant in "traditional" martial arts, at least with newish and less confident instructors. But that initial experience sparked something quite different in me as I asked another and better question: *What if I'm curious at just the right time, might the universe would open up and show me I'm on the right path?*

Fast forward a couple of years, and I'm preparing to test for Shodan – my first-degree Black Belt. At about the same time, one of my parents brought home a VHS cassette of something they thought I would like called *"The Ultimate Fighting Championship"*. Like everybody else at the time, I had never seen anything like it. The UFC captured my imagination the same way my first Karate lessons had, and I wanted more. However, I put this excitement on the backburner as this was not the right time for something new, as I needed to focus on my Black Belt preparation.

The Black Belt Grading was held on July 9th, 1994, on a Saturday afternoon. There were four of us on what would be the first Victoria-based Black Belt test for the B.C. Superkids Karate organization. After a grueling afternoon of everything possible, we left the dojo spent and exhausted. We all knew that we had done well, and our hard work had paid off, but we didn't get our belt that day. Most other dojos will end the test and typically present you with your belt right then and there. Earning your

Black Belt is a rite of passage, and as such, we do a ceremony. A big ceremony! This year to finish earning our belts we would also need to attend a weekend learning and training session that turned out to be the very first Camp Samurai!

The event had Sensei Mueller teaching along with additional training from some special guest instructors. After two days of training, we would finally get the experience we were waiting for – having our new Black Belts tied on for the first time. One of those guest instructors was a former world champion that used to train in the old days with Sensei Mueller. Stan Peterec's seminar was focused on various fighting techniques including ground-based, jiu-jitsu techniques – like the ones I had seen on that VHS cassette my parents brought home for me. It was incredible that at the time I was earning my Black Belt a new door was also opened, - I soaked that up like a sponge! I had so many new questions that needed answers! Questions come quickly, but answers take time.

This curiosity drove me to seek out new ways to train. Everything I learned was always tied back to and grounded in my Karate expertise. What I discovered was my curiosity had a traditional Japanese name – Shoshin. Shoshin is a word from Zen Buddhism meaning *"beginner's mind."* It refers to having an attitude of openness, eagerness, and lack of preconceptions when studying a subject, even when studying at an advanced level, just as a beginner would. It was a perfect fit for me.

Sometimes these different training methods blended with my style well. I would add a takedown and a submission to a combo that we were already practicing. Other times, my Karate and the new thing didn't mesh. Again, I discovered if there was still something missing, perhaps I hadn't asked the right question yet.

Fast forward a decade now, and after a prolonged period of inactivity (life had gotten in the way of training), I found myself looking at the roots of Karate and began studying Kung Fu. After accomplishing a Green Sash in Kung Fu, I still had those same "what if" type questions that went unanswered. The Kung Fu classes were fun, and I was learning some great things. The instructors there gave my previous Karate experience respect, and a certain amount of gravitas as my hard style Karate background demanded respect, especially when I sparred with my Kung Fu teachers.

It was after class one day when my Kung Fu instructor, Sifu Ryan Johnson pulled a video up and asked me if I knew the kata he was about to play. I had fallen out of the habit of watching

Karate videos for quite some time, but this ... this was the most beautiful performance I had ever seen! After that video, my instructor asked me if I had ever heard of a guy named Jesse Enkamp, who called himself *"The Karate Nerd".* I hadn't, but from what I saw, I would add that question to the deep dive of my next adventure. I went back into my Karate Kata's again when I got home that night. Now the universe began to answer me as my love, and passion for Karate was back in full swing.

Looking into The Karate Nerd lead me down a path that had me traveling to London England to another weekend-long seminar that would change my view of Karate all over again. That event – dubbed The Karate Nerd Experience, or KNX – answered questions I had been asking for years. Not only did I punch and kick differently, but I was also able to see applications in techniques in a much more practical manner. That thing I was missing was found, and I couldn't wait to bring it back and share what I had learned. When I got back to CBK, I was thrilled to see that my old Dojo had been curious as well. Sensei Leigh Mueller had sought out the best instructors in various fields and had added Jiu-jitsu and Muay Thai Kickboxing modules to Canada's Best Karate style of training. For me, CBK was and still is unmatched as the best training discipline I've seen anywhere else. I had gone full circle, and now my questions were being answered back where I started. What's interesting is there seemed to be more answers now than ever before and for the most part, I found myself answering the questions with my own training.

I've come to fully appreciate the "what ifs" of training. My many experiences over the past 30 years were created when I looked for the answers to those what-ifs. My Shoshin mindset helped me create some incredible opportunities, and yes, I continue to ask questions. When the answers come, I feel like a kid at Christmas. I also see this in many of the younger students who are getting ready to take that next step into their understanding of Karate. I always remember my original questioning experience where my face found the mat without an answer. I realize now that it was part of my process, and perhaps the young Sempai did me a big favor by teaching me what he didn't know.

I encourage my students to ask those questions of me. I know I'll help guide them to finding the answers for themselves, with only occasionally using the mat as a teaching tool!

BITES, BOYS and BLACK BELTS

BY TINA PARKER

The year was 1997. The principal's office was as stark and uninteresting as the principal herself. I noted that the books that were scattered around haphazardly from the last time I was in there just a week earlier, had been put neatly away as if she was expecting someone important, or had something important to say. She did.

Beside me was a small blonde-haired, 4-year-old boy with paint on his hands, an eternally runny nose, and a defiant expression. He knew what was coming before I did.

"So Mrs. Parker" (the pregnant pause that signaled the right words were about to be selected, hung heavily in the room) "it appears that Troy has bitten 2 teachers this morning and one classmate. That makes 8 over the last 2 weeks I believe?" Actually it was more like 11, but I wasn't about to correct her.

I looked at Troy, who had already zoned out and was idly picking a scab until it bled. *"Is this true, Troy?"* I asked. A second pregnant pause, while the trapped child tried to come up with the best lie possible in the short space of time offered to him for explanation. "I don't know" was the inventive response. I couldn't help but wonder if Montessori teachers tasted better than other teachers. He should know. He had nailed them all over this last term.

With a promise from me to "take care of it", and a delighted look from Troy as he realized he had been expelled from school for the rest of the day, we were disapprovingly ushered out of sterile office.

I actually had no idea how to "take care of it". Sadly, Troy wasn't born clutching a training manual, and the hospital did not give out directions regarding the elimination of biting disorders, which I do think it would be a welcome read. This "geriatric primate" (as I was referred to on a hospital document due to the fact that this was my first child at the ripe old age of 37) was at a total loss.

It was during lunch with a friend shortly thereafter that the subject of martial arts first came up. My friend's grandson had had taken a couple of years of training, somewhere up north where it sounded like the air would hurt to breathe, and it had worked wonders. My doctor suggested the same solution, then a teacher, so I started to pay attention. It sounded like a route I should explore, so with coffee firmly in hand, I let my fingers do the walking through the Yellow Pages.

The first dojo I went into smelled like something had crawled in from a swamp and died there, been resurrected, only to die of the smell all over again. I wondered how long I could hold my breath and smile politely at the same time. Not long enough apparently.

The second dojo was marginally better, however the "master" (to this day I hate that word) weighed almost as much as my car, and I didn't think he moved around much - certainly not enough to keep up with my little spitfire. He did, however appear to have plenty of flesh for Troy to bite, so that was a plus.

The third dojo proved to be third time lucky. It was larger than it looked from the outside, very clean and well cared for. I was greeted by a young man who I instantly liked. He was tall and lanky, with eyes that smiled when he laughed, and crazy spiky hair, that like my child, didn't behave well. He was an old soul in a young body, vital, energetic, fun, and wise beyond his years. Little did I know that he was destined to become one of my best friends, and that to this day he sits beside me in my office in a picture that reflects his silent look of amusement. His name was Tim Bown, and he was one of Shihan Bob Mueller's best young black belts of the time. He had come from Victoria to take on the position of Chief instructor at the new CBK school which Ron Perkio, a friend and colleague of Bob's, had just opened in Langley BC.

Troy loved the Tots Program. He adored his "Sempai Tim" and strived to do well in his class. He was not a natural athlete, which he came by honestly, as his dad and I were about as athletic as a goldfish on a racetrack, but he awkwardly gave it his all. Within a month, the biting behaviors stopped - much to the delight of his teachers and the relief of his mother. We had stumbled on his passion - completely unaware that it would become a lifelong pursuit.

Watching Troy in the dojo was inspirational. So much so, that a couple of months after Troy began, I had a crazy idea to join the adult program. I was tired of running a treadmill to nowhere in the gym while young, thin, women paraded around me in outfits that would barely fit on my big toe. The thought of training in something that mirrored baggy white pajamas seemed really quite appealing. Anyway, what did I have to lose except 10 (ok...20) unwanted pounds, so in I went. The first class was agony. My heart threatened to jump out of my chest, and my legs felt like overcooked spaghetti. And that was only the first 3 minutes of the warm-up. I vaguely wondered how they would dispose of my body if I didn't make it past the next 3, but I survived, albeit barely...then promptly went home and ate the entire kitchen.

The first time I met "Shihan Bob Mueller" was in the spring of 1997 – just a couple of months after I had started. I had heard his name mentioned many times of course, usually spoken in hushed awe, and his anticipated visit to the dojo was one of excitement tinged with a respectful amount of terror. You could have heard a pin drop when he walked through the dojo door. His persona instantly commanded attention, even from those in the class with a runaway tongue. Everything about him exuded power, and he filled the room with his presence without even trying. To this day Shihan still commands the same respect and authority as he did then, but now he is a close friend, and scares me fractionally less.

And so the years passed in the dojo, which was our second home. Ron had an incredibly busy profession outside the dojo and needed help. In 1999 I was offered the position of office manager, developing into role of Director of Operations. It was the beginning of many magical years working alongside now "Sensei Tim". Troy and I were honored to be part of the many "firsts" of the Langley dojo. In 2002, after 20 grueling hours on the floor, I earned my first black belt at the ripe old age of 47, becoming the first adult female in the Langley school to achieve that honor. 4 months later, I became the first student to graduate the Instructor's program. Troy followed the same path 2 years later, earning his first Black belt in 2004. His second degree in 2008 and also graduated the instructor program in 2008. He was Langley CBK's first TOT to earn Shodan, Nidan, and become a full instructor.

In 2008 CBK Langley became Safeguard Martial Arts. The foundation laid through our experience with CBK was invaluable and paved the way for Safeguard to become a healthy and prosperous school in its own right. In December of 2010, to our shock and despair, our beloved Sensei Tim, passed away from a rare and virulent form of cancer. He left behind some enormous shoes to fill. I went back on the dojo floor to fill the gap until Troy, who was Sensei Tim's apprentice at the time of his passing, was ready to fully take on the role of Chief Instructor in his own right.

The years moved on, and the boy whose reputation for biting every teacher in Montessori became a man of strength and character, a much-loved instructor, a mentor, and a beloved role model to his students in the same way Sensei Tim had been to him. In January of 2014, Ron announced his retirement, and in September of that year, Sensei Troy and I became the new owners of Safeguard Martial Arts, seamlessly moving into the new roles which we had been unconsciously preparing for since we first stepped into the dojo 17 years before.

We are forever grateful to have been able to turn our dream into a reality. The journey that began simply because a child liked to taste his teachers, has become our life, our vision, our purpose, and our future.

Almost 25 years ago, we walked through the doors of CBK with nothing to lose, and everything to gain, never imagining what lay before us, or how rewarding it would be. The passion never left us and is stronger today than ever. We have become an epic team, doing what we love and loving what we do, passing the torch to others with dreams that await fulfilment.

Funakoshi once said: "The ultimate aim of karate lies not in victory or defeat, but in the perfection of the character of its participants." He was right.

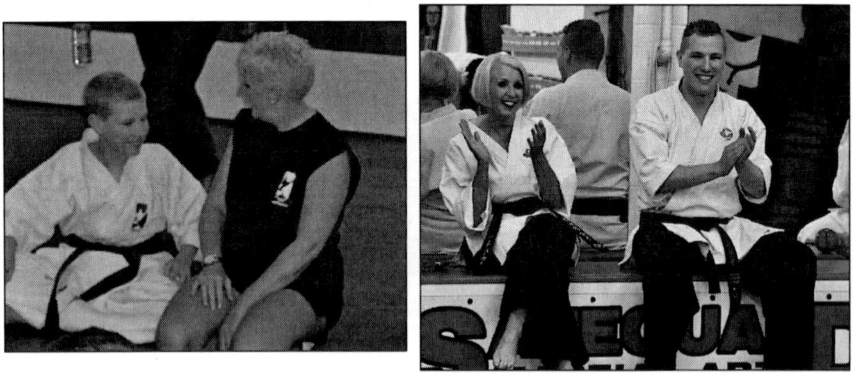

Tina & Troy then and now

I AM WOMAN

BY LUCY PEEL

I am a woman, and not just any woman, but a black woman from Southern Africa, living in an Italian neighborhood, in a predominantly Caucasian country. Fascinating! That makes me an immigrant to Canada. I am also a woman of faith, a martial artist, an entrepreneur and a female leader in my community. I am a dynamic package put together in one. I Am Woman!

Australian singer Helen Reddy wrote the song entitled "I Am Woman" which was released in 1972. The movie "I Am Woman" with Tilda Cobham-Hervey starring as Helen Reddy, was aired on Netflix Canada in 2020. The song became an instant sensation because it spoke to the inner aspirations of women. It empowered women to view their experiences through the lens of strength, and not through a defeated or victimized paradigm.

The song encouraged women to liberate themselves, which at the time was countercultural and magnified the Equal Rights Amendment (ERA). Deep down, women wanted to feel accepted and have the playing field equalized but unfortunately, women were perceived as lessor than men in every aspect and thus treated as such. "I Am Woman" elevated the psychological inclination of women to be seen beyond the stereotypical perception of being the "weaker vessel", domestic and incapable of any leadership, to being seen as "strong" and "invincible" with the ability to do anything if given a chance.

As a young person growing up, my parents empowered me to do whatever I wanted in terms of achievement and career, but also made me very aware of the fact that I was a female and that there were certain expectations required of my gender. I appreciated the empowerment and chose to think and live outside the proverbial gender box.

Immigrating to Canada with my family in 1997 was an adventure in and of itself. I didn't know much about the Canadian geography, but I did know that this was the land of milk and honey. A land of great opportunity. However, the early advice I was given was the painful struggle immigrants face in Canada and the impossibility of breaking through the unseen glass ceiling in the many spheres of life. The advice did not stop there; it went further to state that it would be twice as challenging for me because I was a woman, and I was black. That may all be true, but I have never shied away from difficult situations, which in my view are opportunities in disguise. With this in mind, I set out on my Canadian life journey.

When our children were nearing their early teenage years, my husband and I decided to find a sport that would keep the family together. We chose to explore martial arts because as children, we had watched some of Bruce Lee's movies and the fighting skills had really wowed us. It also looked like a lot of fun. Being proactive, we visited three karate schools before making a final decision. Top priority was a dojo that was family friendly.

One of the karate schools we visited was Canada's Best Karate. We met Sensei Scott Bullard and had a conversation with him. He was encouraging, positive and held the family in high regard. That was the clincher. We decided to embark on our martial arts experience at Canada's Best Karate. For sure, on becoming a part of Canada's Best Karate, we became a part of a wider family community and have made lasting and endearing friendships.

Gichin Funakoshi said "it is important that karate can be practiced by the young and old, men and women alike" which brings me back to "I Am Woman." Funakoshi realized the importance and benefits of equality in the practice of karate-do and was inclusive in its training of gender and age. One might argue that that was because his wife was adept at karate, "and that she sometimes instructed his students when he was late getting home." Or that he knew his trainer, Master Matsumura Sokon had a wife, Yonamine Chiru, who was well known as an Okinawan martial artist, and came from a family famous for their martial arts background. Whatever the case may be, there was an equality in gender view, hence the art being open to women.

This is a view I have held and valued for many years in my own training and experience as a martial artist. When I was on the dojo floor, I wanted to be seen as a karate student and not viewed primarily by my gender. Yes, I am a woman, but I have felt that that did not determine, deter, limit or define my ability or inability as a martial artist. I saw it as a privilege to be on the dojo floor learning a practice that was life itself.

Gichin Funakoshi further said "When you look at life, think in terms of karate. But remember that karate is not only karate –

it is life." The dojo floor represented life with its many forms of challenges and victories, struggles and triumphs. I took the disciplines and principles learned on the floor and applied them to my own life.

Shihan Bullard did not treat me as a woman, but as a student. His famous phrase "suck it up" is known by many of his students. He had the same expectation of each student, male or female regardless of age – "always do your best." That meant your personal best so that you could be better than the day before. That was the standard by which we were held by, and often pushed to achieve more, and in turn gain more, which fell in line with the old adage "no pain, no gain."

Often a guest at the Black Belt Grading Tests, Shihan Bob Mueller would however, first make an appearance at the organized two-hour karate seminars. It was at one of these seminars that I encountered the teaching style as well as the humour of Shihan Mueller. In every story there was a lesson to be learned, a gem that was dropped or a principle to take note of. At one of his seminars, he said: "on the dojo floor there is no gender or age, only the belt." I have never forgotten this statement. In my estimation that made the dojo floor a place of equal opportunity because one was assessed on the belt - on technique and ability, and not on gender capability. I had to own the floor - I Am Woman!

Have you ever been judged by your gender? Have you ever felt like you're being put in a box based on someone's opinion? I have met many people, some being my friends, who have the opinion that martial arts is a man's sport and a man's domain. Women are dainty and are not supposed to participate in the practice.

On the dojo floor some of my male peers were hesitant to spar or do self-defense with me because I am a female. I would usually hear phrases like this: "I don't hit women"; "I don't spar with women" or "I'm looking for a good workout." I immediately recognized that these words came from a place of masculine dominance that viewed the female as weaker. I told my male peers not to look at me as a woman, but as a peer, and spar or do self-defense as they would any other student. The challenge often brought out the best in me, though at times I would walk away wandering how I could have done better or how I could have avoided a particular punch. The view of women not being considered strong enough for martial arts is changing, as women and girls are increasingly engaging more in martial arts and are continuing to break barriers, break cultural biases and challenge the status quo.

Some say leaders are born while others say leaders are made. Whatever side of the quibble we take, leadership qualities are honed and developed with time for specific purposes. A day forever engraved in my mind is the day Bob Mueller asked me this question: *"Would you like to be in a CBK partnership with Scott Bullard?"* Completely thrown off balance after a sleepless night, I managed to say: *"Yes*!"

My poker face hid how I was feeling. How is this possible? An immigrant being given an entrepreneurial opportunity. A woman stepping up into a leadership role. A black woman at that, rising to the occasion. Shihan Mueller confidently answered, "All you do is ask", which he did.

Shihan Bullard has been immensely instrumental in my development as a martial artist, to being a leader in the Canada's Best Karate community. It is a joy to be able to work with someone so willing to give in the karate and business arena. I am grateful that our paths crossed and that he saw beyond my gender, and into the heart of a likeminded karate compadre.

I Am Woman!

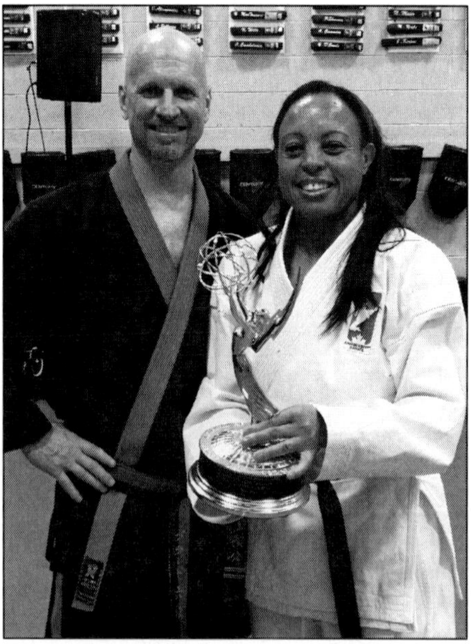

Scott Bullard with Luck Peel holding somebody's EMMY Award

OVERCOMING TRAUMA

BY WENDY FOSTER

Catching the end of the evening news, I was shaken by a report of a sexual assault in Colquitz Park, which was directly across the street from our condo in Victoria. This was my favorite place to walk with our 18-month-old daughter, Kaleigh.

It was obvious to me that I would not be heading back to that park any time soon. I was totally unaware at the time, but a childhood experience from my past had been reawakened by the incident in the park.

One evening, I decided to head across the street to the mall - something that I did on a regular basis. As I was putting on my shoes, I suddenly felt uneasy and didn't want to go by myself. This was the impact of the assault in the park. I realized, at that moment, that I could not let this fear control me.

I began searching for a solution. A couple of days later, I noticed a poster from a local karate school. They were offering an afternoon self-defense workshop for women. I knew this would be a good place to start, so I immediately called to register.

As I timidly walked through the doors of Canada's Best Karate, I was relieved to see 7 other women who seemed just as nervous as I was. Shortly thereafter, an enthusiastic, cheerful young man appeared through a curtained entrance and introduced himself as one of the instructors for the workshop. I breathed a great sigh of relief.

A moment later, an older gentleman with dark curly hair and a very friendly smile came out of his office and greeted us.

"I'm Sensei Kieran," he said in his thick English accent. *"I will be leading the workshop today, and relax. There is nothing to be nervous about."* We looked around at each other, all fidgeting in our seats, and filled the small room with nervous laughter.

The instructors began by asking what had brought us to the workshop and we each gave a brief response. Our situations were slightly different, but the common denominators were fear and feeling unsafe.

It was at this point that I was flooded with images of a scary incident from my childhood. I was 6 years old when our neighbor asked my mom if I could run an errand for her. Mom agreed, and I was sent to the store with a little black change purse and a list of the 4 items I was to buy.

I felt like a "big girl" and was excited about taking my first trip to the store on my own. That feeling quickly changed when 2 large boys knocked me to the ground and stole the little purse. I paced back and forth, not knowing what to do or where to go. I was in shock.

> Trauma is not what happens to you; trauma is what happens inside you as a result of what happens to you.
>
> ***Gabor Maté***
>
> *The Wounded Healer | Victoria, BC | May 2018*

Mom soon came to see what was taking me so long. I cried inconsolably as I told her what had happened.

The trauma I experienced from that childhood incident, as well as a tragic family event, affected me in ways I could not have imagined and wouldn't understand for years to come.

With my love of psychology, my interest in human development, and my child-like curiosity and inquisitiveness, I am an enthusiastic, life-long learner. I've had many teachers and mentors from whom I've acquired much knowledge and wisdom, and Dr. Gabor Mate tops the list. He is the ultimate expert on the effects of trauma, not only on individuals, but collectively and intergenerationally as well. He is my hero.

Dr. Mate has become legendary for his work with the homeless on the East Side of Vancouver, B.C. This work led him to research the causes and effects of early childhood trauma. Without exception, every homeless person, addict, and distressed soul you have ever seen has been traumatized in some way as a child. This trauma, recognizable or not, disrupted their coping skills and altered the course of their development and their lives.

Dr. Mate speaks of his own addictive personality as a struggle that he maintains to this day. He was born in 1944 to a Hungarian Jewish mother in Nazi Germany. She had to hide him and herself from being discovered by the German Gestapo. One day, as a distressed young Mom, she took her baby to the doctor as he would not stop crying. The kindly doctor stated, *"Madam, all the Jewish babies in Germany are crying."* The stress of the times and the imminent constant danger was so stressful on the mothers, that all their babies were sympathetically traumatized. Dr. Mate still carries the trauma he experienced as an infant and recognizes it when it manifests in his adult life.

I have learned a lot about the effects of my own childhood trauma and how those experiences have shaped who I am today.

In my career as an Early Childhood Educator and Teacher Trainer, I was passionate about developing and implementing numerous programs that make a difference in the lives of young people. Perhaps that is why, as I was leaving the workshop, I noticed some photos on the wall of young children in their karate uniforms. I was intrigued and inquired about them.

As it turned out, Canada's Best Karate (CBK) had a Junior's Program. Being the avid researcher that I am, I wasted no time looking into CBK and its programs. I even interviewed a few parents. I then called Bob Mueller, the founder of the karate school, and asked for a meeting.

I told him who I was and that I'd like to come and observe some classes. He agreed and invited me to come the next day. It was obvious that he was very proud of his school and his programs, and I was excited to check them out.

The program consisted of the perfect combination of physical activity, social interaction, and mental stimulation and it was incredibly fun for the children. Even at first glance, it was evident that the foundation of the program was on building confidence, character, cooperation, and respect for self and others.

This whole experience brought me back into "teaching mode" and I asked Sensei Bob if I could volunteer as an assistant.

Knowing my background, he happily agreed and asked if I would offer my professional critique as well. We discussed ways to use my skills to update the original program and to create a new curriculum that expanded on the educational components already in place. The new CBK Junior Program I created was one of a kind. It fulfilled the needs of the children physically, mentally, socially, intellectually, and emotionally. It was like a "Kindergarten Karate School," providing the foundation for a lifetime of learning.

After a few months of implementing the new program, it became clear to me that I needed something more than my current credentials to continue in my role at the dojo. I was the only instructor who was not a karate student, so I asked Sensei Bob to enroll me in CBK. I was about to take my first step onto the dojo floor and into a new phase of my life. Who knew what a journey that would become?

I have never been an athletic person and from day one, I struggled tremendously in the classes and was ready to quit several times within my first year of training. Fear kept rearing its ugly head, but this time I was not going to let it get the best of me. Through the support and encouragement of the instructors, I reached a level of confidence and determination that had me continuously break through my fears and limitations and work my way up through the ranks.

Never, in my wildest of dreams, could I have imagined myself moving past my fears and earning a black belt in karate ...

But that is exactly what I did!

CRITICAL LIFE STRATEGIES

INISIDE & OUTSIDE OF THE DOJO

A constant theme throughout this book is to educate and enlighten the reader with my take on basic martial arts philosophies. Additionally, I want students to understand some of the classical ideas that traditional martial arts training should encompass. Each story adds to the collective narrative to forward both the historical progression of CBK and my own personal understanding of what those events mean. Therein lies the value as I see the stories as a tool to both inspire and educate you about how to achieve and succeed in life.

Life strategies are created by both succeeding and failing, but unfortunately, they can usually only be gained through personal experience. Again, my belief is that you can shorten the learning curve if you learn something that engages at least 2 of the 3 modalities of life. The modalities are mind, body, and spirit. I say that when you take a physical action and combine it with either a definite mental focus or spiritual belief your ability to learn the lesson of your actions is quicker.

This has been my experience. From decades of lessons, I have formulated a few life strategies that I believe can increase your ability to succeed or shorten your time failing. These ideas should be used both inside and outside of the Dojo.

1/ Problem Solving: My Karate Sensei was the first to teach me what I have come to believe is the most important lesson of my life. Problems are part of the solutions. They are, in fact, the crucial first half of success, and action is the key to solving them.

Movement is life. Stagnation is death. Never lock on the problem. Always move, take-action, and focus only on the solution.

The action I take is what I call the <u>30 – minute</u> solution.

I was 26 years old when, after a particularly difficult money problem that keep me sleepless for days, I made a new rule for myself. I decided never again to worry about money! If I ever had another financial problem, I would give myself thirty minutes of 100% worry time. Then, I would decide what to do, then

I'd immediately take the necessary action I deemed appropriate. To this day I have followed my rule to the letter and given myself thirty minutes to come to a decision. Then I take whatever action seems to be the best.

If, on the next day, my action turns out to be the wrong decision, I simply give myself 30 more minutes to come up with a new solution! No self-doubt, no self-inflicted beatings, and no endless worry. Just take the action to move forward and find a positive outcome.

Got a problem? Give yourself about thirty minutes to limit your downside and always think about what you want to have happen.

Never let the problem rule your thoughts.

Problem - Solution – Change

The sweetest word in the English language: Change

2/ Oxygen: My father-in-law was having a heart attack. His adult grandson, seeing his grandfather in distress, was running in circles panicking while the rest of the family of frozen with fear. Being the only non-blood member present I felt less attached to the outcome of the attack. My detached advantage allowed me to be more able to deal with the symptoms I was witnessing.

As a reflex to the trauma, I went over to Opa and sat beside him. Without speaking I put my hand on his forearm so he could feel my energy, and I his. Then looking him in the eye, I began breathing very deliberately – slowly breathing in and out to a paced 4-count. After a couple of repetitions, he began mirroring what I was doing and then I began coaching him. While breathing deeply I simply said *"breathe"*.

When, minutes later the paramedics arrived Opa was calm, and he accepted their help with ease and grace. It turned out he had suffered a "minor" heart attack and recovered over the next few weeks. What I did to help the situation had not gone unnoticed as I was asked why it had occurred to me to help him that way? My answer was simple – my martial arts training. In what was a chaotic moment I didn't know what to do any more than anyone else. No one knew whether it was serious or not - we just knew Opa was in trouble. I reasoned if the attack was serious, I would give him some energy so that he might die peacefully, and if it wasn't serious my actions would help him to not panic. This was a not a conscious thought at the time, but it was my trained unconscious mind that directed me to take this simple action.

You can survive a month or so without food, perhaps a week without water, but only a few minutes without oxygen. When you experience a debilitating physical challenge, your mind also locks up when you panic. The front part of your brain, the frontal lobe houses a collection of cognitive skills that include the ability to self-monitor and regulate yourself. When you feel extreme stress (the fight or flight response) your frontal lobe shuts down and the energy of your mind, through the hypothalamus, triggers the amygdala – (the monkey or reptile brain) which in turn overloads your system with fear.

As a martial artist, well studied in the effects of breathing to perform under labored exercise and the excitement of fighting, I learned to breath effectively while maintaining both my energy and a sense of calm. A relaxed person can be fast and effective, whereas a person tight with anxiety and fear will be slow and unresponsive. For a time, I also studied Neurolinguistic Programing and attended a few workshops with the world-renowned NLP founder, Richard Bandler. Here I learned the basics of self-hypnosis and mind awareness. I have found that Karate has elements of NLP naturally in its training process – but you need to be aware of what they are if you are to use them. If you can connect a physical action to a mental stresser it will help control your reaction so you may assist yourself or help others.

Here is an exercise to help yourself or others to breathe and overcome stress or panic:

a/ Recognize that a situation has developed, and you need to be calm.

b/ Be it yourself or someone else – rub your forehead in a circular pattern (10X in one direction and then the other).

c/ Notice your forehead activated and tingling - now, with your chin down slightly, look up with only your eyes, as if you are trying to see your forehead.

d/ With your eyes up, begin counting slowing backwards from 10 – 1 and at about the count of six begin closing your eyes.

e/ Notice a sense of calm and now take a deep breath in for four counts, hold for a second and then slowly release for a count of four.

f/ Notice your diaphragm moving up and down and your belly going in and out – take the action out of your lungs and put the breathing into your body. Do this for 3 – 5 minutes or until you feel your state change.

Now you can access the panic and make decisions that will help you deal with what is going on. This is martial arts in action and it can become your natural state with an adequate amount of training and concentration. Perhaps this why many people comment that a well-trained martial arts expert seems calm and controlled? Is it confidence or physiology – who knowns and who cares? What I know is it exists, and it works.

For emergencies – if you don't have time to do all of this exercise ... just breathe as slowly as possible!

Over the course of your martial arts training, you will find many strategies for dealing with people and personal panic. These have served me well and I recommend you try them. If you use them as a base for self-control you will discover that your time in the Dojo will provide many other life applications

THE NATURE OF LOVE

IS THERE A MOOSE IN THE GARDEN OF EDEN?

The sign promised 21 KMS to the Confederation Bridge. Another flashing sign said ATTENTION – HIGH RATE OF MOOSE CRASHES FOR NEXT 6 KMS. New Brunswick's portion of the Trans-Canada Highway is known for its accidental interactions between man and nature. However, despite my best efforts and all the moose signs, I hadn't spotted even one of the huge beasts.

At least, not yet.

Something I have noticed about martial artists is, almost to a person, they have a high regard for nature. Perhaps it's the primal themes of training as many styles mimic majestic animals like tigers, dragons and cranes. Or maybe Canadians should invent a Moose or Beaver style of Karate. Chuck, chuck instead of chop, chop! My own love of dogs is common to most people but during my travels I have also found a fascination with squirrels. To be exact I fell in love with little red squirrels. It happened when I drove across North America to take up residence in Canada's Maritimes.

As I crossed the Northumberland Strait, I remembered a question, *"Do you know what the locals say about P.E.I?"*

I was intrigued to hear "*They call it the Garden of Eden – a little piece of heaven.*" With that thought, I touched the island's red dirt for the first time.

The locals are an interesting mix of both inspired independence and practical needs. Anyone not naturally born on the island is thought to be "from away", and as such, they are tolerated for not knowing "the island ways". I enjoyed their peculiarities right away and after getting to know a few people, I found myself asking "the islanders" if they had seen any Moose?

I would carefully explain about my road trip through New Brunswick and how I saw all the signs, but I never saw any Moose.

"And by Jesus, you wouldn't want to! Them fellas are trouble!" was a typical response.

Once into the conversation I would state, *"You know, I haven't seen any Moose here either!"*

Taking a breath, actually more of a sigh, they would carefully explain, *"Well, there aren't any – no big game here at all - just foxes, skunks and squirrels."*

"No kidding?" but as if I had not understood what was said, I'd respond, *"Well, I saw the all signs - but I still haven't seen a Moose!"*

I enjoyed the befuddled reactions.

Perhaps it's my odd sense of humor, but I found it great fun to get such a serious answer to my silly question.

Is there a Moose in the Garden of Eden?

I'm not sure if I believe in the Garden of Eden, but I do believe in the power of intention and the satisfaction of self-determination. You can call it making lemon-aid out of lemons, or the glass is half full mentality, but I call it *"being an artist of life".* When a long-term relationship ended for me, my personal lemonade, was to move away – far away. To start anew, I travelled across the country for love and freedom. I was ready to build a new relationship. My martial arts had always taught me to focus on what you want and it will come to you. Or to quote the movie *"Field of Dreams" – "If you build it – they will come."*

That's how I stumbled on to a little piece of heaven in my Garden of Eden.

It happened one afternoon as I was building a new sun deck on the back of an old house. The home was ringed with Maple and Pine trees, full of morning birds, evening bats, and an occasional fox that would randomly run through the backyard.

I was installing the final pickets on the deck's railing while Wendy, my new lady, was sun-tanning and reading a book. Suddenly, something ran across her feet.

Startled, Wendy screamed, *"What was that!"* as we both noticed a lightning-fast shadow run underneath the deck. Seconds later, we saw a little red tale scamper up the trunk of a big Pine tree and disappear into the fully foliated branches.

"Is that a squirrel or a chipmunk?" I asked.

"Too big to be a chipmunk." Wendy replied, as she ran into the house, *"It's definitely a red squirrel! – I wonder if we have any nuts?"*

Returning with some sliced almonds she asked, *"This is all we have - do you think the squirrel will eat them?"* Sure enough, within moments, the squirrel returned and cautiously took the almond slivers.

Thus began our summer of love with the "little red". Now alerted to the squirrel's existence, we noticed him everywhere. He had gone out of his way to make friends, so we, in turn bought bags of peanuts and quickly the squirrel was eating first out of Wendy's hand, and eventually mine.

We never tired of seeing him and with every visit we experienced an innocence that brought happiness and joy. "Little red" thrilled us with his speed and acrobatic prowess as he collected and distributed nuts around the yard.

After finishing the deck I had some lumber scraps, so I decided to build a home for my new friend. I chose a spot in the big pine tree that was eye level with our sundeck. Carving out two large branches I began construction, not on a squirrel house, but rather, on a squirrel mansion.

I built a two-story home, complete with an insulated bedroom, grand foyer, and a large nut garage. On the front was a canter-levered deck with a safety railing, a streetlamp for the evenings and an outhouse, as everyone knows that squirrels don't use indoor plumbing. Starting with a tar-paper roof, I quickly realized this home needed some a proper roof, so I went to the lumber yard.

"What's the smallest amount of cedar shingles I can buy?" I asked the clerk.

"What's it for?" he inquired

Proudly I stated, *"For my squirrel house!"*

"Whadda got some pests you gotta kill?" he questioned innocently.

My face immediately grimaced with horror, so neither he nor I pursued the conversation any further. He simply pointed to a bundle of cedar shims and I created a "shake roof" for my new pet.

To me this sweet, gentle little friend was a pet, not a pest. That's when it occurred to me that I saw things a little different, not because I was from away, but because I looked at things from within. I had learned years ago to listen to my heart first, before consulting my brain.

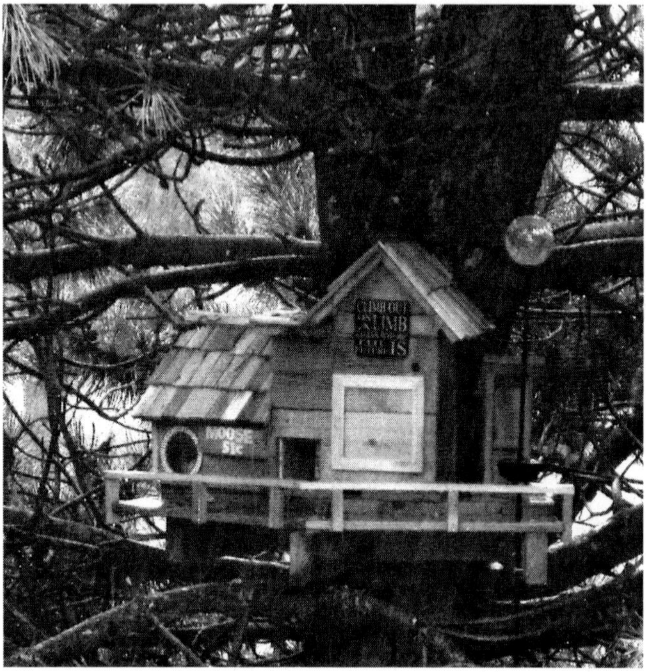

As our joy mounted and feeling like new parents, we decided to choose a name for our squirrel. After some consideration the choice was Rocky or ... Moose!

It was no contest! Moose, the Squirrel, would not only fill our hearts with joy, but now I could declare that, yes, I had seen a Moose on Prince Edward Island.

By spring we discovered that Moose, was actually Moosie, as he was actually she, and had now attracted mates. Soon we were grandparents of twins! To celebrate their birth we added a motivational sign saying: *"Go out on a limb-that's where the future is!"*

Renovations finally concluded when I built a 25-foot suspension bridge from our deck to hers. She, in turn, has continued to reward us with her natural joy and zest for life.

Is Prince Edward Island actually the Garden of Eden?

I can't say for sure, but I know my back yard "Eden" is full of nuts – some shelled, and some not.

For some people, fulfillment may be creating a big event or ending global suffering, but for me it's a little simpler. Becoming "an artist of life" is about noticing the joy that already exists around and inside us. Zen training teaches that it does not matter where or from what you feel joy – what matters is, you embrace it.

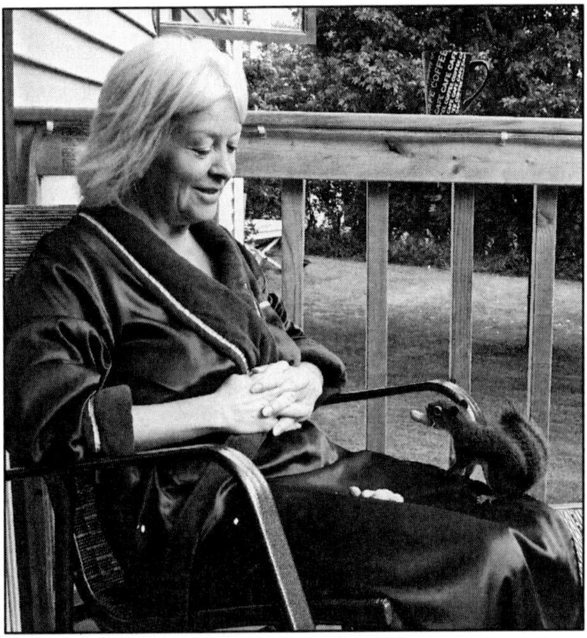

I believe, while this squirrel story doesn't have any practical application for your martial arts training, it can be used as inspiration to notice your surroundings. I say to appreciate and notice what is noticing you. If you can do that then you have learned one of nature's big lessons.

Did Moosie come to me because I needed to experience her joy?

Perhaps, but all I know is, I looked for her every day and I when I saw her, I felt without fail, a joy that is truly enlightening.

My Prince Edward Island Moose didn't crash into my car, rather she became an accidental vehicle for me to find my joy and teach me about love during a challenging time.

NINJA ATTACKS and OTHER METHODS

FOR MOTIVATIONAL TEACHING

Suddenly the eyes of the children widened as a collective wave of panic shot across their faces. Sitting in seiza (kneeling posture), the perfect row of about 20 seven- and eight-year-olds did their best to maintain their composure. Just one more final bow and we would be able to start their Karate class.

I sat facing the kids with my back towards an outside door that had just been breached. I could not see the black-clad masked ninja warriors who had entered and now crawledtowards me.

The children's tension was palpable as I said *"Mokso! Close your eyes, breath in through your nose and out through your mouth - meditation please."* Every fiber of their beings wanted to scream a warning to me – but instead they obeyed. The children closed their eyes and perhaps they prayed!

"Yame! Open your eyes," followed by, *"Rei, final bow."* Then, I very traditionally placed first my left hand, then my right, on the floor to bow as the ninja assassins moved to within striking distance.

At the exact same moment, the ninja leader, his hands gripped tightly on his Samurai Sword, made his move and struck with his sword as I bowed forward the blade narrowly missing my head. The children, frozen in disbelief and still locked in seiza, shrieked like banshees!

My forward bow had saved me, as my assailant went flying over my shoulders, losing his sword in a well-practiced forward roll.

Jumping up, my hands ready to fight, I yelled *"NINJAS!!"* and proceeded to defend the dojo. The screams turned to cheers as I, the Sensei, defeated the would-be assassins. Within a few moments, the bruised and battered Ninjas ran for the exit door and disappeared down the fire escape and into the night.

"Get out of the Dojo! Leave now, you bad Ninjas!" My words of admonishment had chased the Ninjas out the door. Having ensured the enemy was banished and the safety was restored to the Dojo, my satisfied students stood up and we started our class! Without another word, I began teaching the day's lesson and the battle royal was left without discussion.

At the beginning of every kid's class, the evil Ninja attack would happen three more times that day.

Other than saying the Ninjas were defeated, nothing was ever said to the children, including my 5-year-old son, Leigh. It wasn't until the phone calls started coming in from parents later that evening would we know the excitement we had caused! For the rest of the week the phone rang dozens upon dozens of times asking, *"What happened - was there some kind of attack at the school?"* When we told the parents what had happened, we also swore them to secrecy - asking them not to tell the kids that it was just a show.

About 100 excited kids told an unbelievable story of epic proportions. It was great fun for all concerned. Along with my key Black Belts Sweeney, Coles, and Bob Noonan, we had created a fun demonstration that was so real that it captured the kid's imagination for weeks. The fact that we made it real, and without explanation, was the beginning of many legendary performances and teachings.

Many years later Leigh Mueller had Danny Francois, a former Brockville student, visit him at the Victoria dojo. As they reminisced about their childhood experiences at the Church Dojo and the effect it had on their lives, Dan asked, *"Do you remember the day the Ninja's attacked the dojo?"* Leigh knowingly smiled saying *"Yes, but you know it was just a show ... don't you?"* With a wide-eyed honest and astonished look, he retorted, *"No! Are you kidding me? I thought that was real - no one ever told me it wasn't - not for 20 years - damn!"* They laughed and talked about other great demonstrations they had seen at the old dojo!

The world's greatest martial arts demonstrator, Don Jacob says *"When you demonstrate your ability, the important part of the is DO. Demonstrating is doing and when done right it is real!"*

Demonstrating is also an important element for teaching, especially in a Karate Dojo. That said, creating a visual for students to copy is only scratching the surface when it comes to teaching. Capturing the imagination of your class and feeding them, regardless of their age, the philosophy, and meanings behind what they are learning is the key to developing their abilities.

In the case of the ninja attack, the first objective was to entertain and the second was to demonstrate a successful defense. The third element was to offer a graphic moral lesson of good versus bad by protecting yourself and your home.

All CBK classes have a common format. Every class teaches basic skills that have outcomes and meanings. Then they are coupled with a character message about overcoming limitations, and developing a positive self-image, or self-belief. It is the same formula for both adults and children. The first rule is to make the class fun by teaching with joy and setting a standard that can be accomplished within the time frame available. Secondly, control every aspect of the activity with respect and discipline. Every great teacher knows how to reward positive efforts and nullify negative actions.

To teach children effectively I believe it's important to give them big, bold examples to follow. I have found that intricate, or subtle methods of instruction often bore kids, and believe me they do not hold back in showing their disapproval if you fail to keep their attention. If bored, they look out a window, fidget or just plain go on strike and sit down! Kids thrive on big macro concepts, while adults enjoy smaller and more detailed micro-instructions.

I always made a point to show my students both my joy and my displeasure. A good stern "Sensei Look" can accomplish a lot! Children naturally want to please and will work hard for your approval, so it's important to reward them richly when they do the work. The objective is to make accomplishing the skill, task, or drills as being fun.

An effective teacher does not need to play non-karate games to make their classes fun for kids. Accomplishing the skill and rewarding the effort makes learning karate fun. At the same time, bad attitudes or antisocial behavior must be met with immediate disapproval. Learning martial arts requires serious study and endless practice if you want to develop a real skill. However, if you don't engage the student's imagination and mental drive along with the hard work, your students won't succeed.

The three most important things a Sensei does are to encourage, encourage and encourage.

On a class level, I simply rewarded the behavior I wanted and allowed myself to be displeased by what I did not want. A good Sensei will reward an individual's effort with direct praise, and then make general corrections to the entire class so they can be absorbed together. This way the student is always striving to receive individual praise without the fear of personal rejection, or correction. Corrections are an important part of martial arts instruction, but if all you ever do is correct what is wrong, you'll never get what is right.

The simplest and most effective teaching technique I have found is to simply *"catch a student in the act of doing something correctly"* and reward them immediately.

While teaching the entire class I would seek out each person at some point looking to correct their form or technique. Perhaps while adjusting an arm, fist, or foot I'd say *"No, not that, do it like this"*... repeating the request multiple times until they either made the adjustment or made a good attempt at improvement. Then, just as they accomplished what I wanted I'd point to them and yell with a big smile, *"That's it, just like that."* Even if they didn't quite have it right at the time, the positive reinforcement was usually sufficient to encourage them to keep practicing until they acquired the skill and got it right.

Getting it right brings me back to the Ninja attack. CBK has always been an innovator, using showmanship and art to create motivation for its students. While most karate clubs focus only on tournament competition to advance their students' abilities, we have always added demonstrations as a means to create our community.

While this occurred in many forms, the most important demonstrations happened in what we called the Karate Christmas Concerts. This concept started innocently enough in 1985 when I decided that, as a school that taught children, we should have a formal assembly and put on a show for the parents in December. I put together a simple Karate demonstration that involved every member of the dojo and invited the families to come and watch. The admission price was to bring cookies. By the 2nd year, the dojo demonstration was packed with people, and it was standing room only. The following years grew and grew and when I added music to the demonstration it became a concert at Christmas time.

From there, the Christmas Concert needed larger spaces until it became a full-fledged "Broadway-style" two-hour show. My artistic mind reasoned that if you could have ice skating to music for the internationally renowned Ice Capades, you could do the same with karate. The result was themed demonstrations like The Lion King, Phantom of the Opera, and 007 James Bond.

Each year our cast would create a new two-hour show using all our students performing on stage. Along with the entertainment, the idea was to give each student a moment of recognition on stage so they could receive applause. Recognition and applause, particularly for children, is one of the most important teaching tools you can employ. Unfortunately, it is overlooked and underplayed by many.

To that end, even our Black Belt Grading, one of the toughest martial arts tests you will see anywhere in Canada, has an element of showmanship, music, and accomplishment. Again, it was my personal experiences that created the idea of *"a perfect moment"* and applied it to accomplishing your Black Belt. Where others simply give out a belt and certificate, CBK's belt presentation is the most unique in the world. The result creates a warm memory and a feeling for the Black Belt recipients that is usually filled with tears of joy! It is something you to need to experience and see firsthand to understand.

Regardless of what kind of demonstration is being performed it's interesting to remember that all of this began as a secret - a secret Ninja attack!

THE PROBLEM WITH QUITERS

Nobody likes a quitter!

I had stopped to get a coffee at my favorite Victoria corner grocery when our eyes met in a moment of recognition. Admittedly, the young man filling the milk fridge was more certain than me. As he said *"Hi Sensei"* I had an idea who he was. While I couldn't place his name, this adult's childhood face flashed in my mind, but before I could respond he continued, *"It's Jake, Jake Jansen – I was a student of yours when I was a kid."*

"Jake, of course, I remember you". You got your green belt as I recall! Where, at the Douglas Dojo – right?" I said as I was formulating a memory of him.

Jake responded with a big smile. *"Actually, it was Parksville, but you're right about the Green Belt."*

"Wow - Parksville, that's long time ago! I'm always happy to bat 500 in the memory department." I said with some satisfaction as the small talk worked its way towards his job delivering milk, his life, wife, and family. I always enjoy meeting happy people from the past, except when it comes to the end of the conversation where nine of ten times they apologize or justify why they had to quit. Then, like clockwork they say something like, *"I'm coming back! I want to train again! I was in such great shape – I miss it!"*

The fact is almost no one ever comes back. Years before, they had come to the Dojo for a specific reason, during a phase where learning karate was a fit for them. Then something changed in their life, and it moved them on to the next thing.

I get it and I always have.

Furthermore, I think it's terrible that people feel branded as quitters because they didn't get a Black Belt or carry on like me with a lifetime of training. My educated guess is that former students know how good the training was for them, and because it is a high value activity, they wish they had continued. Moreover, they want me to feel good about my program, so they always add that they are coming back. Interesting – yes?

Still, nobody likes a quitter – right?

The problem is where do you set the line between someone who quits or a person who moves on after an accomplishment? To me, earning a Green Belt is a good accomplishment. Truthfully, if you live long enough you will quit everything, including breathing. With that in mind, lets qualify some of the people who have quit Karate.

Perhaps you would like to know who the worst offending quitter I ever experienced was? That's right – ME. Having begun my training at 17 years old, I trained consistently for about 22 years, accomplishing a Yodan, 4th Degree Black Belt while operating a string of Karate schools. However, by my mid-thirties my left knee needed to be repaired again. The second scoping surgery was not to fix a traumatic injury but rather to clean out the joint due to excess wear and tear on the meniscus (cartilage). About a year afterwards I found myself still limping around after teaching class. It was discouraging, as I often wasn't doing anything except walking and talking while I taught. That's when it occurred to me: I'm never going to be world champion – who am I kidding? I've made my mark, and nobody cares whether I train or not. Besides, if I'd like to be able to walk when I'm 50 years old I'd better start thinking about this differently. That's when I quit my active training in hard style Karate.

But did I actually quit? No. Over the next twenty years I lifted weights, rehabilitated my knee with yoga and did every cardiovascular exercise known to man - everything except Karate. At least not the Karate I had known as a younger man – low stances, violent hip rotations, snap back kicks and exaggerated body dynamics. You know, everything that makes you a top-notch karateka. But I did continue to teach seminars, attend gradings, and grow my presence as a leader. But I didn't train my Karate.

So let me ask you a question. Did I quit or did I transition?

Professor Don Jacob teaches that along with your training you must pass three challenges to successfully make martial arts your life. Everyone will at some time be disabled by injury or sickness. They will need to overcome envy or ridicule, and finally they will need to accept that training is a privilege and rank is not an entitlement. Once you experience these three tests and find your way to continue, you can make martial arts a lifetime study.

Overcoming Jacob's three challenges always starts with injuries. Everyone who trains at a high level will injure themselves in some way during their career. It's all a matter of degree relative to your age and your desire, as well as what and why you are training and finally how long the injury lasts.

The second obstacle is overcoming envy or ridicule. Perhaps a well-intended friend or spouse might say, *"Why are you spending all your time at that Karate School? You'll never be a Black Belt – you're too (fill in the blank here: tall, short, fat or skinny)!"* They want you to spend more time with them, so they impugn or ridicule you for your activity. Even in its most subtle form, if left unchecked this can cause irreparable harm and lead people to quit.

Entitlement is a little more difficult to recognize because it develops inside your own psyche. Don Jacob describes it like this: If someone is being helped, even though they can do it for themselves, and the giver asks for nothing in return from the receiver, the receiver may develop a sense of entitlement. The receiver may even attack the giver's character if they decide to stop giving. The receiver starts believing they are entitled to get all they can and give nothing in return.

A great example is people who are given an honorary rank without earning it. This is why the basic rule of any good Dojo is: Everyone works, and nothing is free! You are entitled to nothing except the work. The work is its own reward.

Personally, I worked for everything I ever received. Additionally, I paid over and over in the form of good and bad learning lessons to achieve the success I enjoyed. I'm grateful for a relatively long career with success as a good karate athlete and with knowledgeable skills and a world class Budo mentality. When it was time for me to move into a different phase, I took the road less travelled and moved on.

Muhammad Ali once said, *"The man who views the world at 50 the same as he did at 20 has wasted 30 years of his life."*

So, what is the difference between me, and Jake, the milkman? Nothing. Nothing, except the fact that he transitioned earlier for reasons that made sense to him. No shame there. All this leads a very important skill that all martial arts people and, in truth, everyone should learn. It is the ZEN art of detachment. I can't say when I first learned about the idea of detachment, but I do know that it began making sense to me when I heard a man named Stuart Wilde speak about how to detach by being assertive. As a general guide, I always recommend that people find and purchase his work as he is a tremendous teacher and very entertaining.

The most basic and general way to begin implementing this idea into your life is to first understand your own uniqueness.

The art of Zen begins by aligning you with yourself, rather than being dependent on other people's ideas or opinions about you. What if you could take a bigger view of yourself? If you could step back and watch yourself interact with the world? Would you see yourself in a different way?

Detachment is about becoming free of other people opinions. If something is of value, you use it; if it is not, you leave it. Being free means that instead of reacting to what happens to you, you learn to respond proactively.

No one - not your parents, your family, friends, spouse or even your children - have anything to do with who you truly are. Your true value lies in your uniqueness. A relationship simply means that you can relate to another. You can have a healthy amount of empathy, compassion, love, respect, and trust for another, just like you can have money, possessions and things, but you cannot depend on any of those things as being 100% absolute. You are you. If you lost everything and everybody you had, would you still not be you?

Many people think that if you detach from people and possessions that you will become cold and cruel. The fact is, detaching allows you to trust, feel and engage in a closer, more meaningful way to those around you. Detaching from your possessions does not mean you need to get rid of your stuff. It means you need to own what you have, rather than be owned by it. The way to do this is by appreciating what you have, and if you find that you can't appreciate what you possess, then get rid of it.

All you are really doing is demonstrating to yourself that you recognize your own value and worthiness. Being proactive is to be assertive, and to be reactive is to be aggressive.

Being assertive without aggression is the goal of every martial artist.

Assertiveness is also the understanding that sometimes quitting is how you grow. A lot of growth happens by doing and experiencing new things, especially when you realize that whatever you learn or work at is not an end unto itself. A book is a book, just like a shovel is a shovel and as such they are tools designed to accomplish a job. A tool is only valuable if you employ its function, and in the case of Karate once you have learned or experienced enough for your needs - then it is time to move on.

Even the most serious and dedicated martial artist can only make a lifetime study of the art if they are willing to adjust how and what they do. When you can use what you have learned and apply it to your life, I believe you have maximized your training.

In my case, my Karate training prepared and gave me to tools to put myself on the worldwide stage. Because I spent years crafting my ability to teach and move with confidence, I found myself engaging with many like-minded people. My detached, highly directed, and focused nature allowed me to expand my talents to many forms of art. The result had me tell my story to the world, and it won me an Emmy Award as well as putting me in contact with people and places I had only ever dreamed of. I believe this happened because, when I was in the process of living my dreams, I was not seeking an outcome. By detaching from an outcome, I became free of needing anything from my experience except the joy of doing it. In karate terms, you don't train to get a Black Belt, rather you become a Black Belt because of your training.

On this, I am not alone. Within my own family I have two sons, Leigh and Kieran, who used their training to become successful Karate teachers. But I also have another son, Drew and a daughter, Brittany who accomplished Black Belts as teenagers and took what they had learned and applied it to other interests. Drew travelled world and used his intellect to fund his interests by becoming an expert at online poker. He made a living working for a few hours a day with a lap top computer while sitting on the beaches of the world. My daughter, Brittany, educated herself with her own money, learning to be a hairdresser and then married and had two children. She applied her ability to focus and her drive to succeed to create a dream of a life with her husband, Daniel Adair. Neither Drew or Brittany were quitters, as they used their training to advance themselves and then moved on.

That is the purpose of training. You train to do something with the skills you have acquired. In my mind, a quitter is someone who acquires a skill and then fails to advance themselves with what they have learned.

Among the many Black Belts who have moved on, there are accomplished Doctors, Lawyers, Engineers, Businesspeople and even a Rocket Scientist! One climbed to the peak of Mt. Everest, while another became a world-renowned Opera singer. I have no doubt that their karate training helped them in many ways to accomplish their dreams.

To close, I'll make this blanket statement: Anyone who has ever been grateful for what they learned and used it as a success tool to advance themselves is a winner – regardless of how long they trained. I have no problem with quitters, provided they don't quit on themselves!

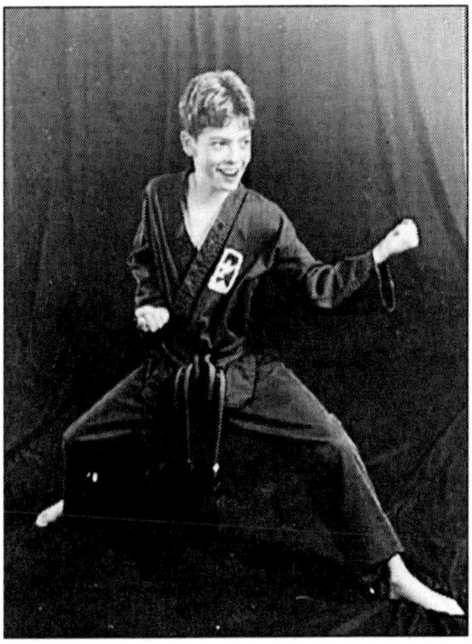

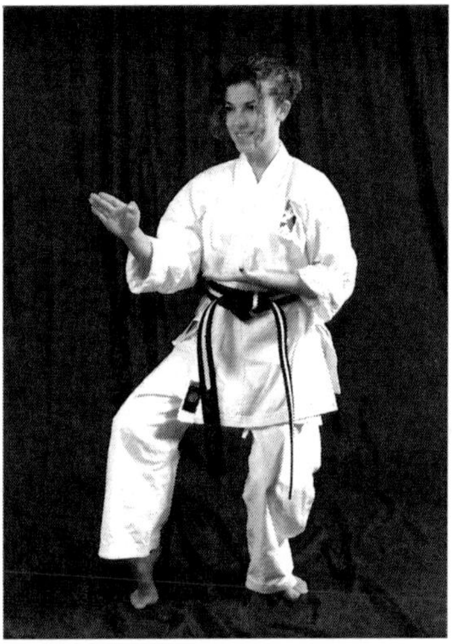

Drew Mueller and Brittany Adair

LEGENDARY BRANDS of DISTINCTION

THE BLACK BELT GRADING

"You have got to see this thing, man!" Professor Don Jacob said proudly from his Trinidad Dojo. *"I'll send you an airline ticket. You must come visit me and see for yourself. It is just a blessed thing, man. It is beautiful!"*

The *"blessed thing"* was the Purple Dragon Black Belt test. Blessed or not, nobody enjoys tests. Tests are always full of anticipation, hard work and worry. The ultimate test for any Karate student is to achieve their 1st Degree Black Belt - *Shodan* in Japanese. It is thought to be a legendary accomplishment, like running a marathon. Perhaps an Ironman competition, with its 2.4-mile swim, 112 mile bike ride and 26.2 mile marathon, is a better comparison.

Like the multiple disciplines of the marathon, *The Black Belt Test* isn't just about competing against others, it's always moving your personal best yardstick. In the end, it's the will to endure that makes it one of the ultimate tests that anyone can experience. It does not matter how much you do or how far you go after earning your first Black Belt. Like witnessing a birth, you will always remember the moment when you had that belt tied around your waist.

The question is "why"? You would think that graduating anything of high value or achieving a long-awaited goal would surely carry the same kind of weight as this simple piece of cloth – but it doesn't. As stated, it is like witnessing a birth: your own birth.

The weight carries with it a worldwide recognition of what a Karate Black Belt symbolizes. Globally, a Karate Black Belt represents people who know how to handle themselves physically. These people can fight, defend themselves and others, have integrity in everything they do; along with all that they are wise, honorable and humble.

Is it fact or fiction? The fact is - it is pure fiction.

There are millions of people who have Black Belts that cannot fight, defend themselves, or have the personal integrity to be honorable and humble. On the other hand, it is also true that earning a Karate Black Belt can be as virtuous a personal journey as you might ever undertake.

The old masters intended this initial accomplishment to be the first step in acquiring the Samurai Budo mindset known as the *"Way of the Warrior"*. The seven commonly accepted tenets of Warrior Bushido are: *Rectitude, Courage, Benevolence, Respect, Honor, Honesty and Loyalty.* These tenets were handed down generationally as Japanese cultural oral history, and were later adopted by Juijitsu, Judo and Karate masters in the early days of the 20th century.

In today's terms, these masters branded their fighting skills by aligning themselves with the oral traditions and the ideals of Bushido. While it has nothing to do with learning kata, kumite or self-defense, branding Karate training with a higher purpose is what helped create the warrior myth that continues today.

To understand what I mean when I say the "branding" of Karate, perhaps it would help to think about some of today's products and services. Gair Maxwell, an internationally renowned branding expert, says that not all brands are created equally. Some are just logos, barely pedestrian in design and meaning, while others become legendary.

Think of what it must be like to be thought of as legendary. The brand makes you feel or associate a value that exceeds what the product actually does. When you have a brand that becomes a legend, you are making your symbol or product mean more than its basic function. For instance, a Mercedes sports car isn't just fast transportation, it represents grace, wealth and status. Apple computers means futuristic innovation, a De Beers diamond ring is forever, and Fed Ex means being on time, every time, etc, etc. A brand makes a "thing" mean something more than it is. Once a brand takes effect, the "thing" takes on an unspoken, subconscious meaning that is accepted globally as being true.

If you are not sure about this, just show up to buy something, say a house or some jewelry, in a Mercedes sports car. The salesperson will immediately think you can easily afford what they are selling. When you have a globally accepted brand its assumed that giving a girl a diamond ring is an eternal act and if a package is sent via Fed Ex that it will arrive at the expected time. Our minds automatically associate the symbols of success with the "actual thing" even before it has become a provable, actionable fact.

An actionable fact happens for me when I first meet someone, and they find out I have a Karate Black Belt. They usually get a funny look on their face and then 99% of the time they say something like *"Hiiyaa"* and make a Karate Chop in the air! The next comment is *"I better be careful around you"* or they make some kind of bowing motion. Now, if that isn't a universal brand in action then I don't know what is! This is my experience, and I can guarantee you, it is what most people who have Black Belts experience as well.

When I add to this the fact that the Black Belt has existed for over a hundred years, I can state unequivocally that the Karate Black Belt is one of the greatest brands ever created. It is truly a legendary brand of distinction. That said, a poor person can own a Mercedes, the diamond ring doesn't make for a long marriage, the package can arrive late and lots of Karate Black Belts couldn't fight their way out of a wet paper bag! What you see isn't always what you get, but as a symbol, it can lead you to become worthy of its designation. The burden to be worthy of your title is like the lump of coal being worthy of being a diamond. It takes time and pressure.

The first time I felt the pressure of my Black Belt designation was two weeks after successfully passing my Shodan test. I was 21 years old and attending a Saturday night party with some high school friends, when word got around about my accomplishment. Gordie Brooks, a genuine tough guy, was one of the partygoers and someone I had always been wary of. I didn't know him, save for his reputation, so when he approached me I was nervous about his intentions. While I don't remember what he said, he let me know that he respected my Bateson Karate Black Belt. I had leveled up in his eyes, but it also made me very uncomfortable that he now saw me as an equal, a tough guy. Believe me, because of that encounter, even though nothing happened, I trained even harder. You see, it was only a few weeks before that I had been a Brown Belt. Nobody cared or even mentioned my Karate, but once I achieved a Black Belt, my accomplishment was acknowledged in many different ways. I didn't really feel any different, but I did feel an unspoken pressure to be more than I was. In truth, I had changed, and it made me want to be worthy of *"being a Black Belt"*, not just getting one.

The next time I felt a similar pressure was when I made the decision to move east to open the Brockville Karate School. Although I had been teaching for over five years and was the

Sensei of the Parksville Dojo, I had never truly accepted this role as being me. To correctly define this for you, I have to say there is a huge difference between doing something and being something. Several people asked me why I would leave my home to travel three thousand miles and start a new Karate School? My answer was simple. I wanted to start fresh, go where no one knew my past and where I would be known only as the Sensei and nothing else. I didn't want to be remembered as a carpenter or a high school friend, so I made a conscious decision *"to be the Sensei"* in every way possible. As such, I always dressed professionally, be it a karategi or a business suit, and I made every action, whether it was noticed or not, lead me to be successful. If I was going to teach others, I needed to commit myself without reservation. In doing so, I became a real Black Belt. I believe people could see, and feel that I was the "real deal" because of the commitment I had made to myself, and ultimately to my students.

Respect, compassion, and gratitude are forged when you brand yourself with the Warrior's Code of Bushido. When you are secure in the integrity of your actions, this is when the universe begins to notice your value. The people I know who have made a similar commitment to their life and training, be them mentors, or students, are the ones I respect and accept as being true Black Belts. Everyone else is simply a pretender.

With that in mind, I accepted Professor Don Jacob's invitation to travel to Trinidad & Tobago to witness his *"blessed thing"* - The Purple Dragon 3-day long Black Belt Test. A month later I spent three days on the hard concrete floor of his Purple Dragon University, located in the mean streets of Port of Spain. He was correct. It was truly something blessed, as he pushed over thirty Black Belt Candidates for an unheard of three full days. His syllabus, already legendary as one of the toughest in the world, was also the most unique grading that I had ever witnessed. Students were expected to work, listen, write essays, and to physically give everything they had for sixteen plus hours a day. I mean everything! They arrived virtually naked and totally dependent, needing their families to bring food, water and support. They were not allowed to leave the dojo at any time or even speak during their ordeal. Silent, save for their determined groans, they also slept for three nights on the concrete floor which they had bled and sweated on. They were immersed 100% in the experience as if nothing else existed or was allowed to influence them during the test. Like tribal ceremonies in more ancient cultures, this was not just a test. It was meant to be a true passage from *"Kyu"*, meaning boy, to *"Dan"* meaning man, as laid out in Japanese terminology.

There, I presented for them my *"Hero"* seminar, speaking of Yoda, Popeye and the Duke - John Wayne. I know it inspired them, but it was I who was truly inspired. During the testing, these students became my new heroes as I saw them pushed well beyond their breaking points. As unbelievably hard as this physical test was, it was also the fairest I had ever seen. It required only the guts to survive and the will to win. Technique, while important, took a second place in this grading. After the first few hours of the first day the participants were already so tired that many would wobble and pass out. Once revived, they knew they still had over two full days of testing to go. *"When the body gives up, use your mind. When your mind gives up, use your spirit!"* Jacob would chant and they, together with him, would *"beat a drum of desire."*

Desire is a word that often gets lost between accomplishment and disappointment. If you are comfortable, prosperous and satisfied, with all your needs met, you may not want for much, but having desire, regardless of your status, is priceless and is what makes life worth living.

After experiencing the Purple Dragon Grading I wanted it for myself and I desired it for my eldest son. When I asked Sempai Leigh, and fellow student Eric Perkio, if they would like to go to Trinidad to train Jiujitsu with Professor Jacob, the answer was a resounding yes! When I told Leigh about the 3-day test he desired that experience more than anything else. Although already a Black Belt, he wanted to prove his worth in another arena.

It was the chance of a lifetime, as not only would Leigh and Eric train full time at the Purple Dragon Headquarters, they would also live directly with and under the care of Don Jacob himself. Living with the master had many unexpected experiences, as he would often wake them without warning at dawn for immediate training, or sometimes keep them up late to see what they could do. He showed them the ghetto of his youth and inspired them to learn about the Black culture there, and in turn to appreciate the good life they had in Canada.

Eric and Leigh both graded in Trinidad. They completed all three days, taking everything that the test had to offer. As the only white foreigners, they were treated with respect but only because they knew to give their all and do the work. No one shirks in this grading, as excuses or minor injuries are all treated with the same answer. If you can't do it, you can quit and leave, but if you are caught slacking in any way you are told to leave without refund or recourse. In a third world country where poverty is rampant, and money is devalued 10 – 1, the cost of the test is $2,500.00. Students and families begin saving for the test almost as soon as they begin training as a white belt. Additionally, with over 20,000 students worldwide, the demand to be considered to grade makes it available for only the best and most dedicated students.

Leigh and Eric knew they was taking someone else's spot, so they respected and treasured the opportunity regardless of the pressure and the pain. Had they not given their all, Don Jacob would have been insulted, and their effort would have garnered them nothing. No respect, no acknowledgment and certainly no belt. Instead, they earned their place as Leigh received a Black Belt Green stripe and Eric a Black Belt White Stripe for their efforts. Leigh returned to Trinidad again the following year to remove the stripe and accomplish his Purple Dragon Full Shodan. In the first grading he was allowed to substitute the Purple Dragon Katas he didn't know with Shotokan Karate forms he was familiar with. When he returned a year later to test again he was required to know the entire PD syllabus and preform it to Purple Dragon standards. He was applauded by Professor for his work and thus earned his full Shodan. Leigh Mueller is the only non-Purple Dragon person to ever be allowed to accomplish this. It's a profound accomplishment of mind, body and spirit and it is a big part of what made him into the man he is today.

Canada's Best Karate adopted the Trinidad Grading format by combining our strengths with the inspired grit and determination that I first witnessed in 1998. Our unique CBK 2 - day grading is now over twenty years old, melding the science of Karate with the art of determination. Our organization is proud that, outside of Trinidad, our Black Belt Grading has also taken on a legendary status. It's tough but fair, and it's an experience where everyone who takes the challenge learns to *"love their life, be unstoppable and become a real CBK Black Belt".* It is a grading like no other. A CBK student who tests for their Black Belt knows, without a doubt, that they earned it and they are worthy. It's something that Leigh experienced, it's what I desired for my schools, and I needed to make our program be worthy of its name – Canada's Best Karate. Once the belt is earned, no one can ever take it away from you, and when the belt is tied around your waist it's guaranteed to burn a moment in your memory that is never forgotten.

Don Jacob was right - the process is a *"blessed thing".*

A hundred years ago, Funakoshi Sensei the ancient master, spoke of the process to find worthiness in a title or an accomplishment. He said, *"When Heaven is about to confer an important office upon a man, it first embitters his heart in its purpose; it causes him to exert his bones and sinews; it makes his body suffer hunger; it inflicts upon him want and poverty and confounds his undertakings. In this way it stimulates his will, steels his nature and thus makes him capable of accomplishing what he would otherwise be incapable of accomplishing."*

To help make Funakoshi's point, a famous Zen story tells of a grandfather walking through the woods with his young grandson. When the little boy finds a cocoon hanging on a leaf, he picks it up to exam it. As he rubs his fingers on the membrane of the cocoon he peels back the layers, and a beautiful butterfly pops out! The beautiful butterfly takes to the air, circling around the little boy's face and then suddenly dies, dropping to the ground – stone dead.

Frightened, the boy looks up asking, *"Grandfather, what happened to the butterfly?"*

Without hesitation the old man tells him, *"You killed it, you killed the butterfly!"*

Tears in his eyes and looking down, the little boy shuffles his feet saying, *"No I didn't, I was careful, I didn't kill the butterfly – I helped it get out."*

Bending his knee, the grandfather reached out and held the boy in his arms, *"Yes, that's true you were careful, but you see, the butterfly needed to struggle to become strong. When you helped it, you took away the butterfly's struggle and it's will to live."*

It is about your will, the will to endure and your drive to succeed. That is where the value lies.

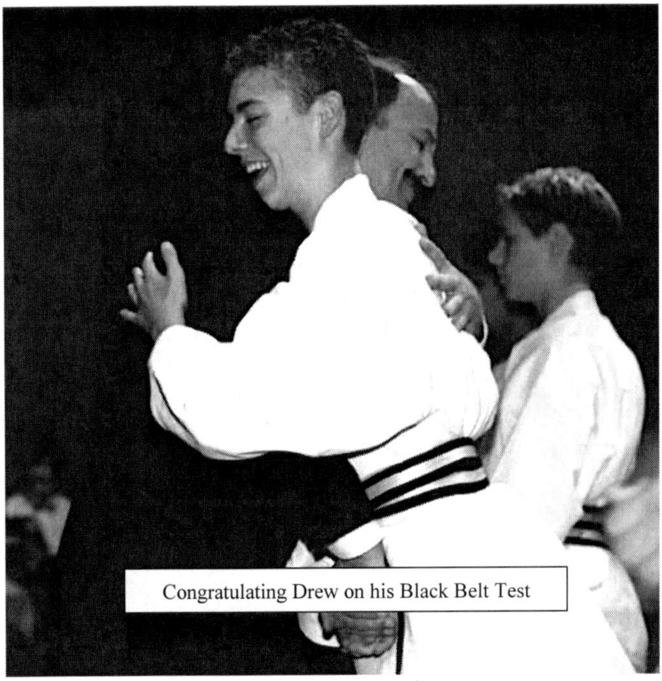

Getting your Black Belt is nothing. Mr. Miyagi, the fictional character from the Karate Kid movies, says he got his from JC Penny. But earning your Black Belt is an entirely different thing. I expect you, like the butterfly, will have to struggle and fight for the right to wear the belt. Just know, when you give all that you have, you get back more than you ever had. I know it will be a life altering experience for you, because it was for me.

To paraphrase an old TV commercial – *"we don't just make you a Black Belt, we make you earn it!"* If having a Black Belt is a brand, then earning a CBK Black Belt makes you one of - and a part of - a centuries-long legend. What made the Black Belt what it was in the past is now passed on to you to embody it in the present. When you take on the burden, to leave it better than you found it, that is when your Black Belt becomes the stuff of legends.

If you can, you must!

TO EVERY SEASON

TURN, TURN, TURN

Music became a fortuitous intersection in the journey for me and Canada's Best Karate. It was game changer, one of the vital continuous links that has allowed our Dojo to bridge the generation gap of progress.

In 1965 The Byrds, a progressive rock band, released their version of a 1950's hymn written by a Lutheran composer named Ed Harris, which was based on a passage out of Ecclesiastes 3 as it is found in the Old Testament Bible. The words and meaning behind the music made it a powerful medium for people of all ages. The Byrds hit song, in turn, powered future generations for decades, proving that music can connect people in ways that words and actions can barely touch. A guitar classic Rickenbacker riff introduces lead singer Roger McGuinn singing;

"To everything turn, turn, turn
There is a season turn, turn, turn
And a time to every purpose, under heaven"

The notes resonated for me during an accidental musical discovery at the center stage of the Royal Theater. The words provided the purpose that led me to years of musical Karate experimentation. Very quickly, through music, I realized the power to transform a meaningful event into a deeper emotional one. When you look behind the melodies to the lyrics of songs you will find many powerful messages. For instance, Bob Dylan's 1960s ballad *"Blowing in the Wind"* became an anthem against the Vietnam War, and Helen Ready's *"I am Woman"* announced to women in the 1970s that they had the power to be and do more.

For me, as a child of the 1960s and a lover of that old music, I needed to up my game and find the right music that could speak to what I wanted to say. As a father with four young children and a Dojo called Superkids, I was constantly immersed in Disney-like movies and themes. When The Lion King movie hit the theaters in 1994, my kids dragged me to the show and that is where I found the connection I was looking for. By the end of the show, I had bought into the animated animal characters, adult themes, and stirring music. After purchasing the CD, I found a little-known piece on side 2 called *"This Land"* and its bitter-sweet orchestration sounded right to me.

Since then, what sounded correct and the *"right of passage"* themes and music of the Lion King have become part of our Black Belt ceremony. It was already a highly intimate and gratifying experience, but when the people heard the music, the tears of joy flowed freely. I can attest that even 25 years later I still get choked up when I witness the belt tying ceremony.

The symbolism and synchronicity of the music were not lost on my then 13-year-old son Leigh. The more I delved into connecting music to our shows, demonstrations, and events, the more he paid attention to how and what I was doing. As the circumstances dictated his emersion into the professional side of Dojo, Leigh, still very young, began helping me, eventually replacing me in just about every way over the next ten years. By the early 2000s, the writing was on the wall and given our family break up, I knew it was time for Leigh to become the Sensei of the Dojo. Although only in his early twenties, he was competent and mature beyond his years, but I still had a few reservations. Could he take over the creative and innovative parts of CBK? And did he have the talent to keep making us different from the average Karate club?

In 2004, as we were preparing to complete the transition to Leigh's leadership, he came to me with a novel idea. *"Dad, I've been working on something new that I think will revolutionize how we end our Black Belt Grading."* He went on to explain what he had in mind. While I had difficulty grasping all of what he wanted to do, I saw the potential of his idea because of the music. He had carefully chosen a musical piece with a narrative that spoke to both of us. He had also added his own "lyrics" and formulated how they could deliver added excitement and meaning to the final leg of the Black Belt test. When he asked if he could show it to me I said, *"No need, I'll see it at the grading next month when you do it live!"* That's kind of how we roll: without safety nets; or as Elvis Presley might say, *"a little less conversation, a little more action."*

With that, we brought in a film crew to capture the grading, and Sensei Leigh presented his *"Remember the Titans"* finale. In what was one of the toughest Black Belt Grading ever, 29 candidates reeled and reveled in the atmosphere, as a packed Dojo saw the most unique finish ever imagined. By the end of the day, I knew that the future of CBK was in good hands and destined to go to unimagined places.

Like the Lion King before, the Titans finale at the end of the test signals that you have made it, and each student feels worthy of what they have accomplished. It is incredible, and if you are a CBK student or a member family, it is something you need to experience before you take the floor on your own Black Belt test.

By using our common love of martial arts, and understanding the power of music we, Leigh and I, have successfully bridged any potential generation gaps. Just like he took over my creativity and leadership, he is doing the same thing with his next-generation teachers and students. Everyone has their time, and purpose. It's what the True North Dojo was designed to do.

"A time to be born, a time to die
A time to plant, a time to reap,
A time to kill, a time to heal
A time to laugh, a time to weep
To everything turn, turn, turn"

A few years before, in 2002, I had used The Byrds words and music to remember Sensei Jimmy Mac who had been lost to cancer. While creating an ambitious CBK tribute film to honor my fallen Sensei, I remembered another Don Jacob lesson: *"Know that people always come into your life for a reason, a season, or a lifetime."*

When someone or something appears in your life for a reason, it is often to meet a need you have expressed inwardly or outwardly. That's often how and why people show up at our Dojo. I say, using an old baseball analogy, that they have a *"hole in their swing"* and the Dojo's role is to fill their need by teaching them martial arts.

Such a reason showed up for me during the writing of this book. The work has spanned two years, ending with the worldwide COVID-19 pandemic of 2020/21. Embracing consistent and never-ending change – CANI - has always been my motto, but the last decade has been particularly tumultuous, as I have lived on both ends of Canada. I moved from Kelowna B.C. to Summerside P.E.I. and back to Victoria, then Nanaimo, and finally, Maple Bay Duncan B.C., where I built my retirement house. During that time, I also found myself caring for my elderly parents. As four new Mueller bundles were born, I also buried my

90-year-old father, which caused me to pause and notice an additional loss - my dog.

I had "*a hole in my swing*" as I had been without a dog for the first time in my adult life. It had been eight years since my English Cocker Spaniel, Pete had died, and I had forgotten how much I missed him. As we transitioned to the new home in Maple Bay I reasoned this need had to be filled. My wife Wendy researched what we considered to be a compromise pet. Her desire for a Border Collie and mine for another "Pete" turned to a solution: a Cavalier King Charles Spaniel would be the pet for us. They are bred especially for love. The Cavalier's temperament is so mild and their ability to give and receive love is so profound that it makes them, even among dogs, the kings of love. Of course, the word Dog spelled backward is God, and as such my ruby red Cavalier King is a God of love.

The lesson of the dog relates to the reason. Choosing to bring the unconditional love of a dog into your life is to know that *"the reason"* is also a lifetime. With a short lifespan of ten to fifteen years, you, as a human being, get to experience the entire circle of life of the dog. My Bubba, the 25lb God named Copper teaches me every day about unconditional love.

Like the Dojo, a dog initially fills your life for a reason. If the fit is right, it becomes a season and if you are fortunate, it lasts for a lifetime – their lifetime. Likewise, what you first learn in the dojo can become a season of experiences and what you retain by earning a Black Belt can last for a lifetime. In my view, the extra CBK efforts to sear a life-altering Black Belt moment into your mind is where the value of the grading lies. The conscious and unconscious message of the test is that you can overcome any obstacle you chose.

It is an archetypical Hero's Journey where the quest to accomplish the goal shapes a future lifetime of self-confidence and self-reliance.

My lifetime participation in the arts, martial and otherwise, has proven to me that we can become the heroes we admire. Part of your own Hero's Journey is to realize that you possess all that you need. Once you accept that the only person who can save you is you, your Black Belt can represent whatever you need it to. My Karate taught me that celebrating everyday heroes, from dogs to gods, allowed me to connect with the extraordinary mythical heroes of my dreams.

Naturally, it's to my mythical heroes, the Duke, Butkus, Sayers, Sabol, MacDonald, and Vollinger, that I owe the greatest debt of gratitude for my Budo nature and indomitable spirit. But more than the old myths, it's the heroes of my own making and the stories I have told that I want you to consider.

It's the heroes of my flesh, my sons and daughters, who inspire and move me forward. And it's the heroes of my experience - the Original Three: Stranges, Sweeney, Coles, with Bullard, Baldwin, and Comeau - who have carried my flag. It's the admiration for my adopted sons like Bassi, Sikora, Emery, Gieble and so many others whose heroic journeys have helped me live and write this book.

These are the ones who are paying it forward and their students are now writing the future chapters that were once just yesterday's dreams. What began many decades ago on a reluctant cold concrete floor has now affected tens of thousands, and none more than I.

As stated, The Bushido Code - the Way of the Warrior - has seven virtues: *Righteousness, Goodness, Courage, Respect, Honour, Honesty,* and *Loyalty*, but there should be one more. I will add *Contemplation* to the code, as the action of looking thoughtfully at something for a long time is an important skill to learn.

As chronicled in this text, I see acts of modern Bushido of every form gracing these pages. But for a long time they went unnoticed. You see, the road was so busy, and the act of doing so intense, that the Budo and its meaning was lost in all the action.

However, fifty years of observing combined with a decade of desire to write it down has become thoughtful contemplation. Funakoshi Sensei once asked, *"The Way, who will pass it on straight and well?"* My rearview mirror reveals that Canada's Best Karate, through its generations, has answered the call of the hero's journey. Wrongs were righted, and each loss found a gain, as the singers sang and the music remained.

"There is a season turn, turn, turn
A time to gain, a time to lose,
A time to rain, a time to sow
A time for love, a time for hate, a time for peace
I swear it's not too late"

Every end brings a beginning. What was right then is still right now, what is wrong remains so.

I close this collection in the year of my 65th orbit around the sun with a wish. "*Starlight, star bright, I wish I may, I wish I might..."* find myself decades from now in a chair alongside my many sons. Perhaps in a rocking chair, seated in a dojo and holding my bubba dog, in an old tattered Karategi. Perhaps I'll catch the eye of the new Sensei, a granddaughter, and as the tears well up in me, she'll smile back, and I'll feel as grateful as I do now.

Once again, I'll witness the grading, feel the energy, effort, noise, and exhaustion of the participants, the Sensei and the students. And, when it all seems like too much, and the goal cannot be attained, the roar of music will break the struggle and announce the end is near.

May I see their tears of joy and their spirits rise as the music spurs them on to *"love their life, be unstoppable and become a real CBK Black Belt"!*

May I feel the anticipation as the crisp new Black Belts are tied around the waists of their beltless bodies.

And may I again taste the salt of my own tears, as I revel in, and share their moment, so I might make it my own, just one more time.

"Turn, turn, turn - Mou Ichido, itte kudasai"

Please do it again, just one more time.

"One day in retrospect the years of struggle will strike you as the most beautiful."

Sigmund Freud

ABOUT THE AUTHOR

Canada's Best Karate founder, Bob Mueller, lives on Vancouver Island with his wife, Wendy, and their beloved dog, Copper (aka, Bubba).

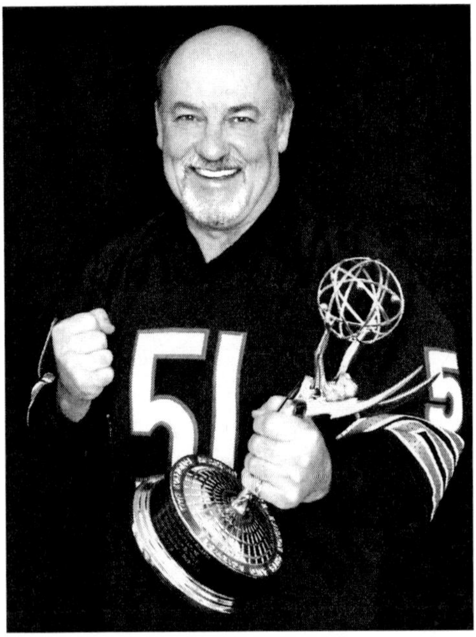

A lifetime of change and adventure had him crisscrossing the country. He lived multiple times in five of Canada's ten provinces before returned to his island home in 2014.

Mueller reached international notoriety when Steve Sabol of NFL Films took an interest in his story called, "Finding Your Butkus". The resulting film about Bob's life story won a Sports EMMY AWARD in 2008.

True North Dojo is his third book. Mueller is also a well-versed artisan carpenter / builder, martial arts entrepreneur, and sports artist. As Canada's Sports Artist© his dynamic work is collectable and internationally recognized. Bob Mueller is also an inspirational speaker who teaches about the power of intention and his belief in magic moments. His desire for others to discover their own personal power is what drives him to continually expand his influence.

If you are interested in finding out more about his work, be it art, speaking or training - please contact him in the following ways:

Canada's Best Karate www.canadasbestkarate.com

Canada's Sports Artist www.bobmuellerart.com

Emmy Award Winning Speaker www.findingyourbutkus.com

Email bmue51art@gmail.com